LOCK, STOCK, AND BARREL

LOCK, STOCK, AND BARREL

The Origins of American Gun Culture

CLAYTON E. CRAMER

 PRAEGER™

An Imprint of ABC-CLIO, LLC

Santa Barbara, California • Denver, Colorado

Library of Congress Cataloging-in-Publication Data

Names: Cramer, Clayton E., author.
Title: Lock, stock, and barrel : the origins of American gun culture / Clayton E. Cramer.
Description: Santa Barbara, California : Praeger, [2018] | Includes bibliographical references and index.
Identifiers: LCCN 2017047557 (print) | LCCN 2017052714 (ebook) | ISBN 9781440860386 (eBook) | ISBN 9781440860379 (alk. paper)
Subjects: LCSH: Firearms ownership—United States—History. | Firearms—United States—History.
Classification: LCC HV8059 (ebook) | LCC HV8059 .C733 2018 (print) | DDC 683.400973—dc23
LC record available at https://lccn.loc.gov/2017047557

ISBN: 978-1-4408-6037-9 (print)
       978-1-4408-6038-6 (ebook)

22 21 20 19 18   1 2 3 4 5

This book is also available as an eBook.

Praeger
An Imprint of ABC-CLIO, LLC

ABC-CLIO, LLC
130 Cremona Drive, P.O. Box 1911
Santa Barbara, California 93116-1911
www.abc-clio.com

This book is printed on acid-free paper ∞

Manufactured in the United States of America

Contents

Preface

For me, the most important novel of the 20th century was George Orwell's *Nineteen Eighty-Four*. Its protagonist, Winston Smith, works for the Ministry of Truth, where Winston changes history books, and even old newspapers, so that the past is continually updated to reflect the ever-changing needs of the Party. "Day by day, and almost minute by minute, the past was brought up to date."[1]

Revisionism, the revising of history, is not always bad. History does change as historians reexamine the evidence. But essential facts seldom change. Even history books published in 1918 agree with recent ones that President Abraham Lincoln was assassinated in 1865. Minor facts, and often theories for *why* events happened, get revised, often after the evidence in support of the new position becomes well established.

This book is in part about some recent historical revisionism. While less dramatic than claiming President Lincoln enjoyed a well-deserved retirement in Springfield, Illinois, it is very close to the Ministry of Truth's slogan: "He who controls the past controls the future. He who controls the present controls the past." The question at the heart of this rapidly changing past is this: how recently did America's gun culture develop? This book aims to demonstrate that the traditional, largely assumed view of America as a gun culture from its beginning is generally correct. The recent revisionist history is chiefly driven by the desires of political activists concerning gun control today.

What is a "gun culture"? While lacking a universally accepted definition, widespread private ownership and use of firearms, a belief that they have some significance beyond their immediate practical need, and the idea that one has a right to possess them certainly seems an adequate starting definition. By analogy, America in the 1960s was a "car culture."

Traditionally, historians assumed that guns were always part of our culture, a consequence of a nation formed from a "howling wilderness,"[2] a necessity in a place where hunting for food and defense against dangerous animals, and sometimes hostile Indians, was needed. In the last two decades, revisionist historians have argued otherwise. In 1996, an Emory University professor of history, Michael A. Bellesiles, published an article in the *Journal of American History*[3] and a subsequent book, *Arming America: The Origins of a National Gun Culture* (2000), that claimed that many long-cherished ideas about violence, guns, and the effectiveness of the militia in early America were incorrect. Bellesiles argued that guns were very scarce and tightly controlled in America before 1840, that there was essentially no civilian market for handguns before 1848, and that few Americans hunted.[4] Initially, many academics responded with fawning reviews of this courageous attack on the "gun lobby" and its "distortion" of American history.[5]

Bellesiles's book was eventually discredited for engaging in fraud. His summaries of probate inventories were clearly erroneous and often completely fabricated. He listed sources in archives that *did not exist* or that he had never visited.[6]

At Emory University's request, a blue-ribbon panel of historians examined the controversy. The committee's comments made it clear that it did not believe Bellesiles's responses. In many cases, the committee members were unable to find Bellesiles's cited documents. Their conclusions included the following passage:

> But in one respect, the failure to clearly identify his sources, does move into the realm of "falsification," which would constitute a violation of the Emory "Policies." The construction of this Table implies a consistent, comprehensive, and intelligible method of gathering data. The reality seems quite the opposite. In fact, Professor Bellesiles told the Committee that because of criticism from other scholars, he himself had begun to doubt the quality of his probate research well before he published it in the *Journal of American History.*[7]

Yet, the graphs produced from Bellesiles's "probate inventories" were a large part of why that article, and the subsequent book, were initially regarded as groundbreaking and persuasive. Who argues with statistics?

In response to the report Emory commissioned, Bellesiles resigned from his recently received tenured position, and Columbia University revoked the Bancroft Prize it had awarded to Bellesiles for *Arming America*—an unprecedented event.[8]

My book *Armed America* (2006) did an adequate job of demonstrating that Bellesiles was not simply wrong, but he had deliberately misrepresented the facts: altering texts, making up texts, and massively misrepresenting his sources. His fellow academics for the most part never noticed because he told lies that led to a very limiting interpretation of the Second Amendment with which they emotionally, and therefore intellectually, agreed.

Almost a decade later, I was astonished to see Bellesiles's false claims rise from the grave, like a vampire not adequately staked. Pamela Haag's study *The Gunning of America* (2015)[9] argues, as had Bellesiles, that the American gun culture, and thus demand for guns, was created in the mid-19th century and was the result of clever marketing by the newly formed mass production gun industry (primarily Colt Firearms and Winchester Repeating Arms). Haag asserts that the industry had created demand for a product that Americans neither wanted nor needed. She also claims that guns were so rare that they were not the primary murder weapon before 1860, according to an 1850s survey based on "eighty-five murders . . . that were mentioned in popular books and pamphlets."[10] If guns were rare, and guns cause murder, this would be a plausible claim. We will later examine the evidence for this claim.

Haag directly acknowledges that she believes Bellesiles's claims about the scarcity of guns and gun culture were correct, and she appears to have no awareness that Bellesiles had been discredited.

This book will explore the following questions:

1. Was gun ownership (and in consequence gun manufacturing and gunsmithing) rare before 1840?
2. Was the civilian market for pistols small or nonexistent before 1848?
3. How did gunsmithing (including gun manufacturing) develop in Colonial and Early Republic America?
4. What role did the gun manufacturing industry play in not only transforming American industry but also creating the modern industrial world across Western civilization?
5. Was American gun culture actually created by gunmakers through clever marketing?

The answers to questions 1, 2, 3, and 5 are provided in the following pages, which will refute the revisionist claims concerning the origins of

American gun culture. Question 4 is an interesting and important part of history that hitchhikes on this larger analysis of revisionist history.

Some of this text and material has previously been published in the *Southern Illinois University Law Journal.*

Acknowledgments

This book would not have been possible without research funding provided by the National Rifle Association of America Civil Rights Defense Fund, at a time when a stroke disabled me from my former profession as a software engineer. Thanks also to Jon Porter, Bob Hunnicutt, Bruce McCullough, and Teresa at the Horseshoe Bend (Idaho) Public Library for locating often obscure sources. John Simutis proofread an early version of the manuscript, and David Golden proofread a late version, dramatically improving every chapter. Carolyn Goldwasser, Eric L. Bainter, Miguel Gonzalez, and Paul Taffel proofread the galleys. The Connecticut Historical Society and Connecticut State Library staffs were very helpful in finding documents from Samuel Colt and his company. Miguel Gonzalez, Kevin McKinley, and John Simutis transcribed the poor 19th-century handwriting in the Colt manuscripts. Thanks also to Michael Millman, my editor at Praeger. And, as always, thanks to my wife, Rhonda, for her editing. It helps to be married to someone with an MA in English!

The recently deceased Don B. Kates, a civil rights activist and dean of Second Amendment legal scholars, played a major role in causing me to study this topic, for which I am very grateful.

A Note on Terminology

Dates

Throughout this book, years expressed in the form 1639/40 indicate dates now in the first three months of the year. In the Julian calendar, used until 1752, the first three months were considered part of the year in which the previous December had fallen. This 1639/40 form was also used in the Colonial period.

Money

I use £10:5:4 as shorthand for £10 5s. 4d. (i.e., 10 pounds, 5 shillings, and 4 pence). In this book, there are many references to the old English money system of 12 pence to a shilling and 20 shillings to a pound. Until you write a spreadsheet to total up and average hundreds of such amounts (as I have), you do not fully appreciate the service Thomas Jefferson did for America by starting us down the decimal money path.

Firearms Terminology

Appendix C explains early firearms terminology.

CHAPTER 1

Gun Culture in Colonial America, 1607–1775

What was the role of guns in Colonial America? Were guns widely owned? If guns were commonly owned and used, then the revisionist claims about the absence of a gun culture in the early American history are highly suspect. Imagine if a historian in 3000 CE wrote a book claiming that there had been no automobile culture in 1960s America (a society in which automobiles had been a substantial part of the average person's use or interest) and no high-powered muscle cars existed. His critics would pull out circulation figures and articles for magazines such as *Car & Driver*, *Motor Trend*, and *Road & Track*. Next, they would point to the number of automobiles registered with the states. Then, they would cite data on the prevalence of gas stations and automobile repair shops. Finally, they would point to literary references to automobiles as common and unremarkable objects of use. At this point, the automobile culture denier would be laughed out of the historical community.

In this chapter, we will take a similar approach by examining the evidence as it exists in the analogous categories for firearms, with civilian uses and possession of handguns given their own special attention. (Because gun registration and ownership licensing is a modern idea (except for nonwhites), there is no firearm analogy to 1960s automobile registration.) In later chapters, we will explore the evidence related to gunsmithing and gun manufacturing because these professions and industries demonstrate widespread gun ownership and use.

Mandatory Gun Ownership and Carrying Statutes

The following laws may seem odd to modern sensibilities; most of the colonies, well into the Early Republic, required individuals to possess firearms as part of their militia duty for defense, at first from Indians and later from slave rebellions and attacks by foreign navies.

Virginia

Virginia's statutes are explored here in greater detail than the other colonies, both because Virginia was the first colony settled and because other colonies, with rare exceptions, followed the same pattern of mandatory firearms ownership and obligatory carrying of firearms to church and other public meetings, as well as government provision of firearms to those too poor to buy their own. Tyler's *Narratives of Early Virginia* contains a 1619 statute that required everyone to attend church on the Sabbath, "and all suche as beare armes shall bring their pieces, swords, pouder and shotte." Those failing to bring their guns to church were subject to a 3 shilling fine.[1]

A 1623 Virginia statute required,

> That no man go or send abroad without a sufficient parte will armed. . . . That go not to worke in the ground without their arms (and a centinell upon them.). . . . That the commander of every plantation take care that there be sufficient of powder and am[m] unition within the plantation under his command and their pieces fixt and their arms compleate. . . . That no commander of any plantation do either himselfe or suffer others to spend powder unnecessarily in drinking or entertainments, &c.[2]

The requirement to work in the fields armed was reissued in 1632.[3] The motivation for the 1623 law and its successor is not hard to find; a surprise attack by Indians in 1622 left several hundred dead, having been killed in the fields.[4]

In 1632, Virginia required that "all men that are fitting to beare arms, shall bring their pieces to the church." This requirement for all militiamen to come to church armed (if requested by the county's militia commander) was restated in a November 1738 statute.[5]

A March 1655/1656 statute prohibited shooting "any guns at drinkeing (marriages and funerals onely excepted)" because gunshots were the common alarm for an Indian attack, "of which no certainty can be had in respect of the frequent shooting of gunns in drinking."[6] It is hard to imagine that such a law was needed, except in the event that guns were widely owned and used as a unusual (by modern standards) form of fireworks.

A 1673 law directed militia captains to "take a strict and perticuler account of what armes and ammunition are wanting in their severall companies and troops." The county courts were empowered to tax the population "for the providing of armes and ammunition for supplying the wants aforesaid, that is to say, muskitts and swords for the ffoote, and pistols, swords and carbines for horse." Militia officers were to keep these arms "for them to dispose of the same as there shalbe occasion; and that those to whome distribution shalbe made doe pay for the same at a reasonable rate." In the 1670s, increasing unease about the Dutch, with whom England was at war, led to concerns that the freemen of Virginia were not adequately armed to resist invasion.[7] An indication of the legal status of firearms and ownership is evident in a 1676–1677 law: "It is ordered that all persons have hereby liberty to sell armes and ammunition to any of his majesties loyall subjects inhabiting this colony."[8]

In 1684, free Virginians were required to "provide and furnish themselves with a sword, musquet and other furniture fitt for a soldier[,] . . . two pounds of powder, and eight pounds of shott." A similar 1705 statute required every foot soldier to arm himself "with a firelock, muskett, or fusee well fixed" and gave him 18 months to do so before he would be subject to fines. Minor changes to the statute in 1738 still required all members of the militia to appear at musters with the same list of gun choices. The militiamen were obligated to supply themselves with weapons, but the ammunition requirement was reduced to one pound of powder and four pounds of lead balls. A 1748 revision obligated militiamen to provide themselves with "arms and ammunition." By 1755, all cavalry officers were obligated to provide themselves with "holsters and pistols well fixed."[9]

A 1748 statute provided that "it may be necessary in time of danger, to arm part of the militia, not otherwise sufficiently provided, out of his majesty's magazine and other stores within this colony." A 1757 version of the statute again addressed the problem of those militiamen who were too poor to buy a gun: "any soldier . . . so poor as not to be able to purchase the arms aforesaid" would be provided with publicly owned arms.[10] Finally, a 1765 statute is the ultimate demonstration of the widespread trust and interest in gun ownership by free Virginians:

That the commanding officer of each of the counties from which the militia has been sent into service in the pay of this colony shall, within the space of three months after the passing this act, sell, for the best price that be had for the same, all arms, ammunition, provisions, and necessaries purchased at the publick expense in the said counties.[11]

The colony was selling off its surplus arms.

Other statutes, while slightly ambiguous, also show that widespread gun ownership was required, not restricted. A 1639/1640 statute is short and simple: "All persons except Negroes to be provided with arms and amunition or be fined at pleasure of the Governor and Council."[12] Who was to provide the arms? Some revisionists have interpreted these statutes as obligations of the government to arm the militia. If the government was required to arm the militia, why would it threaten itself with a fine for failing to do its duty; it would be consistent with the laws of the other colonies that freemen were to arm themselves and their sons, and masters were to arm their indentured servants.

Virginia required masters to supply their indentured servants with certain goods when they had completed their term of service. These "freedom dues" from 1705 onward included "one well fixed musket or fuzee, of the value of twenty shillings, at least." A master who refused to issue the specified goods could find himself ordered to do so by the county court.[13]

This gun culture was increasingly limited to free Virginians, and then only to free *white* Virginians. A 1680 statute prohibited "any negroe or other slave to carry or arme himselfe with any club, staffe, gunn, sword or any other weapon of defence or offence." This would seem to include Indian slaves. (The language is curious because there were free blacks by this point; not every "Negroe" was a slave.) By 1723, Virginia had become increasingly concerned about the growing free nonwhite population of the colony, spurred by a slave plot in 1722. Consequently, it adopted laws that imposed servitude requirements on free children of racially mixed parentage and the prohibition of voting by nonwhites.[14] Unsurprisingly, because bearing arms in the militia was a duty and marker of citizenship, laws adopted the same year also severely limited gun ownership by free blacks and Indians: "That every free negro, mulatto, or indian, being a house-keeper, or listed in the militia, may be permitted to keep one gun, powder, and shot." Those blacks and Indians who were "not house-keepers, nor listed in the militia" were required to dispose of their weapons by the end of October 1723. Blacks and

Indians living on frontier plantations were required to obtain a license "to keep and use guns, powder, and shot."[15]

Even the small number of blacks and Indians who were still members of the militia were no longer trusted with guns by 1738. They were still required to muster, but "shall appear without arms."[16] This limitation of the gun culture to free white Virginians is no surprise and has its present-day equivalents in federal bans on possession of firearms or ammunition by convicted felons, domestic violence misdemeanants, the dishonorably discharged, those who have renounced U.S. citizenship, and those who have been involuntarily committed to a mental hospital or adjudicated mentally ill.[17] Like those feared slave rebellions, when Congress passed the Gun Control Act of 1968, one of the justifications was that

> receipt, possession, or transportation of a firearm by felons, veterans who are discharged under dishonorable conditions, mental incompetents, aliens who are illegally in the country, and former citizens who have renounced their citizenship, constitutes . . . a threat to the continued and effective operation of the Government of the United States and of the government of each State guaranteed by article IV of the Constitution.[18]

Plymouth

A 1632 statute ordered "that every freeman or other inhabitant of this colony provide for himselfe and each under him able to beare armes a sufficient musket and other serviceable peece for war with bandaleroes and other appurtenances with what speede may be." By the end of the following May, each person was to own "two pounds of powder and ten pounds of bullets," with a fine of 10 shillings for any unarmed person. The Plymouth government reiterated this requirement, and the emphasis that "each person" provide these "for himselfe & each such person under him," shortly thereafter.[19]

A 1646 statute directs that

> every Township within this Government before the next October Court . . . shall provide two sufficient snaphaunces or firelock peeces[,] two swords and two pouches for every thirty men they have in their Towneship . . . which shalbe ready at all tymes for service.[20]

Why store two guns for every 30 men, unless the government assumed that the other 28 were already armed, as the 1632 law required?

As in Virginia, mandatory carrying statutes appear:

> It is enacted That every Towneship within this Government do carry a competent number of pieeces fixd and compleate with powder shott and swords every Lord's day to the meetings—one of a house from the first of September to the middle of November, except their be some just & lawfull impedyment.[21]

While not terribly clear writing, it is consistent with other colonial statutes that required all to attend church with guns, and it also implies that at least one person from every home should bring either a gun or sword. If guns were scarce, it would be hard to assume it from such statutes.

The law was rewritten slightly in 1658 to require that a quarter of the militia bring "some serviceable peece and sword and three charges of powder and bullets" or be fined "2 shillings and six pence." This requirement to bring guns to church only applied from March 1 "to the last of November,"[22] apparently because this was when an Indian attack was considered likely.

A 1643 statute specifies which

> Guns Allowed for Service. . . . Musketts fire locks and matchcocks [perhaps matchlocks] so that they have foure fathome of match [a method of lighting the gunpowder on matchlock firearms] at all tymes for every matchcock Caliver Carbines and fouleing peeces so that they be not above four foote & a half long and not under bastard musket or caliver bore.[23]

Limiting which guns were allowed for militia service suggests that there were a lot of obsolete guns in private hands.

Massachusetts

Like its smaller and slightly older neighbor Plymouth, the Massachusetts Bay Colony mandated gun ownership. A March 22, 1630/1631, statute required the entire adult male population to be armed. Every town within the Massachusetts Bay Colony "before the 5th of Aprill nexte" was to make sure that every person, including servants, was "furnished with good & sufficient armes" of a type "allowable by the captain or other officers, those that want & are of abilitie to buy them themselves, others that are unable to have them provided by the town." This suggests that guns were available for purchase.

Those who were unable to arm themselves under the March 22 statute were to reimburse the town "when they shalbe able."[24] It is unclear whether "5th of Aprill nexte" meant the following month or the following year, but in either case, there seems to have been no great concern that guns were in short supply. A March 6, 1632/1633, statute also required any single person who had not provided himself with acceptable arms to work for a master (employer), his wages paying the cost of the arms to be provided to him by the town.[25]

What sort of arms were required? The 1630/1631 statutes were not specific that "arms" meant guns. Certainly, these orders could be read as requiring everyone to be armed with swords, halberds, or pikes. But other statutes adopted in the following years, especially the March 9, 1636/1637, statute requiring everyone to bring their muskets to church, shows that "arms" usually meant guns.[26]

Guns were apparently widely distributed among the population and available for purchase in Massachusetts Bay. An April 5, 1631, directive ordered every man that "findes a musket" to have ready one pound of gunpowder, "20 bulletts, & 2 fathome of match." No person was to travel singly between Massachusetts Bay and Plymouth, "nor without some armes, though 2 or 3 togeathr."[27]

A March 9, 1636/1637, ordinance required individuals to be armed and demonstrates that gun ownership was considered common. Because of the danger of Indian attack, and because much of the population was neglecting to carry a gun, every person above 18 years of age (except magistrates and elders of the churches) was ordered to

> Come to the publike assemblies with their muskets, or other peeces fit for servise, furnished with match, powder, & bullets, upon paine of 12*d.* for every default. . . . And no person shall travel above one mile from his dwelling house, except in places wheare other houses are neare together, without some armes, upon paine of 12*d.* for every default.[28]

The requirement to bring guns to church—but apparently not the requirement to travel armed—was repealed November 20, 1637. A May 10, 1643, order directed the military officer in each town to "appoint what armes to bee brought to the meeting houses on the Lords dayes, & other times of meeting." This requirement was back in force.[29]

A September 3, 1634, order specified that every trained soldier (or militiaman), "as well pykemen as others, shalbe furnished with muskets[,] . . . powder and shott, according to the order for musketeers." While this order is not specific that the militiaman is subject to a fine for failing to furnish *himself* with arms, this is certainly who is obligated by the March 22, 1630/1631; April 5, 1631; and March 6, 1632/1633 laws. At least some towns in the Massachusetts Bay Colony also imposed their own fines for failing to own arms and ammunition.[30]

Guns and ammunition were readily available. An August 12, 1645, law directed the surveyor general to impress "leade, pis[tol] bullets, swan shot, & match, where you can find the same," giving the owners receipts to be redeemed by the treasurer, "according to the rates for which such things are sould in the shops or warehouses in Boston."[31]

Much like Plymouth's limitation on guns suitable for militia duty, Massachusetts, on October 1, 1645, ordered that the only arms allowed "serviceable, in our trained bands . . . are either full musket boare, or basterd musket at the least, & that none should be under three foote 9 inches."[32]

A May 14, 1645, order indicated that the officer of each company would "appoint what arms every souldier shall serve with, so that their may be two third[s] musket." This might indicate that some soldiers did not have guns, but other parts of this law and related statutes suggest that every soldier was expected to own a gun and appear with it, though he might be ordered to use some other weapon in combat. The militia commander was required to view "armes and ammunition" on training days and to verify that "every souldier have one pound of powder, 20 bullets, & 2 fathome of match, with musket, sword, bandilers, & rest."[33]

An August 12, 1645, order also specified that every soldier "have powder, bullets, match, & [bandoleers]," which would not be of much use without a gun. By June 18, 1645, "all inhabitants," including those exempt from militia duty, were "to have armes in their howses fitt for service, with pouder, bullets, match, as other souldiers."[34] It seems likely that the provision allowing the commander to appoint "what arms every souldier shall serve with" was to make it possible to have some soldiers armed with weapons specific to a particular mission. For example, because pikes did not require reloading, pikemen provided a protective shield for soldiers who were reloading muskets.

Another statute on October 13, 1675, exempted from overseas military duty "all such persons as shall be assessed, and shall accordingly provide three fire armes . . . except in extreame & utmost necessity."[35] Clearly, the government believed that there were enough people in Massachusetts who owned at least three guns to draft such a specific statute.

A 1755 order by Massachusetts governor William Shirley to the militia to appear for service provides more evidence that militiamen possessed their *own* arms: "To such of them as shall be provided with sufficient Arms at their first Muster, they shall be allowed a *Dollar* over and above their Wages, and full Recompence for such of their Arms as shall be inevitably lost or spoiled."[36] Clearly, Governor Shirley believed that there were some members of the militia who, contrary to law, did not have firearms appropriate to military service. He also believed that some members would show up appropriately armed, and he was prepared to pay them extra because of it.

Like Virginia, the right (and obligation) of noncitizens to be armed waxed and waned with military necessity. A May 27, 1652, order required all "Scotsmen, Negers, & Indians inhabiting with or servants to the English" between ages 16 and 60 to train with the militia.[37] In May 1656, perhaps after the military crisis had passed, there was an order that "no Negroes or Indians . . . shalbe armed or permitted to trayne."[38]

Connecticut

For the rest of this chapter, we will only give summaries of statutes of a similar nature to the first three colonies, along with detailed explanations of the unique statutes.

Connecticut required most adult males to have guns and ammunition at home, with provisions for providing guns to the poor, who would pay the government for them by working.[39]

We also have many examples of colonists fined for selling guns to the Indians, an unsurprising law considering the frequent wars. The very first entry in *Public Records of the Colony of Connecticut* concerns a 1636 complaint that "Henry Stiles or some of the ser[vants] had traded a peece with the Indians for Corne." In 1640, George Abbott is ordered to pay a £5 fine for "selling a pystoll & powder to the Indeans." (A fine of £5 would have been about 25 days' wages for a laborer.) Fines are repeatedly assessed for selling guns to the Indians.[40]

Much like Virginia and Massachusetts, in 1643, Connecticut ordered that those attending church were to "bring a musket, pystoll or some peece, with powder and shott to e[a]ch meeting."[41]

And these early requirements for most adult free men to own guns did not disappear as the colony became more settled. A 1741 statute reiterates the earlier Connecticut statutes that required every militiaman "and other house-holder" to have a firelock and ammunition and to show these at militia musters.[42]

New Haven Colony

Until its acquisition by Connecticut, New Haven was an independent colony with its own laws. Statutes ordering "every male from 16 to 60 yeares olde" to be armed were in place in 1639, 1643, 1644, and 1646. For New Haven, unlike many other colonies, there are records of fines for failure to be properly armed. (A typical laborers' daily wage at the time was about 4 shillings.) On January 4, 1643/1644, 12 men were fined 2 shillings each "for defect[ive] guns." Four other men were fined 1 shilling each "for defect in their cocks," indicating that their guns would either not cock or not fire correctly, though apparently this was considered a less serious problem than the defects that led to fines of 2 shilling. Of the 12 men, 2 who were fined 2 shillings for defective guns were also fined 6 pence "for want of shott," and two others were fined 1 shilling for "want of shott and pouder." Three men were fined 6 pence for "want of flints" and another, apparently a matchlock owner, "for want of match." Two men were fined 6 pence "for want of worme and skourer" (used for cleaning the channel from flintlock pan to chamber). Eight men were fined 3 shillings and 4 pence "for total defect in armes."[43]

New Hampshire

Like the preceding colonies, New Hampshire required every "Male person from Sixteen Years of Age to Sixty," with a few exceptions, to have a firearm.[44]

New Jersey

New Jersey's 1703 militia statute was similar to New Hampshire's. It required all men "between the Age of Sixteen and Fifty years," with the exception of ministers, physicians, school masters, "Civil Officers of the Government," members of the legislature, and slaves, to be members of the militia. "Every one of which is listed shall be sufficiently armed with one good sufficient Musquet or Fusee."[45]

Rhode Island

Rhode Island required "every man to have so much powder, and so many bullets[,] . . . and that every man do come armed unto the meeting upon every sixth day." Also, "that noe man shall go two miles from the Towne unarmed, eyther with Gunn or Sword; and that none shall come to any public Meeting without his weapon."[46]

There were provisions for determining whether privately owned guns, "his owne proper goods," had been sold to the Indians.[47] This was difficult in an era before guns had serial numbers.

New York

New York required,

> Besides the Generall stock of each Town[,] Every Male within this government from Sixteen to Sixty years of age, or not freed by public Allowance, shall[,] if freeholders at their own, if sons or Servants[,] at their Parents and Masters Charge and Cost, be furnished from time to time and so Continue well furnished with Arms and other Suitable Provition hereafter mentioned: under the penalty of five Shillings for the least default therein[:] Namely a good Serviceable Gun.[48]

Delaware

In 1742, Delaware required "that every Freeholder and taxable Person residing in this Government," with a few exceptions, "provide himself with the following Arms and Ammunition, viz. One well fixed Musket or Firelock." While "every Freeholder and taxable Person" in Delaware was obligated to provide himself with a gun, not all were required to enlist in the militia, only "all Male Persons, above Seventeen and under Fifty Years of Age," with a few exceptions.[49]

The exemptions from militia duty are quite interesting. Quakers were exempted from the requirement to provide themselves with guns, from militia duty, and from nightly watch duty, in exchange for paying 2 shillings and 6 pence for every day that "others are obliged to attend the said Muster, Exercise, or Watch."[50]

Others were exempted from militia musters, but not from the requirement to fight, and the requirement to own a gun:

> All Justices of the Peace, Physicians, Lawyers, and Millers, and Persons incapable through Infirmities of Sickness or Lameness, shall be exempted and excused from appearing to muster, except in Case of an Alarm: They being nevertheless obliged, by this Act, to provide and keep by them Arms and Ammunition as aforesaid, as well as others. And if an Alarm happen, then all those, who by this Act are obliged to keep Arms as aforesaid[,] shall join the General Militia.

Ministers appear to have been exempted from these requirements.[51]

Maryland

Maryland provides similar examples; the government required most of its male population to be armed. Lord Baltimore, the proprietor of Maryland, gave instructions to settlers emigrating to Maryland that provided a very detailed list of tools, clothing, and food to bring with them. On that list, for each man, "Item, one musket[;] . . . Item, 10 pound of Powder[;] . . . Item, 40 pound of Lead, Bullets, Pistoll and Goose shot, of each sort some."[52]

Lord Baltimore believed that most settlers followed his instructions and brought guns with them to Maryland. "An Act for Military Discipline" enacted a few years later required

> that every house keeper or housekeepers within this Province shall have ready continually upon all occasions within his her or their house for him or themselves and for every person within his her or their house able to bear armes one Serviceable fixed gunne of bastard muskett boare.[53]

They were also required to have a pound of gunpowder, four pounds of pistol or musket shot, and "match for matchlocks and of flints for firelocks."[54]

Like other colonies, anyone who lacked arms and ammunition was to be armed by the militia commander, who could force payment at "any price . . . not extending to above double the value of the said armes and ammunition according to the rate then usual in the Country."[55]

While the language is somewhat unclear, it appears that one of the conditions of receiving title to land in Maryland, beginning in 1641, was bringing "Armes and Ammunition as are intended & required by the Conditions abovesaid to be provided & carried into the said Province of Maryland for every man betweene the ages of sixteene & fifty years w[hi]ch shalbe transported thether." The arms required included "one musket or bastard musket with a snaphance lock," ten pounds of gunpowder, and forty pounds of bullets, pistol, and goose shot.[56]

As with most other colonies, a 1642 law prohibited providing gunpowder or shot to the Indians and required "that all housekeepers provide fixed gunn and Sufficient powder and Shott for each person able to bear arms." A 1658 revision of the law required "every householder provide himselfe speedily with Armes & Ammunition according to a former Act of Assembly viz 2 [pounds] of powder and 5 [pounds] of shott & one good Gun well fixed for every man able to bear Armes in his house."[57]

Like Virginia's restriction on nonemergency shooting, "Noe man to discharge 3 Gunns within the Space of 1/4 hour nor concur to the dischargeing Soe many, except to give or Answer alarm." If hearing such an alarm, every housekeeper was obligated "to answer and continue it Soe far as he may." Any man "able to bear arms" was required "to goe to church or Chappell or any considerable distance from home" with a loaded gun.[58]

By the start of the 18th century, Maryland's laws had become a bit more demanding. When an indentured servant received his freedom, a statute passed in 1699 (and reiterated in 1715) directed what goods were to be provided to him by his master. Along with clothes and a variety of tools, the master was also directed to give the newly freed servant,

> One Gun of Twenty Shillings Price, not above Four Foot by the barrel, nor less than Three and a Half; which said Gun shall, by the Master or Mistress, in the Presence of the next Justice of the Peace, be delivered to such Free-man, under the Penalty of Five Hundred Pounds of Tobacco on such Master of Mistress omitting so to do.

To encourage the newly freed servant to keep his gun, "And the like Penalty on the said Free-man selling or disposing thereof within the Space of Twelve Months."[59]

Much like what had happened in Massachusetts, the mobilization of militias demonstrated that at least some (perhaps many) militia members owned their own guns. In 1759, Maryland's Governor Sharpe directed calling up of the militia, offering to provide government arms, but also "That for Every One of such Arms as any of Your men shall bring with them, and that may be Spoiled or Lost in actual Service, I will pay at the rate of Twenty five Shillings a Firelock."[60]

Like other southern colonies, Maryland's trust of the free white population did not extend to slaves. A 1715 Maryland statute directed "That no Negro or other slave, within this Province, shall be permitted to carry any Gun or any other offensive Weapon, from off their Master's Land, without Licence from their said Master."[61]

One other category of Marylanders was not trusted with guns, at least intermittently: Catholics. Catholics were exempted from militia duty because, like blacks almost everywhere in the American colonies, they were not completely trusted. In light of the role that Catholicism played in the recurring attempts to restore the Stuarts to the throne of England, this is unsurprising. In exchange for exemption from militia duty, Catholics were doubly taxed on their lands.[62]

Comparing Maryland law to English law is interesting; English law concerning Catholics and arms after the accession of William I to the throne is at first self-contradictory. A 1689 law prohibited Catholics from possessing "any arms, Weapons, Gunpowder, or Ammunition (other than such necessary Weapons as shall be allowed to him by Order of the Justices of the Peace, at their general Quarter sessions, for the Defence of his House or Person)."[63] The law both prohibited Catholics from possessing arms and yet allowed them, under some restrictions, to have at least defensive arms. Some have argued that "this exception is especially significant, as it demonstrates that even when there were fears of religious war, Catholic Englishmen were permitted the means to defend themselves and their households; they were merely forbidden to stockpile arms."[64]

At times, this law was the justification for disarming Catholics both in Britain and America. In Britain, the death of the queen in 1714 caused orders that "the Lords Leiutents of the severall Countrys were directed to draw out the Militia to take from Papists & other suspected Persons their Arms & Horses & to be watchfull of the Publick Tranquillity."[65]

Despite a thorough search of all volumes of *Archives of Maryland* for the words "Catholic" and "Papist," the only similar example in Maryland seems to be in 1756: "all Arms Gunpowder and Ammunition of what kind soever any Papist or reputed Papist within this Province hath or shall have in his House or Houses" were ordered seized. This suggests that although the 1689 law *allowed* complete prohibition of Catholic gun ownership at the discretion of the government, Catholics were not *usually* prohibited from possession. As part of this same statute, members of the militia were required to swear an oath of allegiance to King George II. Those who refused the oath—thus refusing their legal obligation as British subjects to defend the realm—were not allowed to possess arms or ammunition.[66]

South Carolina

A 1735 statute authorized searches of slave quarters for guns and required any "negro or slave" to have a license to possess a gun. If slaves could be licensed to have guns, this indicates that guns were fairly common.[67]

A 1743 statute, similar to those of Virginia and most New England colonies, required "every white male" to carry a gun and at least six rounds of ammunition for it to church. Other provisions required church-wardens, deacons, or elders to check each man coming in to make *sure* that he was armed. The stated purpose of this severe gun control measure—requiring everyone to be armed at church—was "for the better security of this Province against the insurrections and other wicked attempts of Negroes and other Slaves."[68]

North Carolina

North Carolina passed similar militia laws to Virginia in or before 1715 and in 1746. The 1746 statute obligated "all the Freemen and Servants . . . between the Age of Sixteen Years, and Sixty" to enlist in the militia, and further required all such persons "be well provided with a Gun, fit for Service." Interestingly, unlike other colonies, the definition of a militia member under both statutes did not exclude free blacks, and according to John Hope Franklin, "free Negroes served in the militia of [the State of] North Carolina with no apparent discrimination against them."[69]

Georgia

Georgia's long and poorly written 1773 militia law declared that the governor or military commander may "assemble and call together all male Persons in this Province from the Age of Sixteen Years to Sixty Years . . . at such times, and arm and array them in such manner as is hereafter expressed." But later, "every Person liable to appear and bear arms at any Exercise Muster or Training hereby appointed Pursuant to the directions of this Act Shall constantly keep and bring with them to Such Muster Exercise or Training one Gun or Musket fit for Service." This is followed by a *very* inclusive list of tools required to use a gun in the field.[70]

Members of the militia who were indentured servants, or otherwise subject to "Government or Command" of another, were not obligated to arm themselves, but as in New York and other colonies, their masters were. He "shall constantly keep such arms amunition [*sic*] and Furniture for every such Indented Servant."[71] The militia statute also provided for enlisting male slaves 16–60 years old "as [their masters] can Recommend as Capable and faithful Slaves." Masters were also supposed to arm such slaves when in actual militia service "with one Sufficient Gun One Hatchet powder Horn and shot pouch."[72]

Like South Carolina, in 1770, Georgia required every member of the militia (pretty much the entire free white male population) to come to church armed. The statute is so similar to South Carolina's, including the search of arriving worshippers for weapons, that it would appear to have been borrowed from South Carolina or some common source.[73]

A 1768 Georgia statute "for the Establishing and Regulating Patrols" prohibited slaves from possessing or carrying "Fire Arms or any Offensive Weapon whatsoever, unless such Slave shall have a Ticket or License in Writing from his Master[,] Mistress or Overseer to Hunt and Kill Game Cattle or Mischievous Birds or Birds of Prey." Other provisions allowed a slave to possess a gun while in the company of a white person 16 years old or older or while protecting crops from birds. Under no condition was a slave allowed to carry "any Gun[,] Cutlass[,] Pistol or other Offensive Weapon" from Saturday sunset until sunrise Monday morning. The "Patrols" alluded to in the law's title were for the purpose of "Searching and examining any Negroe house for Offensive Weapons Fire Arms and Ammunition."[74]

Duty to Be Armed

There was a legal duty of individuals to be armed in the colonies of Massachusetts Bay, Plymouth, New Hampshire, Connecticut, New Haven, Rhode Island, New York, New Jersey, Delaware, Maryland, Virginia, North Carolina, South Carolina, and Georgia. The inspection provisions and the requirements to bring guns to church make it clear that these arms were privately owned in New York, Rhode Island, New Haven, Connecticut, Maryland, South Carolina, and Georgia. Fines assessed and requests for exemptions in Connecticut and New Haven demonstrate that these laws were not "dead letters" but actually enforced. Lawsuits in Connecticut concerning defective guns and disputes concerning sales (discussion starting on page 20) demonstrate that privately owned guns existed.

Nearly every free white male was legally obligated to have a gun readily available to him. The only colony that does not appear to have ever imposed such an obligation on its citizens was Pennsylvania.[75] Pennsylvania's exceptionalism was probably because of its Quaker origins and associated pacifism.

First-Person Gun Possession and Hunting Accounts

Virginia

In Virginia, John Hammond's 1656 account tells us that there was little hunting when Jamestown was first settled: "for they durst neither hunt, fowl, nor Fish, for fear of the Indian, which they stood in aw[e] of." But later, the common people felt free "to range the wood for flesh, the rivers for fowle and fish." Referring to his own experiences in Virginia,

"Water-fowle of all sortes are (with admiration to be spoken of) plenti-full and easie to be killed. . . . [Deer] all over the Country, and in many places so many that venison is accounted a tiresome meat; wilde Tur-keys are frequent, and so large that I have seen weigh neer threescore pounds."[76]

Virginia laws also suggest that hunting with guns was common. A 1632 statute licensed hunting wild pigs, but "any man be permitted to kill deare or other wild beasts or fowle in the common woods, forests, or rivers. . . . That thereby the inhabitants may be trained in the use of theire armes, the Indians kept from our plantations, and the wolves and other vermine destroyed." A March 1661–1662 statute prohibited "hunting and shooting of diverse men" on land without the owner's per-mission, "whereby many injuryes doe dayly happen to the owners of the said land." The statute also provided that it was lawful to pursue game shot elsewhere onto private land without permission. A 1699 statute, "prohibiting the unseasonable killing of Deer," complained about how the deer population "is very much destroyed and diminished" by killing "Does bigg with young."[77]

Robert Beverley's 1705 description of Virginia described hunting with guns as a common sport. "I am but a small Sports-man, yet with a Fowling-Piece, have kill'd above Twenty of them at a Shot. In like man-ner are the Mill-Ponds, and great Runs in the Woods stor'd with these Wild-Fowl, at certain seasons of the Year." He described how the "Inner Lands . . . have the Advantage of Wild Turkeys, of an incridible Bigness, Pheasants, Partridges, Pigeons, and an Infinity of small Birds." Beverley lists "Bears, Panthers, Wild-Cats, Elks, Buffaloes, and Wild Hogs, which yield Pleasure, as well as Profit to the Sports-man." Beverley's description of "the Recreations, and Pastimes used in Virginia" includes "Hunting, Fishing, and Fowling." While hunting includes both pursuit with dogs and on horseback, Beverley tells us that Virginians killed wolves with guns, using bait tied to the trigger, "so that when [the wolf] offers to seize the bait, he pulls the trigger, and the gun discharges upon him."[78]

In 1772, Virginia passed a statute regulating deer hunting because of complaints that "many idle people making a practice, in severe frozen weather, and deep snows, to destroy deer, in great numbers, with dogs, so that the whole breed is likely to be destroyed, in the inhabited parts of the colony." The government's concern with this was that "numbers of disorderly persons . . . almost destroyed the breed, by which the inhabit-ants . . . be deprived of that wholesome and agreeable food." Therefore, deer hunting was completely prohibited until August 1, 1776.[79]

Plymouth

William Bradford's account of the Plymouth Colony used an expression that suggests that guns were sufficiently common to constitute a common body of experience: "within pistol shot of the house."[80] *Mourt's Relation*, published in 1622, concerning the Plymouth Colony, used a target shooting practice as a metaphor for his writing: "though through my slender judgment I should miss the mark, and not strike the nail on the head."[81]

French pirates robbed a Plymouth Colony settlement at Penobscot in 1633. The manner in which Bradford describes how the pirates gained the upper hand gives no indication that guns were unusual or scarce:

> Seeing but three or four simple men that were servants, and by this Scotchman understanding that the master and the rest of the company were gone from home, they fell of commending their guns and muskets that lay upon racks by the wall side, and took them down to look upon them, asking if they were charged.[82]

Eyewitness accounts indicate that these laws requiring gun ownership were effective. Issack de Rasieres, a visitor from New Netherlands, described 1627 Plymouth and "the Sabbath-day procession up the hill to worship, every man armed and marching three abreast."[83]

One of the accounts in *Mourt's Relation* described hunting with guns by the first party of Pilgrims to land. Their prey included ducks and geese. Another account described how Miles Standish's party, on an expedition to make contact with the Indians in January 1621, "shot at an eagle and killed her, which was excellent meat; it was hardly to be discerned from mutton." Another description from February 9, 1621, mentioned "the master going ashore, killed five geese, which he friendly distributed among the sick people."[84]

Mourt's Relation, one of the small number of primary sources about early Plymouth, also discussed the abundance of fowl and that they were being hunted with guns. Colonists were encouraged to bring guns with them: "Bring every man a musket or fowling-piece; let your piece be long in the barrel, and fear not the weight of it, for most of our shooting is from stands." Edward Winslow described how when Chief Massasoit was on death's door, Massasaoit asked Winslow to "take my piece, and kill him some fowl, and make him some English pottage, such as he had eaten at Plymouth." Winslow did so, and Massasoit recovered. Issack de Rasieres's circa 1628 account of Plymouth Colony described hunting the birds that stole the colonists' corn: "Sometimes we take them by surprise and fire amongst them with hail-shot, immediately that we have made them rise, so that sixty, seventy, and eighty fall all at once." He also described hunting turkeys and geese.[85]

Emmanuel Altham's 1623 description of the Plymouth Colony described the advantages of this new land, rich in both fish and fowl. "Here are eagles of many sorts, pigeons, innumerable turkeys, geese, swan, duck, teel, partridge divers sorts, and many other fowl, [so] that one man at six shoots hath killed 400." At least some of the Pilgrims hunted deer as well; Altham listed three or four venison brought by the Indians to Governor Bradford's wedding, with another seven or eight provided by the inhabitants of Plymouth.[86]

Massachusetts

Francis Higginson's 1630 description of Massachusetts describes widespread hunting:

> Fowls of the air are plentiful here, and of all sorts as we have in England as far as I can learn, and a great many of strange fowls which we know not. Whilst I was writing these things, one of our men brought home an eagle which he had killed in the wood. They say they are good meat. Also here are many kinds of excellent hawks, both sea hawks and land hawks. And myself walking in the woods with another in company, sprung a partridge so big that through the heaviness of his body could fly but a little way. They that have killed them say they are as big as our hens. Here are likewise abundance of turkeys often killed in the woods, far greater than our English turkeys, and exceeding fat, sweet and fleshy, for here they have abundance of feeding all the year long, such as strawberries: in summer all places are full of them, and all manner of berries and fruits. In the winter time I have seen flocks of pigeons, and have eaten of them. . . . In winter time this country doth abound with wild geese, wild ducks, and other sea fowl, that a great part of winter the planters have eaten nothing but roastmeat of divers fowls which they have killed.[87]

Johnson's Wonder-Working Providence describes how the Massachusetts Bay Colony dealt with the antinomian heresy of Anne Hutchinson in 1637. Hutchinson's beliefs spread rapidly through Puritan society, and some persons being so hot headed for maintaining of these sinfull opinions, that they feared breach of peace, even among the Members of the superiour Court[,] . . . those in place of government caused certain persons to be disarmed in the severall Townes, as in the Towne of Boston, to the number of 58, in the Towne of Salem 6, in the Towne of Newbery 3, in the Towne of Roxbury 5, in the Towne of Ipswitch 2, and Charles Towne 2.[88]

Massachusetts's population was estimated at 15,000 in 1640, and Boston's population at 15.2 percent of the entire colony, or 2,280.[89] Keeping in mind that Hutchinson's followers were a small fraction of the colony, this means at least 2.5 percent of Boston was considered so hot-headed that they needed to be disarmed. This suggests widespread gun ownership.

Other accounts, while not explicit as to how common guns were in private hands, seem to treat large bodies of armed colonists in Massachusetts as unsurprising. A description of a battle at Pemaquid, in Maine, discusses how the people of Falmouth turned out to respond to an Indian attack: "the whole number of Men being all called together had Ammunition delivered them." Because the bullets were the wrong caliber for their guns, "they were forced to beat their Bullets into Slugs."[90]

New Haven Colony

Other evidence that suggests guns were both inexpensive and fairly common comes from a 1645 civil suit. A Stephen Medcalfe purchased a gun from a Francis Linley. "Stephen asked him if it were a good one, he answered yea, as any was in the towne, whereupon they bargained, and Stephen was to give him 17s. As Stephen was going out of [doors] he questioned the sufficiency of the locke, Francis told him indeed John Nash told him she was not worth 3d." (John Nash was the son of the colony's armorer, Thomas Nash, and appears to have also been a gunsmith; Thomas Nash is also a direct ancestor of the author.)

It turns out that John Nash had earlier warned Linley that "the gunne was naught, that it was not worth 3d., that the barrel was thinne and would not bear a new [breech]." The gun was indeed "naught," and when Medcalfe fired "said gunne, the [breech] flew out & struck into his eye and wounded him deepe and dangerously into the head."[91]

At no point was this gun purchase treated as remarkable. The account of how Medcalfe bought the gun from Linley suggests that it was a spur of the moment decision—and unremarkable: "Stephen Medcalfe complained that he going into the howse of John Linley, Francis Linley, his brother, being in the howse told him he would sell him a gunne."[92]

Maryland

An account of 1630s Maryland describes an abundance of wild game. While not explicit that settlers would be hunting, there are recommendations that all settlers should bring supplies that seem most appropriate for hunting. Among those supplies, under the heading "Provision for Fishing and Fowling," are "Leade, Fowling-pieces of sixe foote; Powder and Shott, and Flint Stones; a good Water-Spaniell."[93]

George Alsop's 1666 description of Maryland tells us that while Indians hunted game for sale to the settlers, large numbers of animals were "killed by the Christian Inhabitant, that doth it more for recreation, than for the benefit they reap by it." Alsop describes how his master's house "had at one time in his house fourscore Venisons." What was a delicacy in England had become dull: "plain bread was rather courted and desired than it."[94] Guns were used to protect sheep from wolves and to hunt waterfowl.

Most significantly with respect to how common gun ownership was, Alsop, who spent four years in Maryland as an indentured servant, explained that there was relatively little work to be done in winter, "unless their Ingenuity will prompt them to hunt the Deer, or Bear, or recreate themselves in Fowling, to slaughter the Swans, Geese, and Turkeys. . . . For every Servant has a Gun, Powder and Shot allowed him, to sport him withal on all Holidayes and leasureable times, if he be capable of using it, or be willing to learn."[95]

For 17th-century Marylanders, "Hunting, sometimes for sport but mainly for pot, occupied many hours."[96] Alsop's account is consistent with the Maryland militia laws of 1638, 1642, and 1658, which required every householder to have a gun for every man in the house, including servants,[97] and the other Maryland, Carolina, and Virginia accounts that indicate that guns and hunting by the settlers were common.

Maryland regulated hunting, and the nature of those laws suggests that hunting was fairly common. A 1648 law complained that because previously issued licenses for "killing of Wild Hoggs [and] [e]mploying Indians to kill deere with Gunnes" both by residents and nonresidents of Maryland "hath occasioned some inconvenience & hath given great offence to divers of the Inhabitants of this Province," all existing licenses were repealed. In 1650, the law prohibited foreigners "either English or Indian" from hunting "in any part of this Province or kill any Venison or other Game" without a license from the governor.[98]

A 1654 Maryland law sought to prohibit shooting on Sundays: "Noe work shall be done on the Sabboth day but that which is of Necessity and Charity to be done[,] no Inordinate Recreations as fowling, fishing, hunting or other, no shooting of Gunns be used on that day Except in Case of Necessity." Following prohibitions on drunkenness, swearing, and gossiping, the goal was to improve the morals of the population and was not specifically directed at guns. In 1678, this law was expanded to prohibit a larger list of amusements, but it still prohibited fishing and hunting on the Sabbath.[99]

Scharf's *History of Western Maryland* (1882) described how frontier Marylanders lived at the time of the French and Indian War. He quoted one of the settlers of the time about the early education of boys:

A well-grown boy at the age of twelve or thirteen years was furnished with a small rifle and shot-pouch. . . . Hunting squirrels, turkeys, and raccoons soon made him expert in the use of his gun. . . . Shooting at a mark was a common diversion among the men when their stock of ammunition would allow it.[100]

North and South Carolina

Robert Horne's 1666 description of Carolina (not yet divided into North and South) tells how every freeman who arrived before March 25, 1667, would receive a large allotment of land, "Provided always, That every Man be armed with a good Musquet . . . to serve them whilst they raise Provision in that Countrey." While not explicit that settlers required muskets and ammunition to feed themselves, preceding pages described the variety and abundance of game available in the Carolina woods.[101]

Other accounts of early Carolina were explicit that hunting was a source of both food and sport. Thomas Ashe wrote, "Birds for Food, and pleasure of Game, are the Swan, Goose, Duck, Mallard, Wigeon, Teal, Curlew, Plover, Partridge, the Flesh of which is equally as good, tho' smaller than ours in England." Ashe told merchants to bring commodities, including "all kinds of Ammunition, Guns, Fowling-pieces, Powder, Match, Bullet."[102]

John Archdale's 1707 description of Carolina told how the land contained "vast Quantities or Numbers of wild Ducks, Geese, Teal," and that because there was no need to cut and store winter fodder, one "can employ their Hands in raising other Commodities as aforesaid." Archdale's sentence is unclear, but he seemed to say that in winter, when there were few farm chores, the profusion of wild game meant that the hired hands could be out hunting food[103]—essentially what Alsop had said Maryland servants did in winter, four decades earlier.

A 1738 North Carolina "Act, to Prevent killing Deer, at Unseasonable Times" made it unlawful "to kill or destroy any Deer . . . by Gun, or other Ways and Means whatsoever" from February 15 to July 15.[104]

In 1769, the Cherokees complained to the North Carolina colonial government of "numerous bodys of hunters from North Carolina having this year infested their hunting Grounds and destroyed their game."[105] It is unlikely that the Cherokees were complaining about just a few hunters.

Pennsylvania

William Penn's 1681 description of Pennsylvania included that "Fowl, Fish, and Wild-Deer . . . are reported to be plentiful." Penn warned settlers that for the first year they should plan on buying grain, as they would not yet have productive land. Livestock would be available for purchase at once, and would rapidly increase. But after the first year, "what with the Poorer sort, sometimes labouring to others, and the more able Fishing, Fowling and sometimes Buying."[106] In 1683, Penn described "Fish, Fowl, and the Beasts of the Wood, here are divers sorts, some for Food and Profit, and some for Profit only."[107]

Penn's "Frame of the Government" for Pennsylvania granted to the inhabitants of the province "liberty to fowl and hunt upon the lands they hold, and all other lands therein not inclosed." Almost 20 years later, in 1701, Penn reiterated, "They shall have Liberty to fish, fowle and hunt upon their own Land, and on all other lands that are mine untaken up."[108] This is not direct evidence that hunting was common in Pennsylvania, but it does suggest that Penn considered the ability to hunt an important enticement for settlers.

Gabriel Thomas's 1698 account of Pennsylvania also suggests that hunting was a common activity: "Here is curious Diversion in Hunting, Fishing, and Fowling, especially upon that Great and Famous River [Susquehannah]." Thomas describes purchasing deer from the Indians for gunpowder, and also relates that "there are vast Numbers of other Wild Creatures, as Elks, Bufalos, etc., all which as well Beasts, Fowl, and Fish, are free and common to any Person who can shoot or take them, without any lett, hinderance or Opposition whatsoever."[109]

Alexander Graydon, growing up in Philadelphia circa 1765, gave this picture of his boyhood pleasures:

If furnished, on Saturday afternoon or other holyday, with cash enough for the purchase of powder and shot, or the hire of a batteau or skiff, as the propensity of the day might incline, I had nothing more to wish for. . . .

In my water excursions, the sedgy shores of the Delaware, as well as the reedy cover of Petty's, League and Mud Islands, were pervaded and explored in pursuit of ducks, reed-bird and rail.[110]

New York

Danckaerts, visiting America in 1679–1680, described a marsh near Flatbush, New York, where the inhabitants "go mostly to shoot snipe and wild geese." Danckaerts also described how Shooter's Island in New York (then Schutter's Island) received its name: "This island is so called, because the Dutch, when they first settled on the North River, were in the practice of coming here to shoot wild geese, and other wild fowl, which resorted there in great numbers." On Long Island, "We dined with Jaques; and his little son came and presented us a humming-bird he had shot."[111]

On Staten Island, Danckaerts reported, "Game of all kinds is plenty, and twenty-five and thirty deer are sometimes seen in a herd. A boy who came into a house where we were, told us he had shot ten the last winter himself, and more than forty in his life, and in the same manner other game."[112] Somewhere between New York City and Maryland, Danckaerts tells of a miller with whom he had stayed: "The miller had shot an animal they call a muskrat, the skin of which we saw hanging up to dry."[113]

At a plantation on Chesapeake Bay, Danckaerts stayed the night. In the morning, he and his traveling companion were given directions by "the son, who went out to shoot at daylight." Danckaerts expresses amazement at the number of ducks together in front of the house.

The son was not alone.

There was a boy about twelve years old who took aim at them from the shore, not being able to get within good shooting distance of them, but nevertheless shot loosely before they flew away, and hit only three or four, complained of his shot, as they are accustomed to shoot from six to twelve and even eighteen or more at one shot.[114]

Danckaerts described, a few days later, noise from flocks of waterfowl: "It is not peculiar to this place alone, but it occurred on all the creeks and rivers we crossed, though they were most numerous in the morning and evening when they are most easily shot."[115]

Another incident Danckaerts wrote about was the conflict between a Christian Indian named Wouter and his white uncle, who believed that "a mere stupid Indian, could not shoot." The account described how the two of them, both armed with guns, went deer hunting together in upstate New York. Wouter bagged a deer; his uncle did not.[116]

A search for "gun," "pistol," and "fowling piece" in New York City's wills and estate inventories from 1665 through 1790 found hundreds of matches; some people owned multiple guns.[117] We also have examples, such as Solomon Peters, a prosperous New York farmer and free black at the close of the 17th century. His 1694 will bequeathed his guns, swords, and pistols to his sons.[118]

New Jersey

A 1722 New Jersey "Act to prevent the Killing of Deer out of Season" prohibited deer hunting from January through June. That same law included a provision prohibiting "Persons carrying of Guns, and presuming to Hunt on other Peoples Land," explaining that it was required because "divers Abuses have been committed, and great Damages and Inconveniencies arisen." The same act prohibited a slave from hunting or carrying a gun without the permission of his master.[119]

Connecticut

Were guns rare? While necessarily anecdotal, we have evidence, such as a lawsuit in 1639 by a "Jno. Moody contra Blachford, for a fowling peece he bought and should have payd for it 40s." In 1640, a William Hill is fined £4, "for buying a stolen peece of Mr. Plums man." In 1644, a Robert Bedle is fined for stealing gunpowder from a Mr. Blakman.[120] There is nothing in the reports of any of these cases that suggests that guns were rare or unusual items.

David Humphreys's circa 1740 account of a Connecticut wolf hunt indicated that when a particular wolf's predations became serious enough,

> Mr. Putnam entered into a combination with five of his neighbors to hunt alternately until they could destroy her. . . . By ten o'clock the next morning the bloodhounds had driven her into a den, about three miles distant from the house of Mr. Putnam.

The people soon collected with dogs, guns, straw, fire, and sulphur, to attack the common enemy.[121]

If guns were scarce, or hunting unusual, there is nothing in these lawsuits or Humphreys's account that would indicate so.

Gunpowder Importation

Gunpowder import records also provide some clues about gun ownership and use. The British Board of Trade recorded quantities of gunpowder imported through American ports for a brief period just before the Revolution. We have surviving records for the years 1769, 1770, and 1771 that show the American colonies imported a total of 1,030,694 pounds for those three years.[122] Of course, this only shows gunpowder imported with knowledge of the Crown; Americans smuggled goods quite regularly during those years and may well have made some of their own.

Gunpowder was used not only for civilian small arms but also for cannon, blasting, and (in extremely small quantities) for tattooing. It seems likely that at least some of these million pounds of gunpowder ended up being sold to the British military, colonial governments, or the Indians. Nonetheless, the quantity is enormous. If guns were scarce, the small number of Americans who had guns did *a lot* of shooting. Even if only one-quarter of that million pounds of gunpowder was used in civilian small arms, that is enough for 11–17 million shots over those three years.[123]

How common was hunting in Colonial America? It is difficult to say with any certainty. The evidence, however, suggests what common sense would also suggest: in a country where there were few legal restrictions prohibiting hunting, where game was abundant, and where many settlers had some leisure time in which to engage in a traditional sport, hunting with guns, and therefore gun possession, appears to have been common.

Pistols

Bellesiles claimed that "few pistols had been made in the United States prior to the opening of the [Colt] Hartford factory [in 1848], pistols having found little market beyond the officers in the army and navy."[124] (It important to note that while "handgun" and "pistol" are technically interchangeable terms, common usage today distinguishes semiautomatic pistols from revolvers, both of which are handguns. In addition, "pistol" is often distinguished from "gun" in common usage of the Colonial period: "gun" included only shotguns and rifles.)

Pistols were made in America in the 18th century, but most Americans preferred to buy pistols imported from Britain. A number of surviving pistols were manufactured in America before 1848. Some had sights and rifled barrels at a time when both were uncommon in British pistols, implying that even if small, the American gun industry was cutting edge.[125]

Pistol ads appear in the *Boston Gazette* as early as 1720. Sampling ads from the 1741–1742 period reveal at least two different merchants offering pistols for sale, one of whom, Samuel Miller, identified himself as a gunsmith.[126]

A gang of robbers, having terrorized New York City, moved on to Philadelphia in 1749. A newspaper account of their crimes reported that "two Men, unknown, were lately at Mr. Rush's, a Gun smith, enquiring for six Pair of Pocket Pistols, to make up twelve Pair, having as they said, got the six Pair at some other Place."[127] Colonial statutes regulating misuse of firearms specifically mention pistols as early as 1774.[128] In 1742, Samuel Miller of Boston, a gunsmith, advertised "Neat Fire Arms of all sorts, Pistols, Swords."[129] Perhaps these pistols were intended for military officers—but in 1742, with no standing army, this would not have been a large market. We have the surviving pistols made for William Smith of Farmington, Connecticut, by Medad Hills in 1771, with American-made barrels and apparently English locks.[130] Heinrich Diebenberger advertised pistols in Pennsylvania newspapers in 1772 and 1773.[131]

Gun ownership was widespread, as demonstrated by statutes requiring gun ownership, fines for failure to be armed, lawsuits, criminal cases, literary accounts of hunting with guns, and advertising of guns for sale. Pistol ownership can only be described as common, although perhaps not universal, from literary accounts and ads.

CHAPTER 2

Counting Gunsmiths: Methodological Problems

Along with the preceding chapter's substantial evidence of wide-spread colonial gun ownership, both for hunting and self-defense; gunsmithing; and gunmaking provide a substantial body of evidence for the origins of American gun culture. This is also an insufficiently explored aspect of American economic and industrial history.

In evaluating American gunsmithing capabilities, the first problem to be resolved is the word *gunsmith*, which can include many possible meanings. It can mean a person who repairs broken guns. It can also mean someone who assembles guns from parts produced by others, the manufacture of individual components, or the manufacture and assembly of all components.

The presence of gunsmiths would be an indicator that guns were being repaired and therefore being used by the population of Colonial America. Bellesiles's claim that there were only a handful of gunsmiths in America in the first 150 years of settlement is implausible.

Of course, repairing guns is not the same as making them. While acknowledging that Americans often restocked existing guns (replacing the wooden stock) and sometimes assembled guns from foreign parts, Bellesiles rejects the notion that Americans had the capacity to produce guns in any real quantity, and he consequently argues that the nongovernmental market for guns before 1840 was small.[1]

Other historians hold a different view. Felicia Deyrup, one of the few historians of New England firearms manufacturing, concludes, concerning Colonial New England gunsmithing, that guns were often manufactured and assembled entirely by one person or with an apprentice or two. Even in larger American cities, where there was some division of labor, a single shop would often make all the components of a gun (with the exception of gunlocks, which were usually, although not always, imported). As firearms historian James Whisker explains, "Though apparently few early colonial gunsmiths made their own gun locks, by 1770 the Colonies were probably self-sufficing in the production of hunting weapons."[2]

There *were* large numbers of self-described "gunsmiths" in Colonial, Revolutionary, and Early Republic America, as attested to by contracts, advertisements, city directories, wills, deeds, population censuses, and the surviving guns that they had built (as will be discussed in detail in subsequent chapters). While determining exactly which functions a particular gunsmith performed is difficult, because the information that we have concerning many of these gunsmiths is so scanty, the evidence is clear that gunsmiths were *very* common in Colonial, Revolutionary, and Early Republic America.

Bellesiles argues that gunsmiths had so little work to do that most primarily worked as blacksmiths and described themselves as such.[3] But even if true (and we will demonstrate below that it is not), this is not necessarily evidence that there was little demand for gunsmithing. It might equally be evidence that in an era when most Americans lived in small towns, where narrow specialization would limit one's potential customers, a person skilled at any form of metalworking needed to perform whatever work was in demand. Indeed, works with no ax to grind on the subject of gun ownership in America, such as *Early American Ironware*, are explicit: the two related trades of gunsmithing and blacksmithing were often followed by one man, and for a very good reason:

> It is known that, at times, a gun was made by a number of craftsmen; and that at other times, a complete gun was made by one man. It is also apparent that much forge work was required to forge and weld a gun barrel, to forge and fit the lock parts, and to forge iron mountings such as the trigger guard, the butt plates and other small parts.[4]

This combining of the two trades, or alternating trades from year to year, was apparently common during both the Revolutionary War period and in peacetime. Deyrup also indicates that the combination of gunsmithing and blacksmithing was common throughout New England because gunsmithing as an occupation was limited by population density.[5]

Other combined trades are also in evidence, such as "W. Clevell, a gun- and locksmith who worked in Bushkill Township, Northampton County, Pennsylvania, in 1820." Henry Dippeberger, a Pennsylvania gunsmith, advertised his trade as "making and repairing arms and bleed-ing instruments, also instruments for cupping and for use on the teeth. He sells also pistols, guns, and gun barrels, also all kinds of flint and gun locks." In 1774, Walter Dick of South Carolina advertised himself as "Gunsmith and Cutler. . . . Makes and dresses all manner of [surgical] and other instruments; makes cork screws and Pen-Knives. . . . Gold and other Scales and Beams made and adjusted with the greatest exactness. Locks and keys of all kinds made and mended."[6]

Another expression of this broad approach to metalworking is an ad from the *New Hampshire Gazette* of July 17, 1767, that simply described Joseph Hammond's trade as, "Smith," who "performs all Sorts of the Iron of Boat Work, Chaise and Chair Work[,] cleaning and mending of Guns, Pistols, Locks and Keys, cleans and mends Jacks, Shoes Horses, and makes all sorts of Kitchen furniture, and sorts of Hinges for Houses, &c."[7] It seems doubtful that Joseph Hammond would appear in any list of "gunsmiths," but he certainly found it worth his while to advertise his ability to mend guns.

James Whisker, another historian of the early American gunmak-ing trade, devotes an entire chapter to gunsmiths who worked at other trades, sometimes at different times, sometimes at the same time. While many of the other trades are unsurprising (*e.g.,* clockmakers, locksmiths, blacksmiths), others are quite far removed from the metal trades, includ-ing potters, doctors, and umbrella makers.[8] This combination of trades seems to have been the most unusual of all:

> Ignatius Leitner [describing his new business location]. . . . Where he continues to draw deeds, mortgages, Power of Attorney, apprentice indentures, Bills, Notes, State executor and adminstrators accounts. He will as usual clerk at vendues [auctions] and take inventories and all other instruments of writing done on shortest notice. N.B. He contin-ues and keeps hands at work in his former branches as making rifles, still cocks, casting rivets, gun mountings, etc. at the lowest prices.[9]

To add to the problem of identifying blacksmiths who were also gun-smiths, blacksmiths were by far the most common metal craftsmen in America in the 18th and 19th centuries.[10] If even a fraction of black-smiths also did some unadvertised gun repair, this would be a substantial number of uncounted part-time gunsmiths.

We know about a number of the gunsmiths from tax lists that identify a person by his trade. How many of these craftsmen were primarily engaged in some other occupation (such as blacksmithing) but did gunsmithing as well? James Hadden is identified as a gunsmith in a 1769 City of Philadelphia tax list. On the same page, there are 15 other taxpayers with no trade or occupation listed.[11] It seems likely that many of them were common laborers, but this is only an assumption. Our knowledge of the number of gunsmiths based on tax lists is, at best, a minimum count.

There are some highly ambiguous trades listed as well. A Lewis Brall, "smith," shows up in the City of Philadelphia tax list for 1769. What kind of smith was he—blacksmith, gunsmith, tinsmith, or perhaps all three? In 1776, a gunsmith named Lewis Prahl worked for the Pennsylvania government and made guns.[12] Brall might be an alternate spelling of Prahl. And what about Jacob Brown, who is also listed on that same page with the ambiguous "smith"?

To alleviate this shortage of records, I have gathered information on all gunsmiths for whom I have the years and locations in which they performed their trade. (This appears in an online catalog described in appendix A.) In many cases, we know nothing about them other than that they were a "gunsmith" or apprenticed to a gunsmith to learn that trade. In other cases, we know that they made guns or made guns of a particular type. These gunsmiths were identified from references to them in documents.

There is a large existing literature on early American gunsmiths that was originally created in response to the interests of those who collect early American guns. The quality of the research done for these books varies. Some are primarily lists based on surviving guns that are identified by the maker's marks, which are sometimes ambiguous. These often provide us with nothing more than evidence that a specific person made guns with a technology (such as flintlock ignition) that are present over a period of many years in a particular but sometimes very broad era. Others make extensive use of business directories, census records, and government contracts and are usually properly cited. The catalog described in appendix A is derived from a combination of the most careful of this existing literature and primary sources located during my research.

It does seem likely that at least some of the early American gunsmith literature is in error, failing to recognize that a particular gunmaker may have used different marks or spellings of his name in different records or on different guns. Some of this existing literature is likely erroneous because it was not produced under the exacting standards of citation required of historians.

One measure of the completeness of the various lists of gunsmiths is the amount of overlap. Are there gunsmiths that appear in only one or two sources but are missing from others? If so, it suggests that there is still considerable research to be done to create a comprehensive list. Creating my database makes it clear that there *is* significant overlap—and yet there are still gunsmiths that appear in one, and only one, source. For example, the Buffalo, New York directory published by L. P. Crary in 1832 includes nine gunsmiths—none of whom appear in any secondary lists of gunsmiths. It appears that none of the compilers of these gunsmith lists used Crary's directory. On the other hand, an 1800 Boston directory lists four gunsmiths, three of whom appear in secondary lists and one that appears in none. The same is true for an 1805 Boston directory; three appear elsewhere, and one appears nowhere else.[13] However, it seems likely that for every gunsmith included in the database described in appendix A that should not be there, there is probably at least one gunsmith who actually worked at his craft in early America that is not listed.

If few gunsmiths were able to stay in business, and thus changed professions, why, then, do we find gunsmiths advertising for help? Francis Brooks, a Philadelphia gunsmith, advertised in 1791 for an apprentice. Peter Brong, a Lancaster, Pennsylvania, gunsmith, advertised for "Lock filers: Such as soon apply will receive the highest Wages." Apparently Brong sought craftsmen skilled at filing gunlocks to fit.[14] In 1796, Henry Albright of Chambersburg, Pennsylvania, advertised that he would take on "a Lad from 12 to 15 years of age" as an apprentice for the gunsmithing business.[15] Isaac Price took on at least four apprentices between 1776 and 1787. One of these apprentices, Zenos Alexander, became a gunsmith and took on at least three apprentices in the period 1805–1810.[16] John Gonter of Hagerstown, Maryland, had at least five apprentices in his gunsmithing business between 1794 and 1799.[17] In 1800, Ralph Atmar Jr., a Charleston goldsmith, engraver, and gunsmith, advertised for an apprentice to learn goldsmithing, "and may gain an insight in the Mechanism of Guns."[18] Indentured servant gunsmiths also appear in the records, such as runaway John Kenster, "born in London. . . . He is a gunsmith by trade,"[19] and "William Nicholls . . . is an expert gunsmith."[20]

John Armstrong, a gunsmith who made rifles in Emmitsburg, Maryland, from 1793 or 1794 to at least 1837, had at least four apprentices that we know about. They were bound to Armstrong in 1799, 1801, 1804, and about 1837. There were doubtless other apprentices during Armstrong's career, but because Frederick County stopped recording most apprentice indentures in 1805, the rest are lost to history. At least two of the apprentices show up in other sources as gunsmiths. It is not certain that the George Piper apprenticed to Armstrong in 1801 at age 18 is the same George Piper who worked in Shippensburg, Pennsylvania, from 1834 to 1843. Marine Tiler Wickham, apprenticed to Armstrong in 1799 at age 19, eventually became a government arms inspector and designed the U.S. Model 1812 Musket and Model 1813 Pistol. He also worked as a gunsmith in private practice in later years.[21]

James Whisker devotes 46 pages to an examination of gunsmithing and apprentices, with dozens of examples of orphans, minors, and even adults apprenticed to learn this trade.[22] It seems unlikely that a profession with little or no employment opportunities would induce so many to accept apprenticeship. Similarly, if gunsmiths were short of work, it is a bit odd that so many were interested in taking on apprentices that had to be fed, boarded, and clothed.

Another problem with identifying gunsmiths and gunmakers is the paucity of newspaper advertisements. Many of the early newspapers from which we might gather advertisements are gone forever.

A gunsmith would have advertised when business was slow and he needed more business, or when starting or moving his business. A paucity of ads, rather than being an indication that there was little demand for gunsmiths or gunmakers, might actually be an indication that business was good and word of mouth was sufficient to keep a gunsmith employed in what were, by modern standards, small villages. Only a few "cities" at the end of the 18th century, such as Philadelphia, New York, and Boston, would even qualify as small towns today.

We have evidence that relying on advertising and official records misses a great many such craftsmen. Jacob Dickert is represented in *Early American Gunsmiths* by three entries: a death notice from the Moravian Church Archives that tells us he moved to Lancaster, Pennsylvania, in 1758 and died in 1822; an advertisement on November 10, 1800, announcing the breakup of the partnership of Dickert & Gill, a gunsmithing business; and a rifle marked "J. Dickert."[23]

It seems unlikely that Jacob Dickert was only in the gunsmithing business in 1800, but in the absence of any other evidence, we cannot prove any other years. How many gunsmiths were Dickert's contemporaries, whose guns have not survived and whose ads and records have been lost for all time? We do not know, but it seems likely that there were others, perhaps many others.

Often, we know of gunsmiths by reference but not by name. An 1825 travel account reported "3 gunsmith shops" in Rochester, New York.[24] A history of Lancaster, Massachusetts, lists the various businesses present in 1826 as including "one gunsmith."[25] Similarly, St. Augustine, Florida, had "one gunsmith" in 1837.[26]

We know of James Phips, a gunsmith who settled on the Maine coast in 1643, because his son William became governor of Massachusetts after an illustrious military career. Had Sir William Phips not made a place for himself in history, it is likely that we would not know about his father, a colonial gunsmith. Other early gunsmiths on the coast of Maine are known only by official records that refer to their involvement with the military or Indian trade.[27]

A 1737 advertisement describes where a sale of merchandise would be held: "William Cathcart next door to Mr. Miller's the Gun-smith in Church-street" This is the only reference to Mr. Miller "the Gun-smith." In 1773, Jacob Allen, "Gun-smith," had a shop in Maiden Lane, New York City—and the only clue to his business is that another merchant's ad described his location as "between the House of Mr. Jacob Allen's .. Gun-smith and Mr. John Taylor Brass-Founder." The only known reference to a "Mr. Prevost, gunsmith," is the exhibition of a miniature version of a European city on display in his shop in 1763.

How many other colonial gunsmiths have disappeared from history because none of their neighbors had occasion in an ad to mention the gunsmith next door? We know about gunsmith Daniel Nash (the son of one of my direct ancestors), who worked in Southfield, Massachusetts, in 1699, only because a stolen gun was found in his shop, and thus Nash's shop was mentioned in the consequent criminal case. John Whitten was clearly a gunsmith in 1760 Boston, based on the inventory for which he sought reimbursement ("25 Gun locks . . . 22 Fire Arms" and various gunsmithing tools) after his shop was destroyed, with many others, in the great fire of that year.[28]

A slave gunsmith named Caesar was responsible for cleaning and repairing the arms of the South Carolina militia stored in the magazine in Charleston. How do we know that he was a gunsmith? He was caught by his master with a duplicate key to the public magazine and was deported to a less desirable colony in the West Indies. Whisker has a considerable discussion of black gunsmiths in the Colonial period, both free and slave.[29]

Many gunsmiths we know of only because their occupation is identified in a single document, such as the identification of Peter Elsworth and Samuel Ploug as gunsmiths in a 1775 Continental Army muster roll from New York; or Hugh McCain's entry in the 1800 Pennsylvania state census; or Warren Lyon in the 1824 Providence, Rhode Island, directory;

or Christian Kline's appearance in an 1817 tax list in Dauphin County, Pennsylvania.[30] How many years before and after 1775, 1800, 1817, and 1824 did each of these gunsmiths work at that trade? We do not know, but it seems unlikely that we were fortunate enough to catch each of these gunsmiths in the only year in which they worked.

In other cases, we have records of gunsmiths in two scattered years. As an example, Robert McCartney is listed as a gunsmith at Theater Alley, Boston, Massachusetts, in the Boston Directories of 1805 and 1816. It seems unlikely that he only worked in those two listed years, pursuing some other profession from 1806 through 1815. Did he work as a gunsmith before 1805 and after 1816? Perhaps. But this takes us from the realm of interpolation into extrapolation. When the surviving records demonstrate that a gunsmith was present at his occupation in several different years, it seems a good bet that he worked continuously at that profession throughout that period, absent other evidence.

Jacob Loesch Jr. was a gunsmith in the Moravian community of Salem, North Carolina. We know that he worked as a gunsmith in 1782 and 1783, and that he worked as one before and possibly after those years. The Moravian community prohibited him from working as a gunsmith on December 28, 1781, for fear that it would attract soldiers to town, but it lifted the prohibition on March 5, 1782, at Loesch's request. Loesch died in "Fayittville" in 1821. He had most likely worked as gunsmith in Philadelphia before 1781 and in various locations in North Carolina from 1783 to 1821.[31] But we really cannot confirm any years except 1782 and 1783. It would be foolish to claim that we know that he worked any years *but* 1782 and 1783. But it would also be foolish to claim that we know that he worked for *only* those two years.

We know of some gunsmiths only from a casual reference in other documents, such as John Fraser (or Frazier), "a Pennsylvania gunsmith and Indian trader" who set up shop on the Monongahela River in 1753. In 1771, James Anderson was described as "a blacksmith and gunsmith" who had purchased "Mrs. Campbell's old place" near the Capitol in Williamsburg. By 1777, Anderson had contracted with Virginia to do "Blacksmith's work," but the details of the contract indicate that he was to be paid for the use of tools and vises for gunsmithing as well as the use of two forges. John Cutler advertised himself as a "Black and Gunsmith" in 1757 Boston.[31] A list of soldiers in Captain Andrew Graff's company in 1776 lists Charles Jones, Robert Jones, George Bauer, James Reed, John Gander, and Phillip Wolfheimer as "app. Gunsmith," presumably apprentice gunsmiths.[33]

In 1831, the War Department sent a request to Maj. F. W. Armstrong that he repair all the old rifles belonging to the Choctaws and authorized him to hire "an additional gun-smith" if needed. Similarly, War Department instructions to Lewis Cass specify maximum wages to be paid to gunsmiths providing repair services to the Indians.[34] A comprehensive examination of all documents published before 1840 with the word "gunsmith" would doubtless find vastly more.

A number of gunsmiths worked in the Early Republic, but we know of them only by a few scattered American-made firearms with their names on them and references to them that do not tell us dates. There are many such gunsmiths, such as the Sheetz (or Sheets) family of Lancaster and York Counties in Pennsylvania. We have dates for Philip Sheetz, but for 15 of his descendants and cousins in the Revolutionary period and Early Republic, we know only that they worked as gunsmiths and not the exact years.

Similarly, the Hertzog family produced at least three generations of gunsmiths from 1776 through the 1840s, but we have only partial dates for three of the five Hertzog gunsmiths.[35] The Hawken family of gunsmiths included at least 15 gunsmiths in early America, but firm date information is only available for 10 of them.[36] The Rizor family of gunsmiths suffers from too many cousins with the same first and last names living too close to each other to make sense of who worked as a gunsmith in which years.[37]

Kauffman, a historian of early American ironworkers, lists Christian Paulsey as a gunsmith in Cumberland County, Pennsylvania, but does not provide any dates.[38] Hartzler, a historian of Maryland gunmakers, tells us about the Marker family of gunsmiths—Daniel Marker, George Marker Jr., and Paul Marker, who made rifles that have survived—but gives us nothing more definite than "during the flintlock period."[39]

Similarly, Gluckman and Satterlee's *American Gun Makers*, a list of early American gun manufacturers, lists dozens to hundreds of makers who are known from surviving guns, but we know nothing else about them except that they must have worked in the Colonial or Early Republic periods, based on the design of the gun. As an example, "Follect—or Follecht. Lancaster, Pa. Kentucky rifles, about 1770. . . . Fordney, I.— Unlocated. Flintlock and percussion Kentucky rifles. . . . Millbenz—1825. Unidentified. . . . Miller, W. G.—Unlocated. Late period flintlock and percussion Kentucky rifles."[40] Whisker quotes from William Foulkes's account book for a variety of gunsmithing services provided to a Samuel Harris, sometime between 1763 and 1812, but there is simply not enough information to add Foulkes to our appendix because we do not know the exact years during which Foulkes provided these services.

North Carolina seems to have had a wealth of gunmakers whose activities are known from surviving rifles, but there are no documents. Because these guns can only be dated to general periods, such as "Revolutionary period," their makers have not been included in the database. In North Carolina, these undocumented gunsmiths were often whole families, such as the Kennedy family of Moore County that made guns from the Revolutionary period until after the Civil War.[41]

Similarly, there are some early American-made pistols where the maker is known (some using imported gunlocks and some using American-made ones), but we simply lack the date information required to add them to the database. We have a number of pistols that are unsigned but clearly American-made. While surmises can be made as to their maker, based on similarities to other firearms made by that gunsmith, it would simply be conjecture to add them to the list of pistol makers.[42]

It would be useful to have a population survey with occupations that was sufficiently representative of the population in colonial America that we could sample to determine the number of gunsmiths present. One available sample is the list of men raised for four companies of the Continental Army between July 22 and August 10, 1775. It includes 288 men, two of whom are listed as "gunsmith."

This sample may be atypical because at least two of the companies are from a single county, and it is unclear whether Orange County, New York, was unusually rich in gunsmiths or unusually poor in them.[43] It may be atypical because it would have included those most prone to volunteer for military duty, although there is nothing that would seem to make a gunsmith either more or less prone to volunteer for militia duty. But as a first approximation, it suggests that 0.69 percent of white males in New York were gunsmiths. If this percentage were typical of the United States, it would suggest that there were thousands of gunsmiths in 1775. A somewhat later source of data is an 1823 compilation of the professions of depositors in the Bank for Savings in New York. Out of 1,539 depositors, one was a gunsmith or 0.06 percent.[44]

And yet even the incomplete body of knowledge in appendix A demonstrates that gunsmithing was a common occupation. There are more than a hundred gunsmiths in the Colonial period whose work left some sort of record that survives to the present day. And as we will see, there were far more in the Early Republic.

CHAPTER 3

Colonial Gunsmiths and Manufacturers, 1607–1775

Gunsmiths

How common were gunsmiths in Colonial America? Were they as rare as the revisionists claim? From approximately 1685 to 1700, Charles Town (as Charleston, South Carolina, was then named) had at least two: John Hawkins and John Jones.[1] Other sources list at least two other gunsmiths working in South Carolina before 1700: Anthony Boureau and Augustus Mesmin.[2]

Others who have examined the question of colonial gunsmithing tell a different story:

> The influence of the gunsmith and the production of firearms on nearly every aspect of colonial endeavor in North America cannot be overstated, and that pervasive influence continuously escalated following the colonial era. . . .
> Of all the creative craftsmen identified with colonial America[,] the gunsmith can be considered foremost among them, for he frequently labored with the most basic hand tools under the most primitive conditions to fashion or repair a complex and inordinately vital commodity needed for survival in a pristine and generally hostile environment.[3]

The Plymouth Company "hired London armorer William Pitt[,] who arrived on the *Fortune* in November, 1621." There is no record of him working as a gunsmith, although he was at Plymouth Colony until 1627.[4]

A Massachusetts Bay order of September 8, 1642, directed "that every smith in this jurisdiction, laying aside all other business, do with all speed attend the repairing of the ammunition of the severall townes." While not explicitly gunsmiths, it is hard to imagine that these "smiths" who were asked to repair ammunition were ignorant of the art of gun repair; it certainly makes little sense to expect blacksmiths to repair ammunition (which probably consisted of verifying its effectiveness and perhaps remixing the gunpowder) if they did not have experience with guns. That the order did not list the smiths who were to do this work by name suggests that there were a number of them. The phrase "laying aside all other business"[5] tells us that there were likely other customers seeking gun repair or gunmaking.

Eltweed Pomeroy set up gunsmithing at Dorchester in the Massachusetts Bay Colony in 1630, and male members of his line continued in that line of work until 1849. In 1675, the Massachusetts Colony ordered Captain Timothy Wheeler to "impresse an able gunsmith, who is to repaire to Concorde" to repair guns.[6] There is no evidence that Wheeler impressed a gunsmith, but it seems unlikely that such an order would have been issued if the government did not believe that there were gunsmiths available to impress.

Starting in 1632, Richard Waters operated as a gunsmith in Salem, Massachusetts. Thomas Nash (my ancestor, 19 generations back) "served as town and colony armorer at New Haven," starting in 1640. James Phips worked as a gunsmith on the Kennebec River from 1643 to 1654. Demonstrating the uncertainty of such information, one secondary source lists Phips as a gunsmith as late as 1663. Another says that Phips was dead by 1654,[7] doubtless causing many years of complaints from customers about slow repairs. (There are at least a few guns in existence that purport to have been made by Phips; Demeritt, an expert on Maine guns, believes them to be 20th-century forgeries.)[8]

By the close of the 17th century, gunsmiths had left records in a number of American cities. By 1650, Boston had about 3,000 people living in it—and at least three gunsmiths: William Davies, Herman Garret, and Richard Leader. New York City also had working gunsmiths in the 17th century. Covert Barent was a gunsmith in New Amsterdam from 1646 to 1650. Francis Soleil started working as a gunsmith in New Amsterdam in 1655.[9]

There were at least three gunsmiths repairing (and perhaps even making) firearms in what is now Maryland in 1631–1634. Alexander Toulson was working as a gunsmith at St. Mary's, Maryland, as early as

1663. John Martin billed the Maryland government for "Scowering, Cleansing and fixing of Arms" in 1682. Gabriel Thomas's 1698 description of Philadelphia lists gunsmiths among the professions at work, in a city only 17 years old.[10]

Gunsmiths, and specifically gunmakers, were not in short supply. On February 2, 1688, the Maryland government "ordered that what publick Armes shall be or are Conveyed to Mattapany be put to William Haimes Gun Maker at Harvey Towne to be fixed and made fit for service and he to doe noe other business in the way of his trade till those be done [mended] and finished." Haimes is described as a "Gun Maker," not as a gunsmith. Significantly, with respect to private demand for gunsmithing, Haimes was prohibited from doing any other business "in the way of his trade" until he had finished repairing the government's guns.[11]

The list of Colonial America's gunsmiths goes on and on; M. L. Brown reports that "probably fewer than 100 had arrived prior to 1700."[12] A far from complete list of early American gunsmiths (described in appendix A) shows that *at least* 140, and perhaps 142, gunsmiths were working in America in that first century and a half. How many were there for whom we have no documentary evidence? Five times that number? We really do not know, and the most that we can say is that this is the minimum. Harold B. Gill's survey of colonial Virginia's gunsmiths explains that

> the importance of gunsmithing in Virginia during the colonial period is clear. Gunsmiths were found nearly everywhere: in port towns along the coast, in settled inland areas, and—probably the busiest ones—on the frontier. As with most craftsmen, many of these men remain obscure. They left little trace and the records reveal their names only incidentally.[13]

Gill's list of Virginia gunsmiths and the years that they were active lists eight men who worked in that capacity from 1607 to 1676.[14] Gill lists 16 people as "gunsmiths" active 1677 through 1739.[15]

Another example suggests that gunsmiths were not at all rare in colonial Virginia. During the French and Indian War, George Washington complained to Governor Dinwiddie about the severe problems he was experiencing concerning supplies and gun repairs:

> Six or eight Smiths who are now at Work, repairing the fire Arms that are here, which are all that we have to depend on. A man was

hired the 24th of last Month, to do the whole, but neglected and was just moving off in Wagons to Pennsylvania.[16]

How many gunsmiths have disappeared from history because they were property? The 1749 will of John Milnor Sr., of Charlestown, South Carolina, bequeathed to his son John, "my negro Fellow Prince, a Gunsmith."[17]

Gun Manufacturers

William Henry was a Pennsylvania gunsmith in the Colonial and Revolutionary War era, as were his descendants for several generations. Henry received "of [illegible] Yeats eight Pounds one Shillings six Pence in payment[?] of a filon[?] mounted Rifle made on Account of Mr. John Inglis of Philadelphia. November 9th 1772."[18]

   "McComb and Company" owed to the estate of John Henry, dated August 23, 1774, debts for "6 Rifles at £7. Each" from August 1773 and another rifle at the same price on August 23, 1774, as well a variety of repair services: "repairing a fusee," "cleaning a lock," "stocking 2 fusees & repairing," "stocking a rifle" (multiple examples), "cleaning a rifle," "hardening 2 hammers," "repairing a lock," and parts (ramrods, tumbler pins, locks).[19]

   "George Rathfong" owed John Henry's estate, as of February 8, 1777, for "finishing two smooth Rifles" from December 20, 1774; "39 Musket Scalps [skelps, the pieces of steel fire-welded into gun barrels]" from February 17, 1776; "butting a smooth Rifle" from June 12, 1776; and "butting a Rifle" from July 8, 1776. John Henry's estate inventory and ledger of unpaid bills clearly establishes that he was a gunsmith in the decades before the Revolutionary War.[20]

   A *gunlock* is the trigger lockwork mechanism of a gun (see appendix C). Belesiles emphasized that gunlocks were very complex to make: "No one in America could make the key part of the gun, its lock, until the Revolutionary era."[21] He also claimed that few were made in America until Samuel Colt freed American makers "from the long-term dependence of all American gunmakers on English locks" in the middle of the 19th century.[22]

   It is certainly true that gunlocks on American-made guns in the Colonial period were usually imported. Harold L. Peterson points out that American gunsmiths "had made and repaired military firearms" from the very beginning. In the Colonial period, American-made guns were generally patterned on the English army's standard musket, the Brown Bess, and often reused parts from British or French muskets. According to Peterson,

"The thrifty colonist would not think of throwing away anything so valuable as a gun part, and consequently these parts were used over and over again in many different combinations until they finally wore out."[23] As we will see in subsequent chapters, gunlocks were made in America throughout the Revolutionary War and Early Republic periods.

An article examining the curious history of a musket found in an Arkansas state museum observed that the musket was "assembled by a rural gunsmith" from a variety of recycled parts. Because "firearms components, especially barrels and lock assemblies, were extremely difficult to obtain in colonial America[,] . . . the recycling of the still functional parts from various European produced damaged firearms was a common practice." There is general agreement that gunlocks were far more likely to be imported than made in America during the Colonial period.[24]

The musket in that Arkansas museum was assembled from an early British Long Land Pattern musket barrel, a French Model 1763 Charleville musket gunlock, and British ramrod thimbles. The stock was made from a North American hardwood—the last definitive evidence of American assembly. From a variety of pieces of evidence, including the name scribed into the barrel, a brass plaque on the buttstock, and the report of the person who donated it, the musket appears to have been used during the Revolutionary War by a Massachusetts soldier.[25] Limited gun component manufacturing capacity might then be an indication that while Americans *could* make guns, they preferred to recycle existing components rather than waste them.

Even before examining the question of whether colonial and Revolutionary Americans made guns, or *could* have made guns, it is important to recognize that this entire question of manufacturing capacity is one of the most serious logical errors in the revisionist claim. Even if Americans *manufactured* nearly no guns during the Colonial period, this does not necessarily mean that America was a limited *market* for guns or that it lacked a gun culture. The American colonies suffered a chronic labor shortage, which encouraged skilled labor to be done in Britain, where a relative surplus of labor drove down wages. In addition, British law "sought to inhibit American manufacturing" through laws that promoted mercantilism: the economic theory that the colonies should supply raw materials and purchase manufactured goods from Britain.[26] For these reasons, Britain remained a major source of manufactured goods of all sorts for Americans, right up to the Revolution.

Efficiencies of production in Britain might be another reason why Americans imported guns in preference to building them locally. In the modern context, there are very few American-made consumer electronics products today, but this is hardly evidence that Americans do not buy or want such products or could not produce them if needed. It is simply more cost-efficient to buy them from other countries.

A 1763 sales order from the papers of William Henry, a gun manufacturer, includes "93 Hammers[,] . . . 77 Cocks[,] . . . 81 Cock Pins[,] . . . 90 Bridles[,] . . . 79 Tumblers[,] . . . 2 Gross Gun Bolts[,] . . . 258 Fuzee Main Springs[,] . . . 281 Hammer Springs[,] . . . 263 Cocks[,] . . . 278 Cock Pins[,] . . . 305 Bridles[,] . . . 271 Tumblers[,] . . . [and] 225 Forg'd Breeches." (The spelling has been modernized.) Someone was clearly making gunlock parts, presumably for someone assembling gunlocks.[27]

Whisker claims that John Dandy of Saint Mary's County, Maryland, may have been the first gunsmith to make a gun in Colonial America. According to Whisker, Dandy was paid for having made a gun to order in 1644. Dandy claimed to have made a gunlock in 1639, as discussed in a deposition taken in 1647. (Dandy's career as a gunsmith was cut short by the rope; he was convicted of beating an indentured servant to death.)[28] Certainly, Dandy was a gunsmith; when the colony prepared to go to war, it was ordered that "such Tooles as are Necessary for his fixing of Guns be pressed or otherwise procured from John Dandy for the time of this Service."[29]

Gunsmiths were advertising in the Colonial period, and some of these ads are explicit that they *made* guns. In 1748 New York City, Edward Annely advertised his services as a gunsmith and dealer in imported guns. He also advertised guns made to order: "He likewise makes guns and pistols as any gentleman shall like."[30] John Cookson, a Boston gunmaker, advertised his wares in the April 13, 1756, *Boston Gazette*.[31] Are these merely assemblers of guns from parts or true manufacturers? There is not enough information to know for sure.

Hugh Orr, a Scotsman who settled in Massachusetts, made 500 stands of arms (each stand being a firearm and all its accessories) for the Massachusetts Bay province in 1748, which were stored in Castle William and carried off when the British evacuated Boston at the start of the Revolution. Orr again made small arms once the Revolution began, and he cast cannon as well at Bridgewater. Yet, again demonstrating how inadequate our knowledge of the past is, there are only two sources that I can find that mention Orr's work as a gunsmith[32]—and only one tells us that he made 500 muskets in colonial New England. How many colonial gunmakers were there that made a tenth of that number over a lifetime, for individual nongovernmental customers, and therefore have left no trace?

We have surviving American-made guns. Merrill Lindsay's *The New England Gun: The First Two Hundred Years* shows dozens of surviving guns. While iron was produced in small quantities in New England throughout the 17th century,[33] the first clearly American-made barrels date from the 1730s, when iron from the Salisbury region of Connecticut came into production.

> Before that we find an occasional barrel with no marks, which may have had a colonial origin, or we find a fowler (early shotguns, intended for bringing down fowl) with British marks on the lock and barrel but with ingenious and sometimes unusual furniture nailed onto the cherry stocks.[34]

The New England fowlers of the 1730s, however, are clearly American-made, not simply restocking of existing guns. *Most* surviving American-made guns before the Revolution have French or English barrels. Other parts seem to have been colonially made.

While England's ability to make inexpensive gunlocks meant that these parts were usually imported, and other parts were often recycled from imported guns, "some brass, especially trigger guards, are so heavy and crudely made that they most certainly must be the work of heavy-handed country gunsmiths." Some New England fowling pieces used a mixture of American stocks, French locks, and furniture that was "a mixture of iron and brass[,] suggesting that the gunsmith who put it together made up the parts which he did not have on hand." Another musket, evidently made by a finer craftsman, not only used an American stock but also an apparently American-made gunlock.[35]

In the several decades before the Revolution, the number of surviving firearms that are clearly American-made increases. A 1685 fowler by Gilbert is clearly identified as being of Boston manufacture from the maker's marks. Phineas Sawyer built at least one fowler at Harvard, apparently around 1770; we know because we have one surviving example. Benoni Hills, the father of Revolutionary gunsmiths Medad and John Hills, made at least one fowler, because it exists today. Thomas Earl (or Earle or Earll) made fowlers and muskets at least as early as 1760 because several have survived. These survivors are American-made and sometimes have gunlocks that are "probably English but possibly American." A Medad Hills long fowler dated August 26, 1758, survives, as well as a pair of Medad Hills pistols made for William Smith in 1771.[36]

While some American-made guns recycled parts from European guns, there are both smoothbore fowling pieces and rifles that have American wood for the stocks and barrels that appear to have been made in Colonial America.[37] In March 1775, George Schmidt, one of the Moravian craftsmen of Salem, North Carolina, sold 80 rifle barrels that he had made.[39]

Surviving pistols that were made in Colonial America include a pistol owned by Peter Grubb, who made gun barrels for the Lancaster Committee of Safety during the Revolution. The lock is apparently English-made, but the rest of the pistol appears to have been made in Pennsylvania, perhaps by I. Perkins of Philadelphia or by Grubb himself. While other pistols are uncertain as to the maker, William Antes is clearly the maker of one surviving Colonial period American-made pistol. Antes signed both the barrel and the hand-forged lock, suggesting that he made the entire pistol. Another surviving signed pistol of the Colonial period was made by Matthew Sadd of Hartford, Connecticut, "in the middle 1700s."[39]

North Carolina Governor Dobbs wrote a lengthy letter to the Board of Trade on December 26, 1755, in which he requests a new law regulating the sale of guns to the Indians to require safety testing before sale ("to proof" or "prove" a gun):

> That no Guns should be sold to our Indian Friends or other Indians that were not proved[,] it being a great loss to the Indians in their hunting and maiming many of them, and alienates their affect[tion]s from the English—If the Traders do not follow the Regulations these Inspectors are to acquaint the Board in order to have them prosecuted upon their Return upon their Bonds and Securities.[40]

Britain had required all gun barrels to be proofed since 1637.[41] To prove a gun, the gun was fired with a larger than normal load of gunpowder to verify that it would be safe to fire with normal loads. So, where were these unproofed barrels coming from? One likely source was local manufacture.

Guns had been made in Massachusetts before the Revolution. On December 8, 1774, the Massachusetts Provincial Congress recommended "to the people" that they should enlarge their production of a number of commodities on which they were dependent upon Britain. These included improving sheep breeding, "raising of hemp and flax," the production of flaxseed oil, nails, steel, saltpeter, gunpowder, glass, buttons, salt, stockings, and firearms. Unlike these other commodities, the Provincial Congress was explicit that firearms manufacturing was not new: "As fire arms have been manufactured in several parts of this colony, we do recommend the use of such in preference to any imported; and we do recommend the making [of] gun-locks, and furniture."[42]

That this was not the distant past, but had continued into the present, may be deduced from the Provincial Congress's call of February

15, 1775, for the inhabitants to arm themselves, and it directed the towns to "encourage such persons as are skilled in the manufacturing of firearms and bayonets, diligently to apply themselves thereto, for supplying such of the inhabitants as may still be deficient." Unsurprisingly, the Provincial Congress declared that it would give buying preference to American-made "arms and bayonets." On March 23, 1775, the Provincial Congress directed that its committee on ordnance, in addition to finding out how many cannons were in private hands, also find out "what number of men in the province [were] acquainted with the business of making firearms."[43] The Provincial Congress did not know how many gunmakers there were in Massachusetts, but they clearly believed that they were present.

Stephen Jenks of North Providence, Rhode Island, was a maker of muskets "as early as 1775," and "small arms were at the same time pretty extensively made by several other persons in the Colony." Albany, New York, was engaged in gunstock making as early as 1740, and muskets or rifles were apparently made during Colonial times "in considerable quantity for the Indian trade."[44]

What are we to make of William Grayson's letter to George Washington on the eve of the Revolution? Grayson appears to have been encouraged by Washington to organize an "independant [sic] Company." If gunmaking was almost unknown in Colonial America, why did Grayson report "several of the soldiers had purchas'd muskets in the Country, and that some others had imploy'd our own gunsmiths to make them proper arms"? Perhaps Virginia was uniquely awash in gunsmiths. But Grayson's letter also "return their thanks" to Washington "for your kind offer, and will be much oblig'd to you, to write to Philada. for forty muskets with bayonets, Cartouch [cartridge] boxes, or Pouches, and slings, to be made in such a manner, as you shall think proper to direct; . . . I can venture to assure you, that the gunsmith who undertakes the business, will be paid on demand."[45] If the revisionists are right, Grayson and his friends were remarkable not only in having their "own gunsmiths," but they were under a serious delusion that they would be able to acquire muskets made to order in Philadelphia.

Another letter to Washington, from William Milnor in Philadelphia, the previous month also demonstrates that there were a number of gunsmiths in the City of Brotherly Love, and while guns could still be made to order, time was running out:

I have Applyed to two Gunsmiths,—One palmer tells me he Can make one hundred by May next, And Nicholson says he Can

make the like Number by March, they both agree in the price at
£3..15.. this Currcy. Palmer says Mr Cadvalder had agreed With
him for 100 at that price, a Jersy Musquet was brought to palmer
for a patern, Mr. Shreive Hatter of Allexandira has one of that
sort, which you may see, & if you Conclude to have any, please to
inform me by the first post, as the Gunsmiths I blieve will soon be
preengaged, & there is not one Musquet to be bought in this City
at present, if you should Chose any Alteration, from that Musquet
please to let us know.[46]

In 1774 South Carolina, Burger & Smith advertised themselves as
"Gunsmiths from New York." They offered their services in the making of custom guns. That guns were made in America is also evident in
some accidental references. John Cobb, a gunsmith in Taunton, Massachusetts, was struck dead by lightning in early July 1775. The letter
describing this event called it "a loss to the town as many are unpro-
vided with Arms."[47] (It is not clear whether this indicates that all types of
firearms were in short supply in Taunton, or only military arms, which
would have been in high demand at that time because of the start of the
Revolution.)

We have a number of accounts documenting gunmaking in Colonial
America. Richard Waters emigrated to Massachusetts from England
about 1632. In 1878, a descendant observed that Waters "was by profession a gun manufacturer; married the daughter of a gun maker,
and it is a noteworthy fact that the business of gun making has been
hereditary in some branch of the Waters families almost continuously
since."

His descendants, Asa and Andrus Waters, built a gun factory in Sutton, Massachusetts, at the start of the American Revolution, replacing
the hand-powered manufacture of guns with water power. (They had
apparently made guns at a fairly slow pace before the start of hostilities.)
Asa and Andrus Waters purchased pig iron in Connecticut, had it refined
at a forge in Douglas, and manufactured it into barrels and other parts
of the gun in Sutton.[48]

While gun manufacturing in Colonial America appears to have primarily used hand-powered tools, there were power-driven tools in use
before the Revolution. By 1719, a boring mill was in use at Lancaster,
Pennsylvania, to smooth the interior of barrels after they had been fire-
welded together from strips of iron.[49]

How many guns were made in Colonial America? It is impossible
to say for sure. To say that there were very few made is an arrogantly

certain statement. If only a few guns were made in Colonial America, how is it that collectors have so many still in existence?

To assert that gunsmiths were rare in Colonial America because there was little demand for their services requires sending thousands of ads and documents down *Nineteen Eighty-Four*'s "memory hole."

CHAPTER 4

Repairing Guns during the Revolutionary War, 1775–1783

Were gunsmiths rare not only during the Colonial period but also during the Revolutionary War? Certainly, a number of officials had complained of the difficulty in finding enough gunsmiths to take care of the needs of the army. But this is not necessarily an indication that there were few gunsmiths in Revolutionary America.

First, it is worthwhile to just examine the question of gunsmiths *repairing* guns. (Gunsmiths *making* guns during the Revolution are covered in the next chapter.) It seems likely that the demands of warfare dramatically increased the need for gunsmiths simply because guns were far more regularly fired in battle than would happen in hunting. Guns of questionable reliability, while a nuisance for hunting, would be positively hazardous in warfare. It therefore seems plausible that guns that were marginal for hunting would have been repaired once the owner feared that he had to rely on his gun for his life and not just his dinner. The use of bayonets in combat would also add an opportunity for physical damage to a musket, increasing the demand for repair services. Shortages of gunsmiths by the Revolutionary governments are therefore not necessarily an indication that America had few gunsmiths during the Revolution, only that warfare dramatically increased the need for them.

Another problem is that the Revolution created difficult situations for gunsmiths. Those who were loyal to the Crown, or feared that the Crown might prevail, would have had a powerful reason to not work for the Revolutionary governments. Even those who simply wished to be neutral sometimes found themselves forced to move. The Frederick,

Maryland, area lost at least eight gunsmiths because they were members of religious denominations that refused to serve in the military or pay taxes—and had no interest in choosing sides. Henry Roth Sr. moved to Pennsylvania in 1776 because of increasing disturbances. Jacob Mier and his son Samuel did likewise shortly before the Revolution for similar reasons.[1] Some gunsmiths were driven to inactivity because their denominations sought to remain outside the brutality of war, such as Jacob Loesch, who was prohibited by the Moravians from practicing his trade, discussed on page 36.

Establishing how many gunsmiths there were during the Revolution runs into the same problems that we have previously seen with respect to determining gun ownership. The most complete sources on this subject are those that are official in nature, and that very nature tends to focus on the military's gunsmithing needs, which are different, and more extreme, than the needs of civilians.

As it happens, one of the revisionist claims about gunsmith scarcity during the Revolution is very easy to check in detail. After describing the failures of Pennsylvania to make enough guns to supply an army, Bellesiles claims that

> Massachusetts was somewhat more successful. In June 1775 a special committee of the Provincial Congress reported that there were thirteen smiths and armorers in the state capable of repairing firearms, which they thought "sufficient" for current needs. But they added two significant caveats: all of these smiths are "in want of tools and stock," and all but one "are very imperfect in the business they profess." The exception, Richard Falley, "is a complete master," and the committee recommended his appointment as official state armorer.[2]

But when you look at the cited pages (291, 330, 474, 476, 498–499, 540, 542, 548–553, 562, 565, 590, 592, 595) in *Journals of Each Provincial Congress of Massachusetts*, you find a *very* different story. On page 291, we find out where the number "thirteen" came from:

> The committee appointed to inquire how many armorers were appointed, &c., reported, that the committee of safety informed them that *there were thirteen appointed, and several others nominated*, and that the general officers had agreed that thirteen was a sufficient number, but that they were in want of tools and stock.[3] (emphasis added)

Note the difference between Bellesiles's description, and what the source actually says. There is *nothing* at page 291 that suggests that there were *only* 13 gunsmiths in the state capable of repairing firearms. Indeed, it is clear that there were more than 13 armorers because 13 were appointed and "several others nominated." The appointment of many of these 13 armorers is reported on the pages cited by Bellesiles, but nothing on those pages discusses the number of armorers in Massachusetts or their competence.[4]

In the same journal, on June 12, there is an entry describing the addition of three more armorers, and that may explain the shortage of tools and stock:

> Shuabel and Joseph Sever, of Framingham, entered into the colony service, as armorers, the 10th instant. Capt. Lawrence, in Col. Prescott's regiment, offered to act as an armorer without any pay for his labor, and to return home for some tools which are necessary to effect the repairs of the muskets, it was consented to by the committee, and the said Lawrence was desired to procure his tools as soon as may be.[5]

Lawrence's tools were at home; it certainly would not have been surprising that other gunsmiths were similarly without their "tools and stock" because of the disruptions caused by the war.

A report from May 19 casts even more doubt on Bellesiles's claims that gunsmiths were in short supply: "General Thomas was informed, by letter, that the committee had appointed Messrs. Beman, Shaw, Wood and Dike, as armorers for the forces posted at Roxbury, and [was] desired to acquaint the committee if any further appointments were necessary."[6] Four of the thirteen armorers in the entire province of Massachusetts (if we are to believe Bellesiles) had now been posted to Roxbury, and the committee is asking whether Gen. Thomas would like some more.

On July 8, 1775, the Committee of Safety must have concluded that there were going to be plenty of gunsmiths available to them in the future—many more than 13:

> Whereas, many complaints have been made to this committee, that the armorers frequently deliver the arms out of their shops unfit for service, and delay the work unnecessarily; in order to prevent occasion for such complaints in future, and to hasten the public service in an orderly manner, which has not yet been provided for, it is Resolved, that it be, and it hereby is, recommended to the

honorable Congress, to make an establishment for, at least, four master armorers, each one of whom shall work and superintend one shop, each of which shops, as we apprehend, may well accommodate eight men, including the master.[7]

The committee decided that each of these 4 shops should handle 8 men—or 32 armorers in all. Ten days later, on July 18, 1775, a petition from "Armourers in the service of the Province of Massachusetts Bay" requests some improvements in their working conditions—and there are 15 armourers listed on the petition.[8]

Massachusetts gunsmiths keep appearing at the start of the Revolutionary War, but as bystanders. One of the first warnings that the British were about to march on Lexington and Concord was from "a gunsmith named Jasper[, who] lost no time in informing Colonel Waters of the Committee of Safety." In Concord, there was a gun factory operated by Samuel Barrett. John Cobb, a gunsmith in Taunton, Massachusetts, was struck dead by lightning in early July 1775.[9] What are the chances that 3 of the 13 Massachusetts gunsmiths just happened to be mentioned in documents that came so readily to hand?

In Connecticut, David Trumbull received £100 for "fixing, stocking and repairing &c. about 180 gun-barrels" in late 1775. Other records show that he did repairs for Connecticut in 1776 as well.[10]

The far from complete list of gunsmiths in appendix A reveals that at least 612 were working in America between 1775 and 1783. How many are undocumented? Gunsmiths were apparently present in Pennsylvania; we have records of a number of them being paid for their services repairing guns.[11] This is doubtless a very incomplete list of gunsmiths who were paid by the Pennsylvania Committee of Safety and for only a short period of time: in 1776, 1777, and 1780. (The volumes of *Colonial Records of Pennsylvania* for 1778–1779 on microfiche were unreadable.)

There are other records of gunsmiths who were paid by local governments in Pennsylvania. Lancaster County paid a John Miller £25:17:7 "for repairing public arms" on August 18, 1777.[12] The discovery of this payment was a happy coincidence; an exhaustive search of *Pennsylvania Archives* would probably uncover more such gunsmiths.

In Maryland, there were a number of gunsmiths—in some cases also known to be gunmakers—who had been provided public guns for repair in 1776. Were these the only gunsmiths that the Maryland Council of Safety hired? Unfortunately, there are many other records of payments that provide no information about the services provided.[13]

North Carolina's records show that gunsmiths had been common throughout the state. On December 21, 1775, the Provincial Council appointed 26 officials in 6 different districts to "purchase materials and employ proper persons to make and mend Guns and Bayonets and also to purchase good serviceable Guns, Gun Barrels, Stocks and Locks, Lead and Flints and have them repaired for the use of this province."[14]

When the North Carolina Provincial Congress established a commission to purchase guns—with two commissioners in each of 35 counties—they also provided that firearms not fit for military use were to be repaired, and "that if Armourers cannot be found in each County, sufficient for repairing such Arms, that they sent into such publick Armoury as shall be established hereafter by this Congress."[15] The Provincial Congress directed Col. Nicholas Long to "employ at the Public Expense some Person or Persons to mend and put in fix sundry Guns now in his Possession, and in the Town of Halifax." The assumption was that in many, or perhaps most, counties, gunsmiths would be found capable of repairing guns, and only if a county did not have enough gunsmiths would the government armory have to do the work. New York's Committee of Safety made similar provisions.[16] This does not sound like a severe shortage of gunsmiths.

The records, however, list only a few examples of gunsmiths being paid for their work. The Wilmington committee was reimbursed £83:15:10 for purchasing "thirty-one Guns, stocking four Guns, repairing three Guns, and twelve Gun Locks," and there is a later transaction of £7:1:0 "for two Muskets, repairing one gun and two gun locks."[17]

There are other transactions that indicate that gunsmiths were present; the small number of such transactions suggests that either there were very few gunsmiths present in North Carolina, and the Provincial Council was deluded about this, or, consistent with the other evidence, that the records of publicly paid gunsmithing are very incomplete. One piece of evidence of this incompleteness to the records is that the Wilmington Safety Committee paid Richard Player 5 shillings on January 30, 1776, "for repairing 1 gun more than in the account rendered against the public,"[18] but there is no other record of Player repairing guns.

In 1778, Gen. Washington complained "that there were 5000 Muskets unfit for service in the Magazine at Albany. I most earnestly desire that you will use your utmost endeavours to have them put into repair by the opening of the next Campaign."[19] Why would Washington make a request to repair 5,000 muskets "unfit for service" if gunsmiths were scarce?

We also have gunsmiths moving as groups, as described in this letter from Washington to Henry Knox:

> The Bearer Mr. Buel, who is recommended to me by Governor Trumbull, will undertake to stock a number of the Gun Barrels at Springfield, and repair the old Arms. He has a set of Workmen of his own and will go on with the Business upon Credit, which is a very material consideration. But to prevent the matter being made a job, I think it will be best for you to give orders to the Officer superintending the Laboratory to have the Barrels sufficiently proved before they are delivered to Mr. Buel, as I suspect that they are most of them of the trash kind which Mr. [Arthur] Lee charges Mr. [Silas] Deane[']s Agent with purchasing.[20]

The notes describe Benjamin Buell as "a gunsmith of Hebron, Conn."[21] Clearly, Buell was more than a single craftsman, but an entrepreneur prepared to bring his workmen with him to repair guns.

Were gunsmiths in short supply during the Revolution? In some places, at some times, certainly. But the evidence suggests that the shortage of gunsmiths was comparable to the shortage of soldiers, clothes, and many other commodities rendered scarce because of the sudden change in business conditions induced by the war.

CHAPTER 5

Gunmaking during the Revolutionary Era, 1775–1783

Revisionists would have us believe that Americans not only built almost no guns before the war started, but were unable to correct this problem once hostilities were underway. Others, a bit closer in time to the Revolution, have held different opinions. J. Leander Bishop's 1868 history of American manufacturing reports that cannons were cast in Pennsylvania during the Revolution and that

> Small arms were also made in considerable quantity at Philadelphia, Lancaster, and elsewhere. The general insecurity of the frontier settlements, especially during the French and Indian wars, the temptations of the chase, and particularly the Indian trade, rendered fire-arms a necessary appendage to every household, and created a steady demand for rifles and other defensive weapons. The manufacture received a great impulse during the Revolution. The exportation of firearms, gunpowder, and other military stores from Great Britain was prohibited in 1774. . . . Governor Richard Penn, in his examination before the House of Lords in November, 1775, stated, in reply to the inquiries of the Duke of Richmond on the subject, that the casting of cannon, including brass, which were cast in Philadelphia, had been carried to a great perfection; and also that small arms were made in as great perfection as could be imagined. The workmanship and finish of the small arms were universally admired for their excellence. . . . Rifles were made in many

places in the Provinces at that date, which were thought equal to any imported.[1]

Who is correct, the revisionists or Governor Penn and J. Leander Bishop? We will examine evidence in several categories for each state. First, are there any surviving guns made during the Revolution? Yes, but this turns out to be a bit less helpful to answering the question than it appears. We have surviving American-made firearms, such as Philip Greever's rifle, used at the 1780 Battle of King's Mountain. The gun is marked with "J. Shaffer," probably Jacob Shaffer of Wythe County, Virginia, or possibly Joseph Shafer of Snyder County, Pennsylvania. Robert Young's rifle from that same battle has also survived, and it is also American-made. A pistol and some rifles made by Cornelius Atherton in New England during the Revolutionary War era also exist. And there are pistols made by Henry Mauger of Berks County, Pennsylvania, and a pair of pistols believed to be by William Shenner of Reading, Pennsylvania. (The Mauger and Shenner pistols used Ketland gunlocks imported from Britain.) A Nathan Bailey pistol apparently made for the State of Connecticut also survives. A Connecticut Committee of Safety musket made by Stephen Chandler "seems to be entirely American except for some of the furniture which is British." An Abijah Thompson musket uses a British barrel, but "the rest of the gun—lock, escutcheon, side and butt plates— is American and the stock is American curly maple."[2]

No one denies that at least a *few* guns were made in Colonial and Revolutionary America. If we had some method of estimating the survival rate of guns from that period, the number that remain in museums today might be used to estimate how many guns were originally present. North & Cheney made 2,000 pistols under the 1799 federal contract. About 20 of those 2,000 have survived to the present day—or roughly 1 percent.[3]

Have 1 percent of the American-made guns of the Colonial period survived? Is the survival rate 0.1 percent? We do not know because there really are no complete measures of Colonial and Revolutionary gun production; the survivors are mute witnesses to their brothers since buried or melted down—and they tell us nothing about how many of those brothers once existed.

There is strong reason to believe that nearly all of the guns made during this time were destroyed as they became obsolete or too damaged to bother repairing. But the presence of surviving guns, even in small quantities, does demonstrate that the other forms of evidence are not delusions or errors. As is usually the case, artifacts are interesting and suggestive, but far less conclusive than written sources.

Did Revolutionary Americans believe that guns could be made there? Individuals might be mistaken, or suffering from what revisionists consider patriotic self-delusion. If large numbers of Americans, especially the well-educated and presumably intelligent people in the Revolutionary governments, believed that Americans could make guns, it requires strong evidence to the contrary before we can believe the revisionist claims.

It is important to distinguish between what people *wished* to happen and what they *believed* could happen. Bellesiles writes of the *rage militaire* that swept across America, deluding many Americans into believing that their countrymen were widely armed.[4] But was this a delusion?

The importation of guns from abroad was a difficult situation in the first year of hostilities, at least partly because the United States did not yet exist, and the British government was successful in blocking many European nations from selling munitions to what was still just a bunch of rebels. John Hancock's March 6, 1776, letter to George Washington observes, "With regard to arms, I am afraid we shall, for a time, be under some difficulty. The importation is now precarious and dangerous. To remedy this, a Committee is appointed to contract for the making [of] arms; and, as there is a great number of gunsmiths in this and the neighboring Colonies, I flatter myself we shall soon be able to provide ourselves without risk or danger."[5] Hancock seemed to think that gunmaking was within the capabilities of the American colonists. Was he the only one who thought this?

Lt. Frederick Mackenzie, a British officer stationed in Boston at the start of the Revolution, described how

> the people are evidently making every preparation for resistance. They are taking every means to provide themselves with Arms; and are particularly desirous of procuring the Locks of firelocks, which are easily conveyed out of town without being discovered by the Guards.[6]

That the war with Britain created shortages of gunlocks would appear to be true. The Pennsylvania Committee of Safety on February 9, 1776, asked gunsmith Benjamin Rittenhouse to confer with them "respecting the mode & terms on which he would undertake to carry on a Manufactory of Gun Lock making in an extensive manner."[7] This request can be read in several different ways: that gunlocks were not yet manufactured in Pennsylvania; that they were, but "not in an extensive manner," and more volume was required; or that they were manufactured in large quantities, and the demands of the war, and the cutoff of trade with Britain, required higher volume of production.

Gunlocks were the one significant component imported in large numbers during the Colonial period, and this desire for gunlocks makes sense if the other components of a gun were being made outside of Boston. However, it may also make sense if there were large numbers of existing guns outside of Boston with broken gunlocks. It does seem unlikely, however, that widespread smuggling of gunlocks would be worth the risk unless there were numerous gunsmiths either repairing or making guns. We know of at least one business described as a "gun factory" in Concord, which was operated by Deacon Thomas Barrett.[8]

One of North Carolina's delegates to the Continental Congress, Joseph Hewes, wrote home complaining of the gap between their resolutions and results: "We resolve to raise regiments, resolve to make cannon, resolve [to] make and import muskets, powder and cloathing, but it is a melancholly fact that near half of our men, Cannon, muskets, powder, cloathes, &c., is to be found nowhere but on paper."[9]

It is true that governments have been known to place orders for goods based on incorrect information, and it is entirely possible that there simply was no manufacturing capacity for the guns that the contracts and orders imply. However, it is quite a strong claim to make that the Revolutionary government's knowledge of the state of arms manufacturing was incorrect. A historian today who claims to have a clearer understanding of the true state of Revolutionary arms-manufacturing capabilities than the people who lived at the time needs extraordinary evidence to back up such claims.

If no or few guns had been made in America during the Revolution, Hewes's letter might be a strong piece of evidence to back such a claim. But as we will see, guns were made, though perhaps in smaller numbers than the surviving contracts and resolutions suggest. It is important to also note that the gap between resolutions and results to which Hewes refers includes not only guns but also men and clothing—and no one would seriously argue that men and clothing were in short supply in Colonial America, nor that Americans lacked the knowledge of how to make both! The most that might be said is that the government could not dramatically expand America's manufacturing base or supply of guns, soldiers, and clothing on short notice, nor could it purchase or hire these guns, men, and clothing on terms that it could afford.

It is clear that large numbers of firearms were imported during the Revolution, many of them from France. While "individually owned rifles and fowling pieces" were used, "by far the greater part of the arms used by Continental troops during the Revolutionary War were regulation French army muskets." From existing records, it appears that the vast majority of these imported firearms (of which records exist for 101,918 delivered from February 1776 through August 1781) arrived from 1777 onward—at a time when domestic manufacturing of the Committee of Safety muskets began to taper off.

While Bellesiles portrays this primary reliance on imported arms as a sign of the inability of Americans to make guns in quantity, Gluckman and Satterlee point to a simpler explanation: the guns being imported from France were purchased at an average price of about $5 each, compared to an average price of $12.30 for muskets made in the United States. The lower price for these French guns is not surprising. Although many were unused, they were also obsolete government arms. They may well have been sold at a substantial discount for this very reason and because it suited the French government's foreign policy interests to pull the tail of the British lion.

An inventory of long guns remaining in the arsenals after the war found that most were model 1763 Charlevilles, some dated as early as 1718.[10] If the choice was having new guns made for $12.30 or buying surplus, and sometimes unused, muskets for $5, especially considering the limited finances of the Revolutionary governments, it is no surprise that the American government chose to buy foreign arms, especially from 1777 onward.

We will look at documents that show that guns were actually being manufactured. Contracts may have been drawn up for the making of guns, but if that task were harder than it first appeared, these contracts would have simply been scraps of worthless paper. If we find evidence that necessary and expensive components were being delivered to those who were contracted to make guns, it would be evidence that at least the gunsmiths and government entities involved in the process believed that they were making guns.

Also, we will look at documents that demonstrate that completed guns were delivered and that gunmakers were paid for them. We should not expect that every such delivery was adequately documented; indeed, we will see records showing that guns were made and delivered, while the production of other guns are only known by indirect evidence.

Pennsylvania

Examination of the papers of the Pennsylvania Committee of Safety suggests that Pennsylvania had a substantial gunmaking industry at the start of the Revolution—or at least the people who lived in Pennsylvania thought so. Among the Committee of Safety resolutions of June 30, 1775, is an order to the various counties of Pennsylvania that they were "immediately to provide a proper number of good, new Firelocks, with Bayonets fitted to them"; cartridge boxes with 23 rounds in each box; and knapsacks. A list specifies for each county that it is to supply "not less" than a specified number "of each article" (see table 5.1).

Table 5.1   Pennsylvania Committee of Safety Order for Arms to Be Supplied by the Counties, June 30, 1775

Entity	Count
City and County of Philadelphia	1500
County of Bucks	300
County of Chester	500
County of Lancaster	600
County of York	300
County of Cumberland	300
County of Berks	400
County of Northampton	300
County of Bedford	100
County of Northumberland	100
County of Westmoreland	100

Source: Pennsylvania Colony, *Colonial Records of Pennsylvania*, June 30, 1775, 10:229.

Significantly, this order was to provide *new* firelocks, not used ones and not existing ones purchased from the civilian market. How were these new firelocks to be made? Per the order, "That the Firelocks to be provided as aforesaid, be of one Bore, with Steel Rammers, well fitted to the same, and that Patterns of the said Firelocks, Rammers and Bayonets, be immediately made in the city of Philadelphia, and sent to the different Counties."[11]

A Committee of Safety minute of July 4, 1775, directed the committee in charge of obtaining gunpowder and saltpeter to "procure at the same time two thousand Stand of good Fire Arms."[12] It is not clear whether these were to be newly manufactured or existing privately owned guns. A January 17, 1776, order directs the officers in charge of contracting to obtain "one thousand Firelocks and Bayonets." These actions demonstrate that the Committee of Safety, unless it was partial to passing impossible resolutions, believed that there were private firearms out there that they would be able to purchase or that new ones could be made.[13] Keep in mind that civilian fowling pieces and rifles would have had no provision for attaching bayonets; hence, there was a preference for new firelocks intended for mounting bayonets.

Along with general orders to procure firearms, we also have specific contracts listed, such as a January 17, 1776, order by the Committee of Safety to pay £150 to Gouger, Dunwick, and Kinder, three men making firearms for the colony. In turn, they were supposed to deliver 35 stands of arms.[14] Less than two months later, they delivered "35 Fire-locks, complete, which were made by them."[15]

Bellesiles believes that this production capacity did not exist and that the various orders from governments and private individuals that are documented above reflect delusions about this matter. He tells us that the Pennsylvania Committee of Safety requested 200 muskets from William Henry, and it took 18 months to get them.[16]

Bellesiles has relied on secondary sources for this claim, however, and those sources are wrong on at least one significant count: on March 23, 1776, the Committee of Safety directed negotiating a contract "with William Henry for making 200 Rifles"[17]—not muskets, as Bellesiles says, but rifles—which were considerably harder to make than muskets because of the rifling of the barrels.

There is certainly a minute of June 3, 1778, in which we are informed that William Henry "has about fifty Riffles in his possession," and he was directed to deliver them to Col. Arthur Buchanan. But there is nothing that identifies whether this was a delivery under the March 23, 1776, contract. Henry was also requested to deliver 50 muskets "belonging to this state" that he may have made, stored, or perhaps repaired. William Henry's papers show a very long list of transactions with individuals and the U.S. government for muskets, rifles, and various gun accessories; "100 Rifle Gun locks"; and wages paid to known gunsmiths of the period.[18]

Bellesiles gives no other examples of contracts in Pennsylvania and thus leaves the reader with the impression that muskets were very hard to come by. Not all of the contract details are visible from the available sources, but for at least a few, we can see the sequence by consulting different sources. On July 21, 1775, the Pennsylvania Committee of Safety directed a subcommittee to apply to three gunsmiths, named James Pearson, Tomlinson, and Wiley, to find out "if they can be engaged to advantage" to "Compleating the Fire Arms that may be wanted." On July 27, Pearson and now "Whiley" did contract for the making of gun barrels. Tomlinson apparently engaged in some similar contract because an order to pay Joshua Tomlinson £200 "advanced him towards Gun Barrel Making" appears on July 15, 1776.[19]

On July 22, 1775, the Committee of Safety directed that "a messenger be sent to Joel Ferree, of Lancaster County . . . requesting him immediately to complete the Guns wrote for as patterns and to know how many he can furnish of the same kind and at what price." In July 1776, the Committee contracted with John Kerlin "for fifty Muskets and Bayonets, to be made according to Pattern, at Eighty-five Shillings each."[20]

Bedford County, Pennsylvania, responded to the Pennsylvania Committee of Safety's request that each county make muskets by explaining that they only had one gunsmith, and he was unable to hire sufficient help to make the 100 firelocks required of Bedford County. The request was not absurd, but merely impossible under the conditions of the local labor market. Yet, by 1780, Bedford County had acquired a runaway (apparently an indentured servant, not a slave) gunlock maker, and he was making muskets for the Bedford Committee of Safety. The Pennsylvania Committee of Safety believed that guns not only *could* be made, but *were* being made. On February 13, 1776, they directed that two hundred pounds of brass be supplied to "Lewis Grant . . . for making furniture for Firelocks." Lewis Prahl was to receive 100 pounds of brass "for mounting to the Firelocks making by him for the use of this province." Benjamin Town was also given 200 pounds of brass for making furniture for firelocks being made by "Nicholson and Dunwick." The next day, a Mr. Afflick received 100 pounds of brass for the same purpose.[21]

An August 24, 1775, meeting directed that "Mr. George Gray procure 1500 Brushes and priming wires, for the Provincial Firelocks." On March 26, 1776, Peter De Haven received £150 "for the payment of Fire Arms making for the use of this County." A few months later, he was to receive "100 lbs. Copper, for mounting of Firelocks, for the use of this Province." Northampton County received a quarter cask of gunpowder to proof "the Firelocks making for the use of this Province."[22]

By October 7, 1775, the guns were apparently being made—or there was no point in an order from the Committee of Safety "that Colo. Cadawalader be desired to deliver to the Master at Arms, what Muskets, with the Bayonets, he can spare out of a Number he has order'd to be made; And that this Board pay him four Pounds five Shillings for each, being the price he agreed for." It even appears that there may have been gunsmiths still not busy making guns for the government: "*Resolved,* That the Master at Arms go to the different Smiths in and about this City, who are capable of making Fire Arms & Gun Locks, and desire them that are out of employ to attend this Board."[23]

Another order tantalizes us with evidence that a gunmaker named Nicholson was actually producing muskets, because we find a September 26, 1775, order to deliver "twenty-eight Muskets, made by Nicholson," to Edward Chamberlain. A February 14, 1776, order directs payment of £500 "for the payment of Firelocks, &c." Unfortunately, there is nothing that tells us whether this was an advance toward manufacture or for actual delivery.[24]

An August 15, 1776, order is more explicit: Abraham Moore of Chester County was to be paid £30 "on account of arms to be made for the Service of this State." James Webb was paid £6:0:9 "for stocking Rifles."[25] Thomas Palmer (likely the same Philadelphia gunsmith to whom William Milnor refers in chapter 3, on page 47) was directed to deliver 17 rifles to Robert Towers, and a Mr. Balwin (probably Jacob Baldwin) was similarly directed to deliver 8 rifles on or after July 24, 1776.[26]

Along with these clear orders to make guns, and clear signs that guns were being made, we have considerably more ambiguous records. A November 8, 1775, report from Robert Towers "reports his having received the following articles into store," including a great many muskets, described as "Provincial Muskets." Were these guns owned by the province or had they been made to the province's specifications (as described above)? Some of the goods in this list seem to be items coming from contractors, such as gunpowder, and "Mrs. Ann Gibbs imported Fire-Arms to the amount of forty-seven Pounds." Others are clearly stated as guns purchased from individuals: "1 Musket, bought of Mr. Dunn."[27]

The discouraged North Carolina delegate Joseph Hewes, upset about the gap between resolutions and results, reported that arms were not available for purchase in the Philadelphia area: "These articles are very scarce throughout all the Colonies. I find on enquiry that neither can be got here, all the Gunsmiths in this Province are engaged and cannot make Arms near so fast as they are wanted."[28] Hewes was certainly not suffering from the *rage militaire*, and yet he recognized that gunsmiths in the Philadelphia area were making guns—just not fast enough.

Perhaps Hewes was deluding himself that guns were being made in America. If so, he seems not to have wised up over the next few months. On February 13, 1776, he again wrote about the shortage of guns and powder for the army and the success of the British government in blocking shipments of both from Europe: "Americans ought to be more industrious in making those articles at home, every Family should make saltpeter, every Province have powder Mills and every body encourage the making of Arms."[29] Clearly, Americans *were* making guns; Hewes had stated that in November. They just were not making them fast enough.

The problem of gunlocks, which were largely made in Europe before the Revolution, shows up in Pennsylvania as well. On June 13, 1776, a Col. John Shee sought "thirty Provincial Fire-locks and Bayonets, for which he will give thirty Gun-locks and pay the difference of the value."[30] Gunlocks were apparently the limiting factor on firelock production, and having located 30 gunlocks with which to build more guns, Col. Shee sought to trade them and some money to obtain 30 complete firelocks.

On October 30, 1777, the employees of the Pennsylvania State Gun Factory at French's Creek, Chester County, complained that their wages were too low for stocking guns, and they asked for a raise.[31] It seems most unlikely that if the workmen were not actually stocking guns that they would have asked for a raise, with the approval of their superintendent.

The Pennsylvania government seems to have thought that it had a factory that made guns: "The State of Pennsylvania has for some time past supported a factory for the making of arms, which has been conducted with care and attention by Mr. Peter De Haven and Mr. Benj'n Rittenhouse."[32] On October 10, 1778, it asked Congress whether it wanted to take over the state gun factory, having run out of money to operate it.

Northampton County was given £300 "for the payment of Firelocks ... making in that County for the use of this Province." (It is not clear whether this was an advance to gunmakers or reimbursement for guns already made.) In early 1776, the Committee of Safety paid for 6 pounds of gunpowder "for proving Musket-Barrels made in Bucks County." A minute of February 6, 1776, directs payment of £150 for "Gunlocks & Files." Lewis Prahl did some sort of work for the Committee of Safety that required delivery of "any number of Gunlocks he may find necessary."[33] These are all evidence that the Committee of Safety believed that firearms manufacturing was taking place (although the gunlocks for Lewis Prahl might have been imported).

Committee of Safety muskets were not simply ordered but manufactured. Despite conditions not well suited to their preservation, we have a number of examples that have survived to the present day. It is certainly the case that when arms became available for importation from Europe that these replaced many of these hurriedly manufactured muskets, and the Committee of Safety muskets, which received hard use at the beginning of the war, were unlikely to have survived to be sold off as surplus after the war.[34]

Bellesiles makes much of the low production rates of Committee of Safety muskets, suggesting that Americans simply lacked the ability to produce guns in any quantity. M. L. Brown gives a more detailed description of the problems confronting Pennsylvania manufacturing, which includes not only a shortage of gunlocks but also the low prices offered by the government.

The Lancaster County Committee of Safety complained to the Pennsylvania Committee of Safety on March 16, 1776, that they were having difficulty with making new contracts: "Our workmen universally complain that the sums already fixed are inadequate to their Labours; that the Sacrifice they made in quitting their rifle business is greater than they can bear without some equivalent."[35] The problem was not that Americans could not make guns, but that it was more profitable to make guns for the private market.

How many guns were made? Gluckman asserts that despite the difficulties involved, 4,000 of the 4,500 muskets ordered by the Pennsylvania Committee of Safety were completed and delivered between October 1775 and April 1776. Unfortunately, Gluckman provides no verifiable source for that claim.[36] Attempts to verify this number against the *Colonial Records of Pennsylvania*, the *Pennsylvania Archives*, and the *Minutes of the Supreme Executive Council of Pennsylvania* have been inconclusive. We have records that show that muskets and rifles were made and delivered, but only a few of these records provide any quantities.

On October 27, 1775, the Committee of Safety directed that Mr. Towers

> prove all the Muskets made in this City for the Provincial Service, and to Stamp such of as are proof, with the letters P; and that a Copy of this Minute be handed to the County Commissioners, who are to notify the Smiths they contract with for said Muskets, of this Resolve, and that none of their Guns will be receiv'd or paid for by this Board, but such as have been so proved and Stampt as aforesaid.[37]

In 1776, a Robert Peebles was paid £200 "being in part for 100 muskets made by Col. Peebles" by order of Cumberland County. William Henry, the founder of the Henry gunmaking firm that lasted well into the 19th century, was contracted to make 200 rifles on March 23, 1776. The Committee of Safety "recommended to the Committee of Lancaster, to permit the makers of Rifle Guns in that Burrough, to Contract, under their Care and Controal, with General McKinley, or such person as he shall impower, for Forty Rifle Guns." A rather remarkable contract directs "Mr. Owen Biddle is desired to procure a Rifle that will carry a half pound Ball, with a Telescope sight."[38] This is likely a "wall gun" intended for use against fortified positions, firing a 1.25-inch diameter bullet. This is perhaps the earliest telescopic sighted rifle, if it was actually made.

Matthias Keely, who delivered 31 new firelocks as contracted, was to be given "as much powder as will prove one hundred Firelocks, making by him for the use of this Province." On April 4, 1776, Matthias Keeler (probably the same gunsmith) received £50 advance "towards the payment of Firelocks making by him." In addition, "Robert Towers, Comissary," was told to provide Keeler with 56 musket balls "for proving Firelocks." Towers was apparently purchasing guns. Later that month, he was reimbursed £160:13:4 for "Firelocks, Salt Petre, &c., purchased and paid for by him." Sebastian Keely, perhaps a brother or cousin, also contracted on November 9, 1775, "to deliver six Firelocks per week, until he completes one hundred."[39]

After heaping scorn on state efforts to produce guns, Bellesiles neglects to mention the Continental Gun Factory in Pennsylvania, for which the Continental Congress appropriated $10,000, and which seems, like some of its state counterparts, to have actually produced muskets.[40] Gluckman reports that while muskets were produced by the Continental Gun Factory—despite having to relocate from Philadelphia to avoid capture by the British—"few new arms were made subsequent to 1778 and prior to 1795. There was an adequacy of arms on inventory; what repair work was required, was done at the Congressional arms repair shop at Carlisle, Pennsylvania."[41] Of course, some of the "adequacy of arms" was because of the importation of muskets from Europe.

New York

New York's Provincial Congress was also apparently deluded about the possibility of making guns in America. A series of discussions with Robert Boyd and Henry Watkeys that started June 13, 1775, concerned the making of 1,000 muskets for the soldiers of New York. (As New York was planning to raise and equip 3,000 soldiers,[42] this suggests that the Provincial Congress believed that it already had, or could purchase, at least 2,000 muskets.) At first, the price agreed upon was £3:15:0 per musket.

On June 23, the Provincial Congress negotiated with Robert Boyd to manufacture "Gun Barrells, Bayonets and Steel Ramrods" and with Henry Watkeys to provide gunlocks and then stock and finish muskets within six months. The final contract required Watkeys to manufacture gunlocks on the pattern of one provided to him "marked *Grice* 1760." Watkeys was to be paid £2:5:0 for each musket delivered. Boyd seems to have not been included in this contract.[43] Watkeys apparently failed to deliver on the guns. The following is Bellesiles's description:

> Henry Watkeys appears to have been entirely sincere when he took New York's money in June 1775, but discovered that making guns was much harder than he had initially suspected. Sixteen months later, after producing only six inferior gun barrels, he informed the New York legislature he was "poor and now removed to Brunswick in Jersey."[44]

Why does Bellesiles make a point of saying that Watkeys "appears" to have been sincere? Perhaps it is because one of Bellesiles's sources about Watkeys had pointed out that Watkeys deserted to the British and ended up as a gunsmith in Canada after the war.[45] At a minimum, it gives us a different possible explanation for Watkeys's failure to make guns; his failure may reflect his political sympathies more than technical inadequacy.

While Watkeys failed to make guns for New York, others were more successful. The New York Committee of Safety reported on February 2, 1776, that Jecamiah Allen had provided 100 muskets, and Col. Curtenius "had examined the one hundred Muskets . . . and that they are good and in order." Allen also informed the committee that he had 50 other muskets available as well.[46]

This was not the end of the New York Provincial Congress's attempts. On March 30, 1776, they ordered that "all the public News-Papers in this Colony" run an advertisement asking for "proposals from & treat with any Person or Persons who are willing to engage in manufacturing good Muskets or the Locks Barrels or any necessary parts thereof."[47] New York also provided a bounty for those who erected gunpowder mills and made gunlocks or musket barrels and offered no-interest loans for those purposes.

But New York was also careful to specify that these incentives were not available for gunpowder mills already erected, or for gunlock, musket barrel, or bayonet makers "with whom the Congress or Committee of Safety of this Colony have already contracted, or to any person in their behalf." On this same page, the Provincial Congress also provided very similar loan and bounty programs for the making of "Salt out of seawater"—and no one has suggested that Americans were short of salt, or did not use salt, in the Colonial period.[48]

Clearly, there were already gunpowder mills in operation, and these incentives were intended to create more manufacturing capacity. It appears that the incentives for gunlock makers and musket barrel makers were similarly intended for those not already in the business. This suggests that there were craftsmen in New York already contracted to make gunlocks and musket barrels, or there would be no need to specifically exclude them.

Cornelius Atherton contracted with New York for muskets during this time. We know that a quarter-cask of gunpowder was to be delivered to him in March 1776 to prove the musket barrels that he had made for New York. Atherton apparently delivered at least 22 muskets sometime during this period.[49]

Other evidence that gunsmiths were making guns in New York during the Revolution appears in the minutes of the New York Committee of Safety from March 1776. Gilbert Forbes, a New York City gunsmith, requested the committee's assistance in preventing the removal of William Clarke, "a Lockfiler by trade, and a useful mechanick, employed in his service." A person named Winter from Chester, Maryland (perhaps Elisha Winters, whose gunlock problems will be discussed later in this chapter), had appeared in New York City and demanded the return of Clarke to Winter's service. Winter appears to have believed that Clarke was a runaway indentured servant named William Jones. The committee decided that the bill of sale, lacking any seal, was insufficient proof, and it declined to allow Winter to remove Clarke.[50]

New Hampshire

Other Revolutionary governments, while lacking quite as much detail on their plans to have guns made, also seemed to believe that guns could be made in America. The New Hampshire House of Representatives, in January 1776, discussed "a plan for providing Fire-Arms for a Colony stock." For every musket with a barrel "three feet nine inches long, to carry an ounce ball, a good bayonet with blade eighteen inches long, iron ramrod" (what is generally known as the Committee of Safety specification) "manufactured in this Colony" delivered "on or before the 1st of May next, the owner of such fire-arms [shall] receive three pounds for each."[51] These muskets were to be proofed, and the maker was only to be paid if they passed.

New Hampshire's government ordered "that there be appointed one good man, in each County" to receive and proof such muskets.[52] It seemed to think that there was enough gun manufacturing capacity that within four months there would be so many gunsmiths making muskets, and that they would be so widely distributed, that someone would be required "in each County" to receive and proof them.

Connecticut

Connecticut's government believed that guns could be made in their state, and in large quantities. A May 1775 order directs "that there be procured, as soon as may be, three thousand stands of arms for the use of this Colony, of the following dimensions, *viz.*: the length of the barrel of the gun three feet and ten inches." The terms of this order could include either the purchase of existing guns or the manufacture of new ones. A bounty of 5 shillings was offered for every gun manufactured in Connecticut by October 20, 1775, or 1 shilling and 6 pence for every gunlock manufactured within the colony by that same date.

Were they successful? Not entirely. An October 1775 report informed the Assembly that the committee in charge of arms procurement had "procured a considerable number of said arms to be made in this Colony, which are now in the hands of said committee" and asked for an extension of the bounty to include guns made by May 1, 1776. Another extension of the bounties was requested in May until October 1776, with an increase in the bounty for gunlocks to 2 shillings and 6 pence. The increase in the gunlock bounty suggests that these were the limiting factor in the production of guns. Reports in June 1776 suggest that gun manufacturing was continuing.[53]

It appears that at least Silas Phelps of Lebanon, Connecticut, was successful in making gunlocks. In November of 1776, he was allowed 3 shillings each for 55 gunlocks that he made, but the premium for gunlocks made after June 10 was not allowed to him.[54]

Medad Hills of Goshen, Connecticut, received a Connecticut Committee of Safety musket contract. On February 4, 1776, he delivered 40 muskets and bayonets. Samuel Hall also received a contract from the Connecticut Committee of Safety. While he apparently delivered at least 69 guns, "military duty and sickness" prevented him from completing his contract.[55]

At least one of Medad Hills's muskets has survived, though whether it is one of those made under this contract is unclear.[56] Other Committee of Safety muskets have survived, such as an unmarked musket made in New England (based on the wood) and a Committee of Safety fusil (a lighter form of musket) made by Elisha Childs and Nathan Frink in 1778 in Goshen, Connecticut. Samuel Dewey of Hebron, Connecticut, demanded payment from the Assembly for "46 gun barrels and 21 bayonets, and that they are all in the public service."[57]

Virginia

There are certainly gunsmiths in Virginia who believed that they could make guns. Thomas Worley, Philip Sheetz, and Henry Sheetz "of Mecklenburg in the County of Berkley" signed a document May 28, 1776, offering to make guns for the Committee of Safety, "twenty-four good and well fixt Rifle guns per month, at the rate of Four Pounds and Ten Shillings Virginia Currency each, or in lieu thereof twenty-four good and well fixt muskets with sufficient bayonets at the rate of Four Pounds."[58]

Bellesiles does mention the successful Martinsburg, Virginia, factory of Stephen & Noble, which was "capable of making as many as eighteen muskets in a single week." Yet, rather than acknowledge that this was an impressive performance for a factory of 30 workers, he derides its effectiveness by observing, "If they maintained that rate, they could have armed the Virginia militia in twenty-one years, assuming no gun loss or population growth."[59] There is no reason to assume that a single factory was intended to arm the entire Virginia militia, or that the Virginia militia was devoid of arms when the factory opened.

The Rappahannock Forge in Virginia made guns, without question, because we have some of their production. Nathan Swayze, an arms collector specializing in Rappahannock Forge's production, has found at least 18 surviving guns produced during the Revolution: 10 pistols, 4 muskets, and 4 "wall guns" (a type of very large musket used for defending fixed positions). Unfortunately for its proprietor, the chaos caused in Virginia by the British invasion disrupted production and scattered the Forge's workmen.[60]

North Carolina

North Carolina's Provincial Congress also made provision for the making of guns, naming 18 men in 6 different districts "to direct the establishing of public manufactories in their respective districts, of good and sufficient muskets and bayonets," roughly following the specifications laid down by the Continental Congress. These men were to "collect from the different parts of their respective districts all gunsmiths, and other mechanicks, who have been accustomed to make, or assist in making muskets, or who may in their opinion be useful in carrying on such manufactory." Musket and bayonet together were not to exceed £5.[61] It is unclear how many guns were actually made in such public factories, but it is clear that the Provincial Congress believed that there were gunsmiths living in North Carolina who were "accustomed to make, or assist in making muskets."

There is a curious silence in the North Carolina records about these public gun factories. In November 1776, the Provincial Congress charged three members to "inquire into the state of the Gun Manufacture in the District of Halifax, and make Report thereon." A few weeks later, they reported back that it appeared that muskets could not be made for £5 each, but that it was possible at $20 each. There is no explanation for why the House considered the report and then rejected it. Did the House consider the report as nonsense or extortionate? Did they decide that it was best not to try to make guns in public factories? We do not know. We also do not know whether the problem was specific to Halifax. A few weeks later, Nathaniel Rochester was added to the Hillsborough District's firearms manufacturing commission; the Provincial Congress had not abandoned the notion of making guns.[62]

The Continental Congress clearly believed that guns could be made in North Carolina. A November 4, 1775, resolution directed, "Resolved, That it be recommended to the several Assemblies or conventions of the colonies respectively, to set and keep their gunsmiths at work, to manufacture good fire locks, with bayonets." A November 28, 1775, resolution directed, "That the convention or committee of safety of North Carolina be desired to employ, immediately, all the gunsmiths in that colony, in the making of Musquets and bayonets."[63]

Examination of *Colonial Records of North Carolina* shows surprisingly little discussion of the making of guns. On June 14, 1776, the North Carolina Provincial Congress promised Timothy Bloodworth £5 for each Committee of Safety musket made and delivered within four months. Bloodworth and his workmen were exempted from militia duty, and Bloodworth was advanced £100 to make the muskets and bayonets. (The Provincial Congress raised its offering price to £6 a few months later, with no explanation of why.)[64]

Apparently, Bloodworth's operation was successful, as was that of James Dupre. Factories in Hillsborough and Halifax started in April and

November of 1776, respectively, and made guns until 1778. The arrival of inexpensive surplus French muskets may have contributed to the closing of these factories, but the drought of 1778, by stopping water power at the Hillsborough factory, forced it to stop production.[65]

A curious complaint of May 3, 1776, suggests that guns were being made in North Carolina and that it was not generally important enough to be recorded, unless there was some dispute associated with the guns. An Abraham Childers "in the first troop of Light Horse commanded by Capt. Dickerson . . . had taken seven new rifle guns, with their [bullet] moulds and wipers, from Arthur Morse, of the county of Orange, for the use of the Continental Army." The Provincial Congress resolved, "That the said Abraham Childers has acted without authority, and with violence, evil in its example, and dangerous to the security of private property." The guns were ordered restored to Moore, and Childers was ordered to report to the Provincial Congress "to answer for the said misbehavior." This may have been a misunderstanding; a few days later, Childers apparently escaped punishment, and Moore was given £56 for the seven rifles.[66]

There are other references to guns purchased, repaired, and perhaps made under contract with the North Carolina state and county governments, but what is startling is how few such references there are. On December 22, 1775, the North Carolina Provincial Council (the executive branch, while the Provincial Congress was not in session) reimbursed the Wilmington Safety Committee for £83:15:10 "for thirty-one Guns, stocking four Guns, repairing three Guns, and twelve Gun Locks for the use of the first Regiment." They were also reimbursed £7:1:0 "for two Muskets, repairing one gun and two gun locks, for the first Regiment."[67] One could interpret the very few references to gun purchases as evidence that guns were in short supply; one could also interpret it as evidence that guns were so widely distributed as to not be worth a great deal of discussion.

A number of gun factories operated in North Carolina during the Revolutionary War, and some were continuing manufacturing operations from before the war, such as North Carolina's Charlottesville Rifle Works. It was established in 1740 to produce public arms, and it produced muskets from 1775 to 1777.

The North Carolina Gun Works was established by that state's Committee of Safety in 1776, under the direction of Master Armorer James Ransom. It operated until 1778 and produced muskets and bayonets.[68] Authorized by the North Carolina Provincial Congress, it directed that "all Gunsmiths, and other mechanicks, who have been accustomed to make, or assist in making Muskets," be collected to work there.[69] Perhaps the North Carolina Provincial Congress was misinformed, thinking that there were gunsmiths "accustomed to make, or assist in making Muskets."

Bute County also seems to have had a gun manufacturing facility during the war. On January 26, 1779, the North Carolina government directed that "the remainder of the Guns, Gun Locks and & every other Thing belonging to the Gun Manufactory in Bute County" be sold.[70]

Bellesiles describes North Carolina's Public Gun Factory as having "produced one hundred rifles during the war and then closed shop."[71] A more complete statement—and one that shows that there was a bit more involved than just closing down operations—is that this Wilmington factory, operated by John Devane and Richard Herring, started operations in May 1776 and delivered "one hundred Muskets with Bayonetts, three Rifles and Six Smooth [bore] Guns. That afterwards the said factory, with a quantity of Gun barrels were destroyed by the Tories." Destroyed factories have a hard time operating.[72]

South Carolina

On February 24, 1776, South Carolina's Provincial Congress directed a subcommittee

> to contract for the making, or purchasing already made, any number, not exceeding one thousand stand, of good Rifles, with good bridle-locks . . . not exceeding the price of thirty Pounds each. . . . Also for the making, or purchasing already made, one thousand stand of good smooth-bored Muskets, carrying an ounce ball . . . at a price not exceeding twenty Pounds each.[73]

South Carolina's early and prolonged occupation by the British doubtless contributed to both limited manufacturing and record keeping.

Maryland

Maryland also believed that guns could be made there. An August 1775 Maryland Convention committee was appointed to "inquire into the practicability of establishing a Manufactory of Arms within this Province." They concluded that it made more sense to contract out these services to the existing gunmaking industry. The committee reported that there were at least 12 gunsmiths in the province capable of making guns: 3 in Baltimore, 1 in Georgetown, 4 in Fredericktown, 1 near

Fredericktown, 2 in Hagerstown, 1 in Jerusalem, and "several gunsmiths on the Eastern Shore, and in other places." Each shop was believed to be capable of making 20 muskets a month at a cost of about £4 each.[74]

On August 29, 1775, the Maryland Council of Safety contracted with these gunmakers. Charles Beatty of Fredericktown was "empowered to contract for the making and Delivery of 650 good substantial proved Musquets . . . for a sum not exceeding Ten Dollars and two-thirds of a Dollar in Bills of Credit." A third were to be delivered by January 1, 1776; another third by March 1, 1776; and the final third by May 1, 1776. Beatty had some difficulties with the contracts, but not because there were no gunmakers. Beatty insisted on a slight change in the gunlocks, with "2/3 of the Musketts to be delivered by the first of March next[,] the remainder by the first of May following."[75]

Robert Alexander of Baltimore was similarly empowered to contract for 500 muskets. On September 1, three other officials, apparently in other areas of Maryland, were authorized to contract for "making and Delivery of any number, not exceeding 1000 good substantial proved Musquets" of the same specifications.[76]

Thomas Johnson Jr. was authorized to purchase gunlocks, stocks, bayonets, and ramrods "for five hundred muskets." From the count, it would appear that these items were intended to support Robert Alexander's Baltimore musket making contract. The Maryland Council of Safety was also buying other items required to complete the muskets, such as "one thousand Priming-Wires and Brushes at 7s. 6d. per dozen." Edward Timmins received £7:5:5 for 32 steel ramrods on May 3, 1776. In January of 1776, Charles Beatty and Baker Johnson were advanced £60 for the purchase of gunlocks, and £100 "to enable them to advance for Rifles." Michael Cochinderfer of Frederick County was given £300 "to enable him to carry on a Stocking manufactory."[77]

On August 31, 1775, the gunsmith Isaac Harris of Savage Town contracted to supply musket barrels and bullet moulds at $4 2/3 each. The terms were "agreeable to the one now made and delivered," which shows that Harris had made a sample.[78] Gunlocks stored in Baltimore were ordered delivered to Harris on May 25, 1776,[79] suggesting that he was making guns.

Other contract negotiations show that gunmakers were not in short supply. A letter from Georgetown, Virginia, of October 20, while somewhat unclear, seems to indicate that the Council of Safety of Virginia was prepared to purchase rifles and smoothbores from a Mr. Richardson if Maryland chose not to buy them.[80]

There are other references to the acquisition of rifles that suggest that Maryland's government believed that such guns were available either used or new. A February 1, 1776, order directs that "the Company of Light Infantry, in the regular forces of this Province, be armed with Rifles." John Hanson Jr., Charles Beatty, and James Johnson were "requested to provide and furnish the said Company good substantial and serviceable Rifles."[81]

The existing gunmakers of Maryland did not have enough workers to make the desired number of muskets and rifles; we can find discussions of contract guarantees, such as one from October 21, 1775. The Maryland Council of Safety promised that if William Whetcroft imported sufficient workmen the following spring, and delivered "fifty good substantial proved Musquets" every week for two years, the province would take over the workmen's contracts in the event that peace broke out in the next two years. The first 800 muskets made were to be fitted with imported locks.[82]

Perhaps all these contracts for the making of muskets and rifles were highly speculative—but if so, it seems a bit odd that the Maryland Council of Safety would pay for a great many parts that might or might not be assembled into functioning guns. It is also interesting that there is no comparable purchase of gunlocks, stocks, bayonets, and ramrods to complete the 650 muskets contracted for in Fredericktown or the 1,000 muskets contracted for in other parts of Maryland. These other gunmakers apparently had their own sources for these components.

In any case, guns were being made. By January 20, 1776, there were orders to deliver to John Youst "ten Pounds weight of Gunpowder . . . to prove the Musquets made by the said Youst for the use of this Province." Richard Thompson and Thomas Richardson were appointed to prove those muskets. And the making of guns continued; on February 23, Isaac Harris was directed to request Stephen West to send up "all the Gunlocks . . . now in his Possession." A May 4 order directs delivery of "all the small Arms which were brought from Frederick County" where some of the contractors were based. Jacob Schley, another rifle contractor, was directed on July 30, 1776, to "send to this place, with all the expedition you can, the rifle you made for the use of the Province; also, the ten large rifles contracted by you to be made and delivered on the first day of August next." Major Price is directed to deliver 38 gunlocks "for the rifles made at Frederick County." One the same day, the Frederick Town Gun Lock Manufactory is told to "furnish and make for Jacob Schley ten large Gun Locks agreeable to a pattern they will receive."[83]

There were entrepreneurs who popped up, proposing to make guns and asking for assistance, such as Richard Bond, who announced, "I am setting up a Gun factory, which I expect will be ready to go about [Christmas], where work will be done in the best manner, where gunbarrels may be had ready for stocking—any quality."[84]

Elisha Winters of Kent County agreed to assemble 600 stands of muskets, 40 a month, using barrels and bayonets provided by the government. Winters contracted to make these muskets for £4:5:0 each, purchasing the barrels and bayonets from the government for 28 shillings or £2:4:0. The standard of production was "a sample this day produced to the Convention." It is not clear whether Winters supplied this sample. (This is apparently the same Winters referred to the following year as "Mr. Winters, of Maryland, who has carried on a manufactory of small arms" in the *Journals of the Continental Congress*.) Unlike Hollingsworth, who had required that the government supply gunlocks, there is no mention of them in the Winters contract, suggesting that Winters either had a large supply of gunlocks or could make them.[85]

Winters was certainly making muskets a few months later. The Council of Safety complained that while Winters was "the only person we know of on the Eastern-Shore capable" of repairing an entire battalion's arms, he was "already engaged in making arms for the Province, [and] we should be sorry to take him from that business, unless through absolute necessity." The Eastern Shore Committees of Safety were encouraged to find others to do the repair work required and to apply to Winters for repairs only as a last resort.[86]

There are a number of indications that guns were being assembled, such as payment on April 6, 1776, to Oliver Whiddon of £8:15:0 for stocking 14 muskets; on May 25, 1776, of £10:15:0 for "stocking 20 Musketts & finding 2 Gun Locks @ 12/6 each"; and £5 for stocking 8 muskets on June 8, 1776. Whiddon received another £3:15:0 for stocking 6 muskets on July 8, 1776.[87]

On April 11, Isaac Harris was directed to fit steel ramrods to all the muskets in the magazine. An order on June 29, 1776, directs Harris to "furnish Mr. Samuel Dorsey with the Dimensions, and sizes of the Gun Barrels . . . sufficient for his guidance in manufacturing Bayonets."[88] If Harris was not making gun barrels, the people of the time were fooled.

Perhaps in response to an ad placed in the *Maryland Gazette* by the Maryland Council of Safety, a Henry Hollingsworth of Cecil County, on February 6, 1776, offered to make muskets, "any quantity, from two hundred to two thousand," and promised delivery of 100 by April 10 and another 100 per month thereafter. He apparently could not produce or buy the gunlocks and needed these supplied.[89]

The next mention of Hollingsworth's proposal is May 22, 1776, when the Maryland Convention agreed to purchase musket barrels from him at 20 shillings each and bayonets at 8 shillings each, advancing him £500 for that purpose—enough to pay for 357 barrels and bayonets. Hollingsworth was obligated to provide a bond "in double that sum" in the event that he failed to meet the contract.[90] Did Hollingsworth actually make guns?

Elisha Winters offered to deliver "50 stand of Arms . . . which I think will be highly approved of." After complaining that Hollingsworth was not delivering gun barrels "agreeable to his contract," Winters recommends that Samuel Dorsey could make the barrels.[91]

The council ordered Hollingsworth to deliver musket barrels and bayonets to Winters.[92] Hollingsworth resolved the problem, for a letter from him to the council on August 24, 1776, informed them that "the Guns, Bayonetts and Cartouch Boxes are ready, as also are the Blankets." A letter from Hollingsworth dated September 28, 1776, discusses his forging of barrels and bayonets and that he had now made more than Elisha Winters would be able to use: "as I sent him seventy Bbls and ninety Bayonetts the other day." Hollingsworth was making six barrels a week, but the limiting factor on gun production was the locks.[93] Perhaps this explains Mr. Winters's complaint about his runaway lock maker in New York, as discussed previously in this chapter.

A July 27, 1776, letter from Winters informed the council that he would be delivering 28 muskets "ready to your order by Monday 3d August, making up forty muskets per month, agreeable to my contract."[94] It would appear that Winters had already delivered another 12 muskets that month, although I could not locate documentation to establish this.

As a reminder of the incompleteness of the official records, Isaac Harris, known to have made guns in 1776, receives payment of £155 "due to him per Account," but there is no explanation as to the nature of the account.[95] A more thorough examination of the *Archives of Maryland* might reveal even more evidence of Revolutionary gunmaking there.

An August 24, 1776, letter to Col. William Richardson states that a Capt. Dames had "an order on Mr. Winters for Forty Musquets which will completely furnish his Company and enable him to supply Captain Dean's with some."[96] Winters made another 40 muskets, and that this would "completely furnish his Company" and leave some left over suggests that most of Dames's company was already armed.

Other gunsmiths contracted with the Maryland Council of Safety to make guns, but the records for whom are incomplete and confusing. For example, on July 8, 1776, Oliver Whiddon was paid £3:15:0 for stocking six muskets. James Boyd of St. Mary's County contracted to make muskets "completely fitted in the usual manner" for £4:5:0 each, "the Council engaging to take any quantity of him, & find Powder for their Proof." On July 7, John Yost contracted to make 300 muskets at £4:5:0 each and 100 rifles at £4:15:0 each, "to be delivered at the times and in the proportions expressed in his bond." Yost was advanced £150 "to enable him to comply with his contract."[97]

Less than a month later, Yost responded to a July 23 request to know what arms were available: "I have them all ready of the first contract, including the bayonets, which I expect this day with an express which I have sent for them. I have also been much detained in the last contract, by repairing old arms for the Militia, the Colonel finding it very necessary." Yost hoped to dispatch all the arms of the first contract by "the latter end of this week."[98]

It seems unlikely that Yost had made 300 muskets in less than a month, so this shipment of "the first contract" would seem to refer to some previous arrangement, perhaps the "November last" contract referred to on August 10. On that date, Yost was paid "£50, common money, being the balance due him on his contract . . . in November last." On the same day, he was advanced £400 for his next musket contract.[99]

A letter from Yost on September 13, 1776, reported that he had built a horse-driven mill for boring gun barrels; "that I am now employed with all the Workmen I have in making Locks, Screws, Mounting and forging Barrels ready for boring, but cannot proceed to that Part of the Work before I receive the Materials (Steel in particular,) which I purchased at Philadelphia sometime ago." A merchant who was supposed to deliver them had failed to do so.[100] Yost had significantly expanded his operations, but gunmaking was clearly *not* a new activity. Yost was making guns, or at least parts for them.

He was not alone. An August 16, 1776, meeting of the Maryland Convention had resulted in an order "that the Council of Safety be directed to purchase of the Managers of the Gun Manufactory of Dorchester County, all the Muskets they have by them, both finished and unfinished."[101]

A less successful operation was a publicly owned gunlock factory in Fredericktown. A committee of the Maryland Convention appointed to look into "the state and condition of Manufactories" reported that it had been a disappointment, with £1200 advanced, but no more than

£82:19:7 "has been returned in work, valued, in the opinion of your Committee, at high prices, and only thirty-eight gun-locks have been produced." The Committee believed that the results did not justify the investment.

The committee did, however, recommend that the convention accept Elisha Winters's proposal to take over the factory, install his own workers, and produce muskets for the state. Winters would be obligated to produce at least 125 muskets monthly at £4:5:0 per musket. The barrels for Winters's factory would be provided by Henry Hollingsworth of Cecil County, at a price of "twenty shillings common money per barrel." The proposal seems to have been rejected, with no explanation as to why.[102] The committee's report, however, establishes that while slow, gunlocks were being made in the public factory. At least to the committee members, Elisha Winters had established his ability to make muskets, and 125 muskets per month seemed in the realm of possibility.

Yost's letter of September 13 told a somewhat different story about the Fredericktown gunlock factory. "I was told by the Manager of the Gun Lock Manufactory at Frederick Town, that they forge Gun Locks much faster than they can finish them off; as that is the Case, I should be glad to furnish myself from thence with 300 ready forged Locks, provided the Terms are admissible."[103] If the manager of the Fredericktown factory was telling Yost the truth, it appears that the Fredericktown factory was capable of forging the parts for gunlocks but not assembling them; Yost seems to have had workmen capable of assembling the parts into gunlocks.

Hartzler presents evidence that matches the Yost letter; the Maryland state gunlock factory did forge the required parts, but it was unable to quickly assemble these parts into completed gunlocks. Other correspondence quoted by Hartzler suggests that financial difficulties more than technical problems caused its demise.[104]

Unsurprisingly, gunlocks appear to have been the limiting factor in the making of guns. A letter to the "Gun-Lock Commissioners" (apparently those in charge of the public gunlock factory in Fredericktown) several weeks earlier had asked "how many locks you make per week. We have barrels enough here and in Kent for the locks you can make."[105]

We do not know the actual production total of muskets. It seems to have been less than the optimistic projections. There are letters suggesting that guns were not being produced as fast as desired, though still within contract. A letter to John Youst (as his name was now spelled) asked him "to be as expeditious as you possibly can in supplying the Muskets."[106]

Other letters demonstrate that some of the contractors were failing to meet their contracts; and by the absence of such letters to the other contractors, we can infer that either they met those contracts or those letters did not survive. A letter to Henry Yost (perhaps a relative of John Yost, or Youst) of Frederick County complains about his failure to fulfill his contract for 75 muskets: "We are much surprised that we have not had some Guns delivered us heretofore from your Shop." A similarly scolding letter to John Unseld of Fredericktown complains about how his original contract for 80 muskets with bayonets and bullet moulds had so far yielded only "Twenty nine Muskets very roughly made . . . and one Bullet Mould have been delivered but not one Bayonet." Unlike other makers, Henry Yost's and John Unseld's muskets were returned to them "as unfit for Service." Whatever Henry Yost's deficiencies as a musket maker, he was paid £100 on January 30, 1781, for the repair of muskets.[107]

Other gunmakers appear out of nowhere (or at least it would appear so from examining official records) to make small quantities of muskets. Thomas Smith of Chestertown wrote to the Maryland Council of Safety, introducing a Robert Read, "a blacksmith of this town, who waits on the Council to sell them seventeen muskets which he has made, and carries with him. They seem to be strong and substantial. He proposes contracting with your Board for a good many. He bears the character of an honest man; has some real property in this town, and, I believe, would be pretty punctual."[108]

At least some of the accessories made for the muskets were only serviceable. Stephen West's letter of May 4, 1776, criticizes competitors' products: "Your Rammers and Bayonets of your Country-made Arms I am told are rough Trash, & the Rammers fly out in Exercise." West emphasized that while the guns he makes are better than his London-made carbine, "we cannot make them so cheap as [the country craftsmen] do," and he asked for £6 each, plus a supply of gunlocks, as "it would expedite matters." To justify this price, he pointed out that Pennsylvania gunmakers received £5:6:3 from Virginia, "and their Guns are not equal any way to those of mine."[109]

Hartzler's *Arms Makers of Maryland* shows a flintlock musket made in the style of the English Brown Bess, but it has a proof mark believed to have been used by Ewing and Gist for the musket barrels made in Maryland—and this is not the only musket known with this proof mark and Maryland government ownership markings. Ewing apparently was in charge of proving the 127 muskets made by Keener, Messersmith, and Riddick.[110]

Perhaps few of these contracts were fulfilled. But if so, where are the records of upset governments demanding their money back? There are certainly much smaller financial transactions recorded, such as £10 "to be deducted out of William Niven's Account against the publick, for not enrolling agreeable to the Resolutions of Convention."[111]

Baltimore gunsmiths delivered at least 131 Committee of Safety muskets (some of which were clearly part of the 127 muskets made by Keener, Messersmith, and Riddick) that we know about because the proof test results were reported on February 12, 1776.[112] Bellesiles, who would have us believe that the manufacturing of guns was an entirely new activity for Americans, reports that Maryland's inspector "tested seventy-two muskets from the shop of Baltimore's leading gunsmith, Peter Lydig. Eight of them promptly burst."[113]

The gunsmith's name in the source that Bellesiles claims to have read is Lydick, not Lydig. While the spelling of Lydick's name changes in various places in the *Archives of Maryland*, the spelling is consistent on the page of the *Archives of Maryland* that Bellesiles cites. When you read James Whisker's description of the failure of Lydick's muskets, you can see that the spelling and the claim of burst barrels comes from Whisker's account, not the source that Bellesiles cites.[114]

The report in the *Archives of Maryland* that Bellesiles cites does not say that 8 muskets burst. It says that there were "64 good, 8 bad," out of 72 guns. Proofing might indeed cause a musket to "burst." But there are other forms of failure besides bursting that would cause a gun to fail the proof test. Bellesiles apparently uses "burst" because it creates a negative image in the reader's mind and because a secondary source made that claim,[115] and with no more information than the source that Whisker cited.

But even if Bellesiles did look up the source he cited—the *Archives of Maryland*—he must not have read it very carefully, or we can presume that he would have mentioned the even higher failure rate of Sam Keener's muskets, "13 good 19 bad," that appears within three lines of the Lydick musket failure report.[116] Apparently, these failures were not considered a big problem. As late as 1837, without the supply problems of the Revolutionary War, the U.S. government's Springfield Armory experienced a 12.15 percent failure rate for gun barrels, and considered this acceptable.[117]

A Peter Littig (probably an alternate spelling of Peter Lydick) was paid £50 for making muskets on May 31, 1776,[118] and another £281:5:0 on his arms-making contract the following year. Keener was also paid £187 "on his Contract for making Arms." Both agreed to contracts for more muskets: 150 from Littig and 100 from Keener, at a price of £3:15:0.

The government was to supply both the locks and the barrels, so Littig and Keener were apparently more assemblers than gunmakers. If the barrels that failed in 1776 had been supplied by outside vendors, this might explain the willingness of the Committee of Safety to again contract with Littig (or perhaps Lydick) and Keener for more guns.[119]

Other suppliers of muskets and rifles to the Maryland Committee of Safety included John Yost and Richard Dallam. At least some guns were made on the Eastern Shore of Maryland as well, at £4:5:0 each, "and probably in several other parts of the Province."[120]

On April 4, the Commissary of Stores was directed to supply five pounds of powder to Isaac Harris "to prove Musquets." Again, on July 6, 1776, Harris was given two pounds of powder "to prove his rifles and Musquets." Maryland's Council of Safety paid the partnership of John Shaw and Archibald Chisholm £22:6:8 for stocking muskets. On May 8 and June 19, 1776, the Council of Safety paid them for assembling guns from 50 barrels made by Isaac Harris and stocks made by Chisholm. On July 5 and July 16, 1776, the Maryland Council of Safety ordered delivery to Harris of "one Faggett of steel" and "half a faggot of Steel," respectively, apparently for the making of guns, "also, eighty-four Muskets, to be repaired."[121]

Elisha Winters informed the Council of Safety on July 27, 1776, that "I shall have twenty-eight muskets ready to your order by Monday, 3d August, making up forty muskets per month, agreeable to my contract." Thomas Smyth's letter of May 23, 1776, reports that Robert Reed of Chester Town had already made 10 muskets, and was prepared to sell them, with bayonets, at "85/ each."[122] (This may be a typo for £5—a typical price for the time.)

Richard Dallam of Harford County, Maryland, reported on July 16, 1776, that he had finished 22 muskets and had "fifteen more ready for stocking, six of which will be finished this week." Dallam apologized for his slow production based on "Harvest & sickness of two of my best hands and the bursting of twelve or thirteen of my barrels." A week later, Dallam reported that five more guns were complete, and by the following week, he would have made enough to complete his contract. Dallam was reluctant to make any more muskets at the contracted price and complained that the Committee of Observation had paid £4:10:0 "for guns worse than mine." On August 11, a Col. Ewing reported that "Dallam had thirty more stand completed."[123]

Apparently, the Council of Safety was willing to pay a higher price for subsequent guns from Dallam. A July 27, 1776, letter to Dallam informed him that "the price you ask is high for Guns, but we want them at present, and therefore will take any number you may make in six Weeks from this time, and give you four pounds ten shillings currency for them completely finished."[124]

Even as late as April 18, 1777, when guns were being delivered at bargain prices from Europe, there were still guns being made in Maryland. George Gordon received £4 for a musket, and Richard Bond signed a contract to make 1,000 gun barrels for the state, "not less than sixty two Barrels per month." More than a year later, Bond was still making gun barrels.[125]

Gunlocks

As discussed earlier in the chapter, gunlocks were largely imported before the war and generally the limiting factor on gun production. On March 9, 1776, it appears that a Pennsylvania "Committee appoint[ed] to direct the Manufactory of Gun Locks" existed, and it was provided with £300 with which to carry on this apparently strategic effort—and one that only made sense if there were guns being made that required those gunlocks. As previously mentioned, the Maryland Council of Safety similarly appropriated funds with which to establish a gunlock factory at Fredericktown, though in this case, the factory was unsuccessful and was closed in 1778. Instead, a gunsmith named Messersmith presented samples of gunlocks that he had made, and he offered to make 10 a week at $3 each.[126]

The New Jersey Committee of Safety "established the State Gun Lock Factory at Trenton late in 1775. . . . The State Gun Lock Factory was forced to close shortly after December 8, 1776, when Washington hastily retreated beyond the Delaware River, hotly pursued by Lord Cornwallis. Hessian and Highland troops occupied Trenton."[127]

A March 6, 1776, letter from the Newark Committee to President of Congress John Hancock makes references to two prisoners of war named Brown and Thompson who were working for a Mr. Alling in the making of guns and gunlocks. Apparently, there was some interest in moving these POWs away from Mr. Alling's gun manufacturing operation, and the Newark Committee was attempting to keep them. "Alling, in consequence of the leave obtained from Congress, had contracted to supply upwards of two hundred gun-locks for the use of the United Colonies, which contract was in part executed, but he would be very unable to fulfill his contracts, if Thompson should be taken from him." Alling was making gunlocks; his contract "was in part executed."[128]

Samuel Wigfal and Marmaduke Blackwood contracted with the Provincial Council of Pennsylvania "for two hundred Gun-locks to be made according to Pattern."[129] Samuel Kinder and James Walsh were described as "Philadelphia gunlock-makers" in December 1776.[130]

In the July 17, 1775, *Pennsylvania Packet*, "Sarah Jones, widow," advertised for the return of a runaway servant, William Jones, described as "by trade a gunlock maker." The servant's last name, Jones, matching the upset mistress, suggests that he might have been a slave. The name is the same as the runaway indentured servant sought in New York, which was previously discussed on page 70.

Duncan Beard, while better known as a clocksmith and silversmith, also made gunlocks for Delaware, as did Frederick Shraeder, of Wilmington, Delaware.[131] Samuel Boone manufactured gunlocks in Maryland before June 1777, and he continued to make gunlocks and firearms as late as 1782. At least one surviving European pistol bears a Revolutionary War era gunlock made by Rappahannock Forge, and arms collectors are of the opinion that at least some surviving muskets used gunlocks made by Rappahannock Forge. There is a late flint lockwork made by P.A. & S. Small of York, Pennsylvania, which could be colonial or as late as the Early Republic. A Charleville pattern flintlock made by Evans, with a Philadelphia or Pennsylvania proof mark, survives, demonstrating early gunlock making in America.[132]

The evidence is clear: guns were manufactured during the Revolution, and the surviving records, which are necessarily fragmentary, suggest that there were considerable numbers of such manufacturers who each made dozens to thousands of guns at the start of the Revolution. How many total were made? We really do not know. We do know that there are a surprising number of surviving guns that were made in the United States during the Revolution, under conditions of invasion, labor shortages, and shortages of gunlocks, which had been largely imported before the Revolution. Revisionist claims that Colonial America lacked a gun industry and was unable to correct this problem during the Revolution fail to match the available sources.

CHAPTER 6

Gun Culture in the Early Republic, 1783–1846

This chapter looks at evidence of gun culture in the Early Republic as expressed in travel accounts, advertising, and newspaper reports. Michael Bellesiles's *Arming America* claims that most Americans, even on the frontier, did not hunt until the mid-1830s, when a small number of wealthy Americans chose to ape their upper-class British counterparts.[1] An even more amazing claim is that, until 1848, when Samuel Colt mass marketed the revolver, violence between whites was somewhat unusual and murder was rare.[2] As evidence for these two related claims, Bellesiles asserts, "Generally stated, an examination of eighty travel accounts written in America from 1750 to 1860 indicates that the travelers did not notice that they were surrounded by guns and violence."[3] This sentence can be read in at least two ways: that travelers did not notice that they were surrounded by gun violence, or that they did not notice that they were surrounded by guns *and* violence. Because Bellesiles repeatedly denies widespread gun ownership, he implicitly claims guns were rare in these accounts.[4]

Unintentionally, Bellesiles marshaled a list of sources that demonstrate a strong gun culture in the Early Republic. But he falsely claimed the opposite.[5] The remainder of this section uses eyewitness accounts of early America to demonstrate the opposite of Bellesiles's claims, many of them in his list of sources for his gunless America.

Bellesiles did not include in his list accounts that clearly describe atypical occupations and travels, such as George Frederick Ruxton's *Life in the Far West*, describing fur trapping in Utah, New Mexico, and

Colorado in 1847, which was awash in guns and violence. Likewise, Bellesiles excluded John Palliser's *Solitary Rambles and Adventures of a Hunter in the Prairies*, which reports an 1847 hunting trip similarly awash in guns and violence. Both books took place within the United States, but where few Americans—other than the Indians—yet lived.[6] The presence of guns in *these* accounts tell us nothing about gun ownership in American society.

In every region between 1789 and 1846, memoirs and traveler accounts either treat gun ownership as common or explicitly tell us that it was common. No account that I have found even *implied* that hunting was unusual or rare. There is no evidence that hunting was in any sense an upper-class phenomenon; many of the following accounts are explicit that it was common or nearly universal among the lower classes.

When Aaron Burr was tried in 1807 for his criminal conspiracy to detach the Southwest into its own country, one of the pieces of evidence used against him was a meeting of a Mr. Blannerhassett with a number of his coconspirators—all of them armed.[7] Burr's defense attorney argued there was nothing suspicious about being armed because gun ownership was the norm in the Early Republic:

> Arms are not necessarily military weapons. Rifles, shot guns and fowling pieces are used commonly by the people of this country in hunting and for domestic purposes; they are generally in the habit of pursuing game. In the upper country every man has a gun; a majority of the people have guns every where, for peaceful purposes. Rifles and shot guns are no more evidence of military weapons than pistols or dirks used for personal defen[s]e, or common fowling pieces kept for the amusement of taking game. It is lawful for every man in this country to keep such weapons.[8]

In 1781, Perkins & Coutty of Philadelphia advertised that they were making guns and pistols "in all its branches, where Gentlemen may be supplied with Guns and Pistols of the neatest and best quality on the shortest notice." Gunsmith John Nicholson offered a variety of firearms for sale in November of 1781, including "pistols . . . upon the most reasonable terms."[9] Both of these ads *could* have been for the military officer market, but the Revolutionary War hostilities had ceased by this point.

In 1796 and 1797, Francis Baily traveled through America. He describes an "excellent tavern" on Chesapeake Bay, "which is frequented by parties in the shooting season, for the sake of the wild fowl with which the Susquehannah so plentifully abounds."[10]

He described his visit to Washington, D.C., which was still largely wooded. To emphasize how far the new capital had to go before it would be a large city, Baily reports, "Game is plenty in these parts, and, what perhaps may appear to you remarkable, I saw some boys who were out a shooting, actually kill several brace of partridges in what will be one of the most public streets of the city." It was not boys out shooting that was remarkable to Baily, but that they were shooting in what would be one of the main boulevards of America's capital.[11]

Baily describes his visit to Fredericktown, Maryland, which was a "large and flourishing place" with a "large manufactory of rifle-guns carried on[,] . . . but so great is the demand for them, that [they] could not meet with one in the whole place." Baily notes the rifle-guns sold "in general from 15 to 25 dollars each, according to their style of being mounted." Past the Allegheny Mountains, Baily and his party came to Hager's-town, which "like Frederick's-town, [wa]s a place of great trade, and also a manufactory for rifle-guns, of which [they] bought two at twenty dollars each."[12]

During Baily's trip down the Ohio River, he describes how, each day, his party moored their boats together, "so that there were fourteen or fifteen of [them] in company: and [they] every day sent out some of them into the woods with their guns to hunt for deer, turkeys, bears, or any other animals fit for food." Baily describes a plantation in the wilderness where they asked for food, but they could not help because "they were, in fact, in the same destitute situation in which [Baily and his party] were—obliged to depend upon their guns for subsistence." Following a serious boat accident, his party became more desperate for food. With their stock diminishing, they were forced to take turns and "go out every morning with [their] gun and shoot whatever [they] could find; and many a time would we lay ourselves down at night without a prospect of anything wherewith to break our fast the next morning, save what [their] guns might procure [them] the next day."[13]

Baily's description of frontier Columbia, Ohio, emphasizes hunting as a source of food: "The inhabitants live[d] a great deal upon deer and turkeys, which they sho[t] wild in the woods." Baily went hunting there with Dr. Bean, a settler on Little Miami River, in which they "mounted on horses, and had each a gun." Baily explains that black bears were hunted in Ohio by cutting down trees in which bears had climbed, "and three or four of the party with loaded rifles" would shoot the bear as he climbed out of the fallen tree. Baily also makes casual references to guns, such as an "old man, accompanied by his dog and his gun." As his party floated down the Mississippi, the first boat in the expedition fired a gun as a signal to the others. Baily also describes Long Island's villages, which were "much frequented by different parties from New York [City], which go over to hunt, shoot, and fish."[14] The accounts from Baily's book certainly demonstrate he was surrounded by guns and hunting.

Edward Pole advertised his "Military Laboratory," where "Owners and Commanders of Armed Vessels may be supplied, for either the use of Small Arms or Cannon, at the shortest notice, with every species of Military Stores." Among items advertised were "musket's [sic] and pistol's [sic]." That there were customers other than ship captains is suggested by the offering of "musket cartridges in blank, for the exercise of the militia."[15]

Isaac Weld's description of his trip through North America in the years 1795–1797 describes how "German mechanics" of Lancaster, Pennsylvania, manufactured a variety of goods, "principally for the people of the town and the neighborhood. Rifled barrel guns however are to be excepted, which, although not as handsome as those imported from England, are more esteemed by the hunters, and are sent to every part of the country."[16]

Weld describes how rifles worked for his British audience, many of whom were unfamiliar with rifled weapons:[17]

> An experienced marksman, with one of these guns, will hit an object not larger than a crown piece, to a certainty, at the distance of one hundred yards. Two men belonging to the Virginia rifle regiment, a large division of which was quartered in this town during the war, had such a dependence on each other's dexterity, that the one would hold a piece of board, not more than nine inches square, between his knees, whilst the other shot at it with a ball at the distance of one hundred paces. This they used to do alternately, for the amusement of the town's people, as often as they were called upon. . . . Were I, however, to tell you all the stories I have heard of the performance of riflemen, you would think the people were most abominably addicted to lying.[18]

Weld discusses the manufacture and use of rifles for hunting and compares Canadian hunters to their American counterparts:

> The people here, as in the back parts of the United States, devote a very great part of their time to hunting, and they are well skilled in the pursuit of game of every description. They shoot almost universally with the rifle gun, and are as dexterous at the use of it as any men can be.[19]

The difference between Americans and Canadians, according to Weld, was that Americans used American-made rifles and preferred smaller calibers.[20]

Another of Bellesiles's 80 gunless accounts is Fortescue Cuming's *Sketches of a Tour to the Western Country*, which describes Cuming's journey through Pennsylvania, Ohio, and Kentucky, from 1807 to 1809.[21] Throughout his journey, and with no surprise, Cuming mentions gunsmiths, gunpowder manufacture, widespread use of guns for sport, subsistence hunting, self-defense, and the occasional murder. Cuming describes the abundant wildlife of Kentucky, even after settlement, and notes "that little or no bread was used, but that even the children were fed on game; the facility of gaining which prevented the progress of agriculture."[22]

Even though Cuming was a hunter, he expressed his admiration for the superior marksmanship of Western Pennsylvanians and Virginians:

> Apropos of the rifle.—The inhabitants of this country in common with the Virginians, and all the back woods people, Indians as well as whites, are wonderfully expert in the use of it: thinking it a bad shot if they miss the very head of a squirrel, or a wild turkey, on the top of the highest forest tree with a single ball; though they generally load with a few grains of swan shot, with which they are equally sure of hitting the head of the bird or animal they fire at.[23]

Rev. William C. Smith's frontier account, *Indiana Miscellany*, describes settlers who were armed with guns and prepared for self-defense against Indians. Smith also describes the morality of the early Indiana settlements by telling how "it was a rare thing to hear . . . the report of a hunter's gun on the holy Sabbath day."[24] Smith's statement thus implies that gunfire was *not* rare during the rest of the week. During the War of 1812, Smith told of a shortage of provisions for the settlers, who had fortified their villages,

> but usually they had plenty of meat. All the men were excellent hunters—some of them real experts. The country abounding in game, they kept the forts well supplied with venison and bear-meat. . . . When considered at all admissible to venture outside the fort to labor, the men went in company, taking their trusty rifles with them. . . . Some of [the women] could handle the rifle with great skill, and bring down the game in the absence of their husbands.[25]

Robert Carlton's memoir of frontier Indiana life, cited by Bellesiles, written as a pseudonymous novel (as was common at the time) describes how hunting was a common part of life, done partly for sport and partly for low-cost fresh meat:

> Let none think we western people follow rifle shooting, however, for mere sport; that would be nearly as ignoble as shot gun idleness! The rifle procures, at certain seasons, the only meat we ever taste; it defends our homes from wild animals and saves our corn fields from squirrels and our hen-roosts from foxes, owls, opossums and other "var ments." . . . The rifle is a woodman's lasso. He carries it everywhere as (a very degrading comparison for the gun, but none other occurs,) a dandy a cane. All, then, who came to our tannery or store came thus armed; and rarely did a customer go, till his rifle had been tried at a mark, living or dead.[26]

After listing a variety of wild game that were hunted in the uninhabited land between settlements, Carlton lists "'the neighbours' hogs,'—so wild and fierce, that when pork-time arrives, they must be hunted and shot, like other independent beasts." Carlton's many hunting references with guns, usually with rifles, suggest it was ordinary; guns were also used for catching criminals.[27]

Carlton uses the imagery of guns to describe the height of the trees in the forest: "till their high heads afforded a shelter to squirrels, far beyond the sprinkling of a shot-gun, and almost beyond the reach of the rifle!"[28] In describing how life on the frontier expanded a person's talents relative to those who stayed in the East, Carlton compares the double-barreled shotgun with the rifle, which was common in his region:

> Does the chap shoot a double-barrelled gun?—so can you, if you would—but you transcend him, oh! far enough with that man's weapon, that in *your* hands deals, at your will, certain death to *one* selected victim, without *scattering* useless wounds at a venture in a little innocent feathered flock.[29]

Carlton's America was steeped in a gun culture. Carlton devotes an entire *chapter* to the joy of target shooting with rifles, opening the chapter as follows: "Reader, were ever you *fired* with the love of rifle shooting? If so, the confidence now reposed in your honour will not be abused, when told my love for that noble art is unabated."[30]

Carlton also describes target shooting matches as common, and he took pride in participating in a match where the prize was a half-barrel of whiskey. As president of the local temperance society, his goal was to shoot "for the fun of the thing," and if he won, he would pour the whiskey into the local stream. The local blacksmith was also a rifle maker, and, according to Carlton, his rifles were better than those made back East.[31]

The rifle was so common an implement, and target shooting so common a sport, that when Carlton went out evangelizing in a sparsely settled part of Indiana, one of his fellow preachers switched in mid-sermon to a metaphor involving rifle matches to sway the audience: "My friends and neighbours don't you all shoot the rifle in this settlement?" They were becoming restless with analogies that meant nothing to them, but they understood the preacher's analogy to a rifle match. Carlton also describes Pittsburgh, in a whimsical style with literary allusions, as a place where guns are made: "some here make tubes of iron, with alternate and spiral 'lands and furrows,' better by far to shoot than Milton's grand and unpatent blunderbusses."[32]

Carlton describes what would have been a fatal gun accident that was narrowly averted and gives no indication that this was a shocking event. Carlton refers to pistols on several occasions with no indication that they were either rare or regarded with any particular concern.[33] Yet Hall's references to pistols are far exceeded by his mentions of rifles and shotguns.[34] Hall's discussions of hunting, use and misuse of guns, and target shooting occur throughout the book and are treated as common events.[35]

Abraham Lincoln's autobiographical sketch, prepared in 1860, describes his family's movement from Kentucky to Indiana around 1816, and how "a few days before the completion of his eighth year, in the absence of his father, a flock of wild turkeys approached the new log-cabin, and [Abraham] with a rifle gun, standing inside, shot through a crack, and killed one of them." Lincoln was not much of a hunter,[36] but even his family, which was not wealthy by any means,[37] owned a rifle, and hunting was an acceptable action for a seven-year-old.[38] Lincoln's poem "The Bear Hunt," written around 1846, states, "When first my father settled here / 'Twas then the frontier line: / The panther's scream, / filled night with fear / And bears preyed on the swine. / But wo[e] for Bruin's short lived fun, / When rose the squealing cry; / Now man and horse, / with dog and gun, / For vengeance, at him fly."[39] Another line of the poem is "Bang,—bang—the rifles go."[40] Hunting and guns were common on Lincoln's frontier.

In *Fordham's Personal Narrative*, cited by Bellesiles for gunless America, upon his arrival at St. Vincennes, Indiana, in 1817, Pim Fordham

describes what was considered appropriate paraphernalia for traveling in the Indiana wilderness: "guns and tom[a]hawks, and all things
necessary to encamp in the woods." Fordham also mentions Indiana's
"back-wood settlers, who are half hunters, half farmers."[41] He divided
the frontier population of Illinois into four categories, of which the first
two relied upon hunting for their survival:

> 1st. The hunters, a daring, hardy, race of men, who live in miserable
> cabins, which they fortify in times of War with the Indians, whom
> they hate but much resemble in dress and manners. . . . But their rifle
> is their principal means of support. They are the best marksmen in
> the world, and such is their dexterity that they will shoot an apple
> off the head of a companion. Some few use the bow and arrow. . . .

> 2d. class. First settlers;—a mixed set of hunters and farmers.[42]

Suggesting it was the norm in the Illinois Territory, Fordham's letter to
his brother back in Britain describes his style of dress when traveling: "I
wish you could see your brother mount his horse to morrow morning. I
will give you a sketch. A broad-brimmed straw hat,—long trousers and
moccasins,—shot pouch and powder horn slung from a belt,—rifle at his
back, in a sling." Fordham observed that "should a war break out on our
frontiers, I hope that there is not nor will be, a young Englishman among
us, who would hesitate to turn out with his gun and blanket." Fordham
assumed that every "young Englishman" in the Illinois Territory owned
at least one gun.[43]

Fordham describes people who hunted at least partly to sell game to
others, and he also indicates that hunting for one's own table was common. His account of a Christmas Day village feast lists wild turkeys
being cooked.[44] That the game was hunted, not trapped, may be inferred
from the following description:

> The young men had their rifles out, and were firing *feux de joi*
> almost all the preceding night, all the day till late into the evening.
> It reminded me of Byron's description of the Moslems firing at the
> feast of the Ramadan in Constantinople:—but we backwoodsmen
> never fire a gun loaded with *ball into* the town,—only from all
> parts of it, out towards the woods.[45]

Fordham fills his account with descriptions of settlers (including himself) engaged in hunting for sport and for food. Most significantly of

all, with respect to the supposed rarity of firearms in America, Fordham wrote a letter to potential immigrants telling them what they should and should not bring to America: "Do not bring with you any English rifles, or indeed any firearms but a pair of pistols. A good rifle gunlock would be valuable." While pistols might have been expensive or rare, firearms in general were readily available; bringing a gunlock (which weighed little and took up little space in luggage) for assembly into a rifle in America was a wise decision. It seems likely that guns in America (other than pistols) were as cheap, or cheaper, than in Britain.[46]

Anne Newport Royall's description of 1818 Alabama, cited by Bellesiles as another gunless America account, discusses the use of guns for self-defense and hunting as completely ordinary and incidental. Royall also describes bear hunting in her native Virginia.[47]

Henry Rowe Schoolcraft's 1818 journey through the Ozarks also provides evidence that firearms ownership, sport hunting, and subsistence hunting were common. Schoolcraft's description of the frontier settlement of Sugar-Loaf Prairie shows that guns and hunting were the norm:

> These people subsist partly by agriculture, and partly by hunting.... Hunting is the principal, the most honourable, and the most profitable employment. To excel in the chace [sic] procures fame, and a man's reputation is measured by his skill as a marksman, his agility and strength, his boldness and dexterity in killing game, and his patient endurance and contempt of the hardships of the hunter's life. . . . They . . . can subsist any where in the woods, and would form the most efficient military corps in frontier warfare which can possibly exist. Ready trained, they require no discipline, inured to danger, and perfect in the use of the rifle.[48]

At least some of Sugar-Loaf Prairie's hunting was commercial fur trapping, and so perhaps this was atypical of the region—but Schoolcraft's description of other frontier settlements shows that hunting was a common part of how settlers obtained their meat. By the time frontier Ozark children reached 14 years of age, they "[had] completely learned the use of the rifle, the arts of . . . dressing skins and making [moccasins] and leather clothes." Early in his journey, much to Schoolcraft's chagrin, he attempted

> to engage our hostess and her daughters in small-talk, such as passes current in every social corner; but, for the first time, found I should not recommend myself in that way. They could only talk

of bears, hunting, and the like. The rude pursuits, and the coarse enjoyments of the hunter state, were all they knew.[49]

At one isolated cabin that Schoolcraft and his companion visited, the lady of the house was home alone while her husband was on a hunt. Schoolcraft expressed amazement that the lady of the house instructed Schoolcraft and his companion about not only "errors in our dress, equipments, and mode of travelling," but also "that our [shotguns] were not well adapted to our journey; that we should have rifles." Schoolcraft and his companion were astonished "to hear a woman direct us in matters which we had before thought the peculiar and exclusive province of men." Ozark women as hunters surprised a New Englander like Schoolcraft, but his comments also imply that the sex of his instructor was surprising—not widespread hunting and firearms.[50]

New Yorker John Stillman Wright's acidic *Letters from the West* (1819), describe the early farmers of Cincinnati as "mostly, of indolent slovenly habits, devoting the chief part of their time to hunting, and drinking whiskey." While Wright does not expressly say the farmers hunted with firearms, his description of them implies that hunting was *not* an upper-class phenomenon, nor was it rare. Richard Flower's *Letters from the Illinois* describes the Illinois Territory in the early 1820s. At the frontier village of Albion, Sunday amusements included "the backwoodsmen sh[ooting] at *marks*, their favourite sport."[51]

A circa 1820 Du Pont gunpowder packaging illustration for Hagley Mills (as Du Pont gunpowder was marketed after 1814) also suggests that the market for gunpowder included some significant numbers of hunters. While not conclusive evidence, the hunter's attire suggests a rustic, not a member of the upper class.

Merchants advertised gunpowder in ways that gave indications that hunters were a significant market: "Eagle Powder, for Sportsmen, Coarse and Fine, for Land or Sea shooting."[52]

William Blane, in another gunless America account, mentions guns and hunting several times throughout his book *An Excursion through the United States and Canada, during the Years 1822–23*. On the road across the Allegheny Mountains, he describes his first encounter with rifles in the hands of some hunters:

As one of them, an old man, was boasting of his skill as a marksman, I offered to put up a half-dollar at a distance of fifty yards, to be his if he could hit it. Accordingly, I stepped the distance, and placed the half-dollar in the cleft of a small stick, which I thrust into the ground. The hunter, slowly raising his rifle, fired, and to my great astonishment struck the half-dollar.[53]

Rifles were common in the backcountry, as Blane could go to any house, and "the people were always ready to lend [him] a rifle, and were in general glad to accompany [him] when [he] went out hunting." Blane describes squirrel hunting with an American on an island in the Ohio River and how the Americans were in a losing battle to exterminate them: "In parts of Ohio, the people attempted to destroy them by means of guns, dogs, and clubs. One party of hunters, in the course of a week, killed upwards of 19,000. . . . The people are very fond of the flesh of the squirrel, roasting it, and making it into pies, soups, &c."[54]

Blane's description of the backwoodsmen observed that "every boy, as soon as he can lift a rifle, is constantly practicing with it, and thus becomes an astonishingly expert marksman. Squirrel shooting is one of the favourite amusements of all the boys, and even of the men themselves." Blane also wrote about the impressive marksmanship skills of the American militiamen, remarking, "in these immense forests, where every tree is a fort, the backwoodsmen, the best sharp shooters in the world, constitute the most formidable military force imaginable."[55]

Americans hunted birds as well, and Blane describes the normal procedure by which Americans hunted the prairie fowls: "They are delicious eating, and are killed in great numbers by the unrivalled marksmen of this country. After driving up a flock of these birds, the hunter advances within fifteen or twenty paces, raises his long heavy rifle, and rarely misses striking the bird on the head." He admits that he was not as good a shot and had to resort to shooting the prairie fowls in the body instead of the head: "the Backwoodsmen regarded my unsportsmanlike shooting with as much contempt, as one of our country squires feels, when a cockney shoots at a covey of partridges on the ground." Blane also describes the astonishment when he informed Americans that British game laws prohibited hunting deer in public lands, and even limited hunting on one's own land, unless of a certain wealth, of which "such flagrant injustice appeared to them impossible."[56]

Karl Bernhard, the Duke of Saxe-Weimar-Eisenach, visited America in 1825 and 1826. Another gunless America account, he references hunting and guns on many pages, which is always treated as ordinary. He describes how emigrants "supported themselves by hunting" and relates one occasion when he was invited to dinner in which a wild turkey brought home from a hunt was to be eaten.[57]

Sandford C. Cox's *Recollections of the Early Settlement of the Wabash Valley* describes 1820s and 1830s Indiana using the journals and memoirs of the early settlers, who used guns for hunting, entertainment, defense of their country, and assisting law enforcement.[58]

English naturalist Philip Gosse, another of Bellesiles's gunless America citations, visiting Alabama in the 1830s, provided one of the more complete descriptions of the attitude of the population toward hunting and firearms:

> Self-defence, and the natural craving for excitement, compel him to be a *hunter*; it is the appropriate occupation of a new, grand, luxuriant, wild country like this, and one which seems natural to man, to judge from the eagerness and zest with which every one engages in it when he has the opportunity. The long rifle is familiar to every hand; skill in the use of it is the highest accomplishment which a southern gentleman glories in; even the children acquire an astonishing expertness in handling this deadly weapon at a very early age.[59]

Gosse's account also emphasizes the high level of marksmanship in America:

> But skill as a marksman is not estimated by quite the same standard as in the old country. Pre-eminence in any art must bear a certain relation to the average attainment; and where this is universally high, distinction can be won only by something very exalted. Hence, when the young men meet together to display their skill, curious tests are employed, which remind one of the days of old English archery. . . . Some of these practices I had read of, but here I find them in frequent use. "Driving the nail" is one of these; a stout nail is hammered into a post about half way up to the head; the riflemen then stand at an immense distance, and fire at the nail; the object is to hit the nail so truly on the head with the ball as to drive it home. To hit at all on one side, so as to cause it to bend or swerve, is failure; missing it altogether is out of the question.[60]

Gosse also describes widespread hunting of squirrels, wild hog, and varmint, including opossum and raccoons, with rifles. Alabamans hunted for sport, food, and to protect crops from damage.[61]

Alexis de Tocqueville's *Journey to America*, his account of the travels that led to writing *Democracy in America*, quotes a Tennessee farmer in 1831:

The dweller in this country is generally lazy. He regards work as an evil. Provided he has food enough and a house which gives half shelter, he is happy and thinks only of smoking and hunting. . . . There is not a farmer but passes some of his time hunting and owns a good gun.[62]

Tocqueville also describes a usual "peasant's cabin" in Kentucky or Tennessee: "There one finds a fairly clean bed, some chairs, a good gun, often some books and almost always a newspaper."[63] Guns and hunting were not unusual in Kentucky or Tennessee, according to Tocqueville; they were typical.

Robert Baird's *View of the Valley of the Mississippi*, another gunless America account, reads like a real estate promotional guide, emphasizing the enormous benefits of moving to these largely unsettled states. But he still admits some unsavory aspects of the frontier. A few instances of violence appear in Baird's promotional work—such as St. Louis and its dueling problem—but they are usually in conjunction with a positive statement, such as "a great moral change is going forward here." Baird also reports a dispute at cards aboard a steamboat: "Pistols and dirks were drawn!"[64]

While Baird sometimes mentions gun violence, he repeatedly mentions hunting—and in a manner suggesting that the abundance of game would be an important factor when deciding where to settle.[65] Baird describes Michigan's advantages:

The wild game of this territory is similar to that of Indiana, and the adjoining unsettled parts of Ohio. Deer, bears, beavers, otters, wolves, foxed &c. are numerous. Geese, ducks, and other aquatic fowls are exceedingly abundant. Wild [turkeys], pheasants, prairie hens, &c. &c. are to be found in great numbers and afford delicious food to the settlers in the autumn and winter.[66]

Baird made similar remarks about the wild game of Illinois, Missouri, and Florida. In Missouri, Baird told of the abundance of game, describing a "semi-barbarian population" that lived off the game: "I have seen some of these men who could spend hour after hour in detailing their achievements with the 'rifle.'" Baird also describes steamboat passengers, including "the half-horse and half-alligator Kentucky boatman, swaggering, and boasting of his prowess, his rifle, his horse, and his wife."[67]

Harriet Martineau's supposedly another gunless America account describes the mid-1830s. Her America shows that firearms and sport hunting were common occurrences along the Mississippi and unsurprising to her:

> While I was reading on the morning of the 12th, the report of a rifle from the lower deck summoned me to look out. There were frequent rifle-shots, and they always betokened our being near shore; generally under the bank, where the eye of the sportsman was in the way of temptation from some object in the forest.[68]

Gert Göbel's description of the Missouri frontier in the 1830s tells us that there were no religious observances at Christmas, and no gifts were exchanged:

> There was just shooting. On Christmas Eve, a number of young fellows from the neighborhood banded together, and, after they had gathered together not only their hunting rifles but also old muskets and horse pistols from the Revolutionary War and had loaded them almost to the bursting point, they went from house to house. They approached a house as quietly as possible and then fired a mighty volley, to the fright of the women and children, and, if someone did not appear then, another volley no doubt followed. But usually the man of the house opened the door immediately, fired his own gun in greeting and invited the whole company into the house. . . . After everyone had chatted for a little while, the whole band set out for the next farm, where the same racket started up anew. In this way, this mischief was carried on until morning, and since, as a rule, a number of such bands were out and about, one could often hear all night the roaring and rattling of guns from all directions.[69]

Accounts of similar practices—apparently of German origin—appeared in many states, both frontier and settled in the 1830s.[70] It appears that "Christmas shooting" took the same place on the Missouri frontier that Christmas caroling did in the America of the author's youth.

Rebecca Burlend's narrative of the Missouri frontier in 1831 describes bird hunting, and she implies that it was not only common among British emigrants but also Americans. Her husband had successfully hunted a turkey—or so he thought. Rebecca had it mostly cooked for Sunday dinner when their guest arrived and expressed surprise, "as those birds are difficult to obtain with a common fowling-piece." Mr. Burlend had bagged a buzzard, not a turkey—definitely not fit for the table![71]

Frances Wright is certainly one of the most pro-American British visitors of the Early Republic, and her claims should be regarded with greater care than many of the other visitors. Nonetheless, her assertion that "every man, or nearly every man, in these states knows how to handle the axe, the hammer, the plane, all the mechanic's tools, in short; besides the musket, to the use of which he is not only regularly trained as a man but practised as a boy"[72] suggests that the use of firearms in America was widespread, even granting some romantic hyperbole on Wright's part.

The Anglo-Irishman Thomas Cather described emigrants headed to the frontier while crossing Michigan in 1836. Rifles were the norm, not the exception:

> Emigrants from the old states on their way to settle in the Western forests. Each emigrant generally had a wagon or two, drawn by oxen. These wagons contained their wives, children, and *rest of their baggage.* The man walked by the side of his team with his rifle over his shoulder.[73]

British naval officer and novelist Frederick Marryat visited North America and described North Carolinians emigrating west in 1837:

> These caravans consist of two or three covered wagons, full of women and children, furniture, and other necessaries, each drawn by a team of horses; brood mares, with foals by their sides, following; half a dozen or more cows, flanked on each side by the men, with their long rifles on their shoulders; sometimes a boy or two, or a half-grown girl on horseback.[74]

There are references to guns other than when used for hunting or dueling, but they are always treated as ordinary. Marryat's account of his journey frequently mentions Americans hunting and shooting in a way that suggests that there was nothing particularly unusual about it. He describes how hunting was the "principal amusement of the officers" at Fort Snelling. (There would have been few other entertainments on the frontier.) Captain Scott, one of those officers, had a reputation as a very great marksman, based on his ability to throw two potatoes in the air and puncture both of them with a single rifle bullet. Captain Scott's hunting did not seem to be a peculiarity of Fort Snelling being on the frontier. Marryat recounted Scott's hunting anecdotes involving bear and buffalo as well as when Scott was a 12-year-old in Vermont; these accounts indicate that both hunting and gun ownership were common in Scott's youth in Vermont. Marryat also devotes a bit of his book to discussing dueling with guns and his disgust at how widely this was accepted behavior in America, even among congressmen.[75]

British immigrant Mary Clavers's book shows that guns and sports involving guns were widespread on her 1839 frontier. Discussing the problems of church attendance, she writes, "Many of the neighbours always make a point of being present, although a far greater proportion reserve the Sunday for fishing and gunning." Clavers mentions long guns, pistols, and hunting in a manner that suggests they were normal parts of frontier life. Hunting was unremarkable. Kirkland comments on a neighbor whose husband's love of hunting left her alone and neglected. She also reports that, in the woods, "the division of labour is almost unknown" and "in absolutely savage life, each man is of necessity 'his own tailor, tent-maker, carpenter, cook, huntsman, and fisherman.'"[76]

Harriet Williams Sawyer of Maine described 1840s Indiana life. Unlike Rev. William C. Smith's somewhat earlier version of Indiana, described on page 91, Sabbath-breaking was a problem: "The Sabbath in the West is much desecrated; trades are transacted; labor, it is true, is generally suspended, but the Sabbath is regarded by most as a day of recreation. Hunting and intemperance are common."[77]

John James Audubon's *Delineations of American Scenery and Character*, another gunless America account, describes a society awash in guns and hunting and traveling along the Ohio River:

> The margins of the shores and of the river were at this season amply supplied with game. A Wild Turkey, a Grouse, or a Blue-winged Teal, could be procured in a few moments; and we fared well, for, whenever we pleased, we landed, struck up a fire, and provided as we were with the necessary utensils, procured a good repast.[78]

Audubon's preparations for a trip in the forests of Pennsylvania, included "25 pounds of shot, some flints . . . my gun *Tear-jacket*, and a heart as true to nature as ever." [emphasis in original] (This speaks to America as a gun culture: who else names their guns?) The results of this particular hunting trip included "juicy venison, excellent bear flesh . . . that daily formed [his] food." Audubon describes what this area must have been like before settlement: "Bears and the Common Deer must have been plentiful, as, at the moment when [he wrote], many of both kinds [were] seen and killed by the resident hunters." Audubon witnessed an incident in which eight bears wandered into a clearing; the bears driving away the woodsmen: "Down they all rushed from the mountain; the noise spread quickly; rifles were soon procured and shouldered; but when the spot was reached, no bears were to be found."[79]

Audubon's chapter on "Navigation of the Mississippi" describes how boatmen would stop along the way when logs blocked their path: "The time is not altogether lost, as most of the men, being provided with rifles, betake themselves to the woods, and search for the deer, the bears, or the turkeys, that are generally abundant there." The flood stages of the Mississippi and Ohio Rivers trapped "Bears, Cougars, Lynxes, and all other quadrupeds that can ascend the trees." The animals were "fatigued by the exertions which they ha[d] made in reaching the dry land, they will there stand the hunter's fire, as if to die by a ball were better than to perish amid the waste waters. On occasions like this, all these animals are shot by hundreds."[80]

Audubon describes a squatter's cabin and how squatters "like most of those adventurous settlers in the uncultivated tracts of our frontier districts . . . [were] well versed in the chase, and acquainted with the habits of some of the larger species of quadrupeds and birds." Audubon went cougar hunting with a party of squatters: "Each hunter . . . moved with caution, holding his gun ready." Audubon tells of a young couple's home in the backwoods where their clothes and their furniture were "homespun" and "of domestic manufacture," and a "fine rifle ornamented the chimney-piece."[81]

Another family (in the Louisiana bayous) was composed of runaway slaves. Their food supply consisted of wild plants and bear: "One day, while in search of wild fruits, he found a bear dead before the muzzle of a gun that had been set for the purpose. . . . His friends at the plantation supplied him with some ammunition."[82]

In a chapter about how the burning of forests changed the nature of the trees that grew there, Audubon describes an immense forest fire in Maine and how the settlers responded to the fire that awakened them one night:

We were sound asleep one night, in a cabin about a hundred miles from this, when about two hours before day, the snorting of the horses and lowing of the cattle which I had ranging in the woods suddenly wakened us. I took yon rifle, and went to the door to see what beast had caused the hubbub.[83]

Another chapter on Kentucky sports describes how Virginians moved into the Ohio frontier: "An axe, a couple of horses, and a heavy rifle, with store of ammunition, were all that were considered necessary." Kentucky sports included target shooting with rifles, and Audubon spent four pages describing a sport similar to Gosse's account of "driving the nail," discussed on page 98, and in *Mourt's Relation*, discussed on page 18. This was apparently not a new practice, nor specific to the New World.

Audubon was clearly a gun enthusiast. When a new acquaintance offered to show him the new percussion cap method of firing a gun, Audubon was keen to see it. His friend demonstrated that it could fire underwater by loading and firing it in a basin of water—inside the house.

Guns were a fundamental part of how Audubon was able to produce his beautiful works on natural history: "I drew and noted the habits of every thing which I procured, and my collection was daily augmenting, as every individual who carried a gun always sent me such birds or quadrupeds as he thought might prove useful to me."[84]

Audubon devotes a whole chapter to "Deer Hunting" with rifles, distinguishing "Still Hunting" from "Firelight Hunting" and "Driving." "*Still Hunting* is followed as a kind of trade by most of our frontier men. To be practi[c]ed with success, it requires great activity, an expert management of the rifle, and a thorough knowledge of the forest." Another section describes alligator hunting, where by a "rifle bullet was now and then sent through the eye of one of the largest." Audubon titled another chapter "The Moose Hunt," which took place in 1833 Maine, and, of course, the hunt was with guns. Similarly, an entire chapter is devoted to "A Racoon Hunt in Kentucky" using rifles, with a detailed description of rifle loading.[85]

Another gunless America account is Ole Rynning, who wrote that those considering immigrating to America should bring "some rifles with percussion locks, partly for personal use, partly for sale. I have already said that in America a good rifle costs from fifteen to twenty dollars."[86] One should bring guns both to sell (indicating that there was a demand for guns in America) *and* because one would need them.

Another gunless America account, Charles Augustus Murray, came from Britain to America in the 1830s to hunt. He reported that both firearms ownership and sport hunting were common in rural Virginia. Murray tells us that these Virginia hunters were not members of the upper class, but ordinary farmers:

I lodged the first night at the house of a farmer, about seven miles from the village, who joined the habits of a hunter to those of an agriculturalist, as is indeed the case with all the country people in this district; nearly every man has a rifle, and spends part of his time in the chase. My double rifle, of London manufacture, excited much surprise among them; but the concluding remark of almost every inspector was, "I guess I could beat you at a mark."[87]

The frontier would have more reason for firearms ownership than the East, but even from the most settled parts of pre-1840 America, the advertisements, memoirs, and travel accounts show gun ownership and hunting were unremarkable. Jonathan Vickers advertised in a Cleveland newspaper in 1821 that he had opened a "Gun Factory" where "New Rifles and Fowling Pieces will be furnished cheap, for cash."[88] Another ad in the same issue lists "Best Eng. Powder, Com. Amer'n [ditto] Shot & Lead."[89]

Haswell's *Reminiscences of New York by an Octogenarian* describes New York City life from 1816 to 1860. Haswell's entry for November 1830 describes shooting a "ruffed grouse" at 144th Street and 9th Avenue in Manhattan, "and it was believed by sportsmen to be the last one to suffer a like fate on the island." Haswell also describes the opening of commercial hunting clubs on the island of Manhattan.[90] This suggests that sport hunting on Manhattan was already common at a time when Bellesiles argues that sport hunting was still unusual in America.

American merchants after the Revolution, such as John Jacob Astor, went into the fur trade, exchanging American-made rifles for fur. Starting in the 1830s, Astor's American Fur Company contracted with Pennsylvania gunmakers. From 1835 on, the Henry family of Nazareth, Pennsylvania, became the only contractor for American Fur, and they manufactured about 2,300 rifles for this trade.

The U.S. government also contracted for trade guns, many of them rifles, to satisfy treaty obligations associated with the westward removal of Indian tribes. At least 18 manufacturers contracted with the U.S. government to make thousands of Indian trade rifles in the period 1800–1809. Henry Deringer contracted to make 8,500 rifles in 1837 and 1840; 2,500 of these rifles were explicitly "Indian rifles," and some of the remaining 6,000 may have been Indian rifles.

How long did firearms last in Indian hands? Because of the difficulties of repair on the frontier and the absence of Indian gunsmiths, one might assume that Indian guns would be short-lived. Yet, the evidence suggests otherwise. H. E. Leman of Lancaster, Pennsylvania, contracted to make 500 Indian rifles for the U.S. government during the 1830s; when the Sioux and Cheyenne surrendered most of their firearms in 1877, four decades later, 94 were Leman rifles.[91]

In addition to guns produced under government contracts, we have scattered surviving guns that demonstrate that there were a number of gunmakers in New England that seem to have escaped Bellesiles's jaundiced eye. Welcome Mathewson made both fowlers and rifles in the early 19th century. Lindsay shows dozens of clearly American-made sporting guns and military-style long guns from the late 18th and early 19th century made in New England (though often with imported English locks).[92]

Concerning Bellesiles's claim, "Few pistols had been made in the United States prior to the opening of the [Colt] Hartford factory [in 1848], pistols having found little market beyond the officers in the army and navy." We have advertising evidence of pistol manufacturing after the Revolution but before 1848. Anthony Desverneys Jr., of South Carolina, advertised in 1785 that he "continues to make and repair all sorts of guns, Pistols and generally everything that belongs to the Gunsmith's Business." A 1791 Philadelphia newspaper advertised a merchant as a "Pistol Maker." A similar 1798 advertisement in the *Pennsylvania Packet* advertised "Gun and Pistol Manufactory. . . . Where Merchants, Captains of vessels, and others may be supplied with all sorts of small arms, on the lowest terms and shortest notice." In 1812 Pittsburgh, Aaron Hart advertised his ability to furnish "Rifles, Fowling pieces, and Pistols, equal in goodness and workmanship to any made in the state." Isaac King advertised in the January 8, 1818, *Somerset Whig* that "He has and expects to have on hand, for sale, GUNS of all descriptions, Pistols. . . ."[93] Perhaps the market for pistols was not as narrow as revisionists claim.

A November 9, 1807, letter from the superintendent of the Springfield Armory to Secretary of War Henry Dearborn shows that pistols were being made in America for nongovernmental purposes. Prescott responds to Dearborn's request for pistols: "I believe Pistols . . . can be made here as advantageously as in any other part of the country and I think I may venture to say better."[94] If not being made at the government's own armory for the military, then who was the intended market?

There are many surviving pistols of the Early Republic, apparently *not* made under government contract nor for military purposes, including dueling pistols. Lindsay shows a number of these survivors from the first few decades of the 19th century, unmistakably American-made, by makers such as Silas Allen, Asa Waters, and Simeon North. While some have English-made gunlocks, the Asa Waters pistol is signed by Waters on the lockplate, suggesting that Waters made the lock, along with the rest of the pistol.[95]

Hartzler's *Arms Makers of Maryland* agrees with Bellesiles that "the great majority of gunsmiths who made longrifles in America used flintlocks, and later percussion locks, that were made in Europe." But Hartzler's description of John Armstrong's practices shows that importation was driven more by economics than technical limitations:

> John Armstrong stands out as a gunsmith who usually made and signed his own flintlocks, contrary to the usual practice. His apprentices learned to make gun locks as well as the other parts of the rifle and the apprentice indentures make specific mention of the lock making instruction. It is noteworthy that Peter White, who probably worked with Armstrong and who possibly apprenticed under him, also made most of his own flintlocks until his later years.[96]

At least part of why gunlocks were generally imported was not because Americans could not make them—because we know that Americans did make them—but because there was no advantage to doing so. Jacob Dickert and other Lancaster County, Pennsylvania, gunmakers, in their 1803 letter to Congress requesting that the tariff on guns not be reduced, describe how they were just completing 20,000 guns for Pennsylvania. They make a point of describing how "gun locks, and every other article in a gun, have been made in the best manner."[97] (Bellesiles cites this letter, but he seems to have missed this detail.) George Moyer of Lancaster Borough, Pennsylvania, is listed as a "Gun Lock Maker" in tax lists from 1819 and 1821.[98] Andrew Klinedinst, a York, Pennsylvania, gunsmith, advertised in 1825 that "he also makes locks,"[99] which would seem to indicate gunlocks.

Robert McCormick advertised for "Lock forgers, lock filers" among other "Gun-Smiths wanted" in the *Pennsylvania Herald and York General Advertiser* of May 25, 1798. Daniel Sweitzer advertised for mechanics to work at his "Gun Lock Manufactory" in a Lancaster, Pennsylvania, newspaper on August 23, 1808. One surviving pistol with a Sweitzer gunlock still exists. When Daniel Borden was apprenticed to "Philip Creamer of Tancy Town, Gun Smith," in 1799, one of the terms of the contract required Creamer to supply 40 of the gunlocks that Creamer made. Similarly, Peter Piper was apprenticed in 1801 to "John Armstrong of Frederick County, Maryland, Gun Smith and Gun Lock Maker, to learn the said mystery and occupation of a Gun Maker and Gun Lock Maker."[100]

Gunlocks were made in America for military arms as well. A surviving musket, apparently made by Adam Angstadt for the Pennsylvania militia at the close of the 18th century, shows a maker's mark of AA inside the gunlock—suggesting that Angstadt not only made the musket but also the gunlock. Hicks reports that gunlocks made by Samuel Dale for Springfield Armory were not, as some have believed, imported from England. Samuel Dale was at one time employed at Springfield Armory.[101]

Along with documents that indicate that gunlocks were made by American gunsmiths, we also have surviving guns. A percussion rifle apparently made by Jacob Kunz of Philadelphia was marked with his name on both the barrels and the gunlock, strongly implying that he was the maker of both. (I will only say "implying" because we know that some importers had gunlocks stamped with their name, either in America or at the factory in England.) Kunz was certainly working in Philadelphia in 1817; this one surviving rifle is the only evidence we have for his work as a gunlock maker.[102] It certainly suggests that there were other gunlock makers in America during this time whose guns did not survive.

James Haslett made muskets for Virginia as well as pistols and sold imported pistols in Baltimore as early as 1806. He advertised in the November 12, 1806, *Federal Gazette & Baltimore Daily Advertiser* that he offered dueling pistols for sale, some made by him and others that were imported from London. His pistols were apparently of very high quality, and his customers included the governors of both Maryland and Virginia. Halbach & Sons sold imported pistols, and a number of pistols have survived from the period 1824–1833 with gunlocks stamped "McKim and Brother Baltimore." As was common at the time, some gunlocks imported from Britain were stamped with the American importer's name. These gunlocks were made into pistols for the civilian market after arrival in America.[103]

Francis D. Poyas advertised his services as a gunsmith in 1825 Charleston, South Carolina—but Poyas apparently made pistols as well. The Charleston Museum has a pair of percussion lock pistols stamped with Poyas's name on the frame. It seems likely that they are his manufacture; they are not government contract pistols.[104]

Debts owed to the estate of James Ross, a Steubenville, Ohio, gunsmith who died in 1816, showed that, along with debts for repairs of guns and apparently for purchases of guns, there was also $45 owed by a customer named John Miller for a "pair of pistols." S. E. Dyke's *Thoughts on the American Flintlock Pistol* shows 91 flintlock pistols unquestionably of American manufacture before 1840; they do not appear to be government contract pistols.[105]

J. Bolton and J. McNaught advertised in 1816 Richmond that their services included "all kinds of GUNS and PISTOLS made, altered and repaired in a perfect manner." The inventory of James McNaught's estate in 1826 shows a "pair of dueling pistols[,] . . . 6 pair small dirk pistols[,] . . . 2 pair best round stock pistols with flints[,] . . . 2 pair percussion pistols, plain secret triggers[,] . . . 3 pair rifle barrel pistols[,] . . . 5 pair secret trigger pistols."[106] It seems a good assumption that these were unsold inventory; the descriptions of the pistols do not sound like they were intended for military use.

Jacob S. Baker advertised in *Whitely's Philadelphia Annual Advertiser* of 1820: "All orders for Rifles, Pistols, Fowling Pieces and Muskets will be punctually attended to." A Cleveland, Ohio, gunsmith in 1823 advertised that "Rifles, Fowling pieces, and Pistols will be furnished on short notice." While the ad is ambiguous as to whether Andrews made all of these items or simply sold and repaired them, it is clear that he sold pistols and considered that there was enough demand to bother listing them for sale.[107]

In 1831, Francis Areis advertised as follows: "Manufacturers and Repairer of all kinds of Fire Arms; Pistols, Guns, Swords, Gunlocks." This can be read as either manufacturing or repair of pistols; either way, it appears that there was either enough demand for pistols or enough pistols in need of repair that Areis considered this ad worth running. Henry A. Cargill, a Nashville merchant, advertised pistols for sale for almost two months on the front page of the Nashville *Daily Republican Banner*. A few months later, A. W. Spies advertised in every issue of the *New York Morning Herald* for several weeks: "Hardware, Cutlery, Guns and Pistols . . . 500 Guns, 300 Rifles, 2,000 pair Pistols/Gun and sporting implements of every kind/Gun materials for Gunsmiths."[108]

In the same paper, on many of the same days, S. M. Pike was advertising "Particular Notice to Sportsmen—A choice assortment of fine double and single barrel guns, rifles and pistols." A B. Ferguson of Huntsville, Alabama, advertised in May 1837 that he was a "Gun and Locksmith," offering repairs and that "I also have on hand some Guns and Pistols for sale, and also a variety of gun and pistol locks."[109]

In Louisville, Kentucky, Fletcher & Reeves advertised in an 1837 business directory: "Dealers in Watches, Jewellery [*sic*], Silver Ware, Military Goods, Pistols, Surveyor's Compasses, Piano Fortes, Music, &c." In St. Louis that same year, Meade & Adriance described themselves as "Importers and wholesale dealers in . . . *Guns, Pistols*, Cutlery, Military and Fancy Goods, generally"[110] [emphasis in original].

Isaac Weld's account of travels between 1795 and 1797[111] discuss how in the backcountry of America and Canada, "the people all travel on horseback, with pistols and swords." While Pym Fordham was staying in Princeton, Indiana, from 1817 to 1818, he also described the prevalence and use of pistols. He observed, "Yesterday 8 men on foot armed with pistols and rifles came into the town from Harmony. They had been in pursuit of an absconded debtor from Vincennes." Fordham reported nothing surprising about eight men armed with pistols and rifles to pursue a mere debtor. He also describes an associate judge as carrying "a pair of pistols at his saddle bow; and altogether look[ed] more like a Dragoon Officer in plain clothes, than a Judge." Fordham did not report that the pistols themselves were remarkable; what was worth noting, at least to a transplanted Englishman, was that a *judge* was carrying them.[112]

Fordham also describes a party in the Illinois Territory that had excluded some "vulgar" party crashers. At this party, on July 4, 1818, Fordham reports that "some young men armed themselves with Dirks (poignards [daggers] worn under the clothes) to resist [any] intrusion" by party crashers. Attempts were made by "the rabble" to interrupt the party, "but the rumour that they were armed with dirks and pistols prevented serious mischief." While the antecedent of "they were armed" is unclear, that it prevented serious mischief by "the rabble" suggests that pistols were weapons commonly carried as a realistic deterrent to "the rabble."[113] According to Fordham (and many other travelers), the boatmen who worked the Mississippi River were a wild and dangerous population. Fordham advises for "all travellers going alone down the river, to get one man at least that they can depend upon, and to wear a dagger or *a brace of pistols*; for there are no desperadoes more savage in their anger than these men"[114] [emphasis added].

The Methodist preacher Peter Cartwright traveled through the Allegheny Mountains to Baltimore in April 1820. The presence of pistols lying in the road was not startling:

> In passing on our journey going down the mountains, on Monday, we met several wagons and carriages moving west. Shortly after we had passed them, I saw lying in the road a very neat pocket-pistol. I picked it up, and found it heavily loaded and freshly primed. Supposing it to have been dropped by some of these movers, I said to brother Walker, "This looks providential;" for the road across these mountains was, at this time, infested by many robbers, and several daring murders and robberies had lately been committed.[115]

Cartwright also recounts his use of this pistol to defend himself against a robber. On his return, he used a pistol to defend himself from robbery during a toll gate dispute. The owner of the tollgate "called for his pistols," apparently with the aim of shooting at Cartwright. In other incidents from the 1820s, Cartwright mentions pistols with no hint that they were at all unusual items, even if the *use* of them was dramatic.[116]

Cartwright describes two young men reduced to deadly enemies as a result of rivalry over a young lady: "They quarreled, and finally fought; both armed themselves, and each bound himself in a solemn oath to kill the other. Thus sworn, and armed with pistols and dirks, they attended camp meeting."[117] Cartwright found neither the pistols nor the threats of death surprising.

In 1820, two young men were competing for the affections of a young lady in Lawrenceburgh, Indiana. Mr. Fuller offered Mr. Warren the chance to write a note disclaiming any interest in her, or engage in a duel. Mr. Warren declined to do either, at which point Fuller shot and killed Warren with a pistol. The report emphasizes that Warren was "highly respected," and Fuller, his murderer, was "pleasing in his address, intelligence, and communicative." The report closes with, "Great God! Is this human nature? When the restraining power of offended Heaven is withdrawn, man becomes desperate, and dies by his own hand."[118] The newspaper editorialized about the murder, but nothing indicates that the presence of a pistol was remarkable.

William Oliver Stevens describes 1820s Georgia:

No adult male ever went abroad unarmed. Whether it was to attend church, a social affair, or a political meeting, the Georgians carried loaded pistols, bowie knives, and sword canes. The pistols rested in the breast pockets of the coat and could be drawn quickly by both hands.[119]

Two days before Christmas, in 1828, Mayor Joseph Gales of Washington, D.C., issued a proclamation that shows pistols were common:

WHEREAS it has been too much the habit of idle and inconsiderate persons, on Christmas and New Year's Day and Eve to indulge in firing off guns, *pistols*, squibs, and crackers, and burning of gunpowder in divers other ways, to the great annoyance of the peaceable inhabitants of this city, and to the manifest danger of their persons and property—all which practices, where they are not contrary to the express ordinances of the corporation, amount to "disorderly conduct," and as such are punishable by law:

Now, therefore, with a view to prevent such disorderly practices, I, Joseph Gales, jr. Mayor of Washington, do enjoin upon all Police

Constables, Ward Commissioners, and others, whose duty it is to preserve peace and good order, to be diligent in the execution of their several duties, and to apprehend and bring to justice all persons so offending against the laws.[120] [emphasis added]

Charles Haswell described a widely reported 1830 incident. Prominent Washington newspaper editor Duff Green at the U.S. Capitol drew a concealed handgun to deter attack by a New York City newspaper editor. Haswell's account of subsequent events suggests that instead of regarding the carrying of pistols as dastardly, criminal, unrespectable, or surprising, Green's acquaintances good-naturedly ribbed him about the incident. Green appears to have not suffered for his actions; two years later he published the 1830 census for the federal government.[121]

Pistols repeatedly appear in private hands and in acts of violence at the highest levels. The U.S. House of Representatives tried Samuel Houston for "a breach of the privileges of the House of Representatives, by assaulting and beating Mr. Stanbery, a member of that House." The testimony includes that Rep. Stanbery

had a consultation with some of my friends, who agreed with me upon the answer which was sent. It was the opinion of one of my friends (Mr. Ewing, of Ohio,) that it was proper I should be armed; that, immediately upon the reception of my note, Mr. Houston would probably make an assault upon me. Mr. Ewing, accordingly, procured for me a pair of pistols, and a dirk; and, on the morning on which the answer was sent, I was prepared to meet Mr. Houston if he should assault me.[122]

Even *slaves* had pistols—or at least newspapers reported that they did. The Chickasaw, Mississippi, *Union* reprinted an article from the *North Alabamian* that reported the following: "And many of our Negroes . . . fancy that, in defence of their *honors* [sic], they must carry loaded pistols and long knives! We do things on a magnicent [sic] scale here in Pontotoc!—Negroes going armed." The *North Alabamian* also reprinted the Chickasaw *Union*'s report of "little boys, just out of swaddling clothes, wielding dirk-knives and pistols with as much *sang-froid*, and manifesting as familiar an acquaintance with their use, as if they had been born with weapons in their hands."[123]

Another news account shows that pistols and murder were unsurprising:

Mr. B. D. Boyd, a highly respectable and correct young man, and an officer in the Commercial Bank, together with an [sic] another young man in the room, interfered to prevent further aggressions by either party. Stewart, however, drew a pistol, and, in mistake we presume, shot Boyd in the lower part of the abdomen. Stewart is said to be from Mississippi, and about 17 years of age.

We regret the necessity that calls for the publication of these facts, but public opinion must be made to bear upon the common practice among our young men of carrying deadly weapons in a peaceably [sic] community.[124]

The editorializing is clear: young men carried pistols far too freely. The presence of pistols was not startling; indeed, it was all too common.

A February 1837 Alabama newspaper reported a quarrel in Columbus, Georgia, between "Col. Felix Lewis and a Doctor Sullivan, the latter drew a pistol and attempted to shoot the former, when Lewis produced a Bowie knife, and stabbed Sullivan to the heart, who died in two minutes."[125] In Missouri, an Alexander H. Dixon drew a sword cane on a man named Flasser, who drew a pistol and shot Dixon to death.[126]

Searching the Library of Congress's "Chronicling America" Web site of historic American newspapers in the period 1836–1847 for "pistol" returns 12,216 matches.[127] Not all such occurrences are necessarily evidence of pistols in civilian hands in America. Newspapers in this period often carried fiction, and some references are to foreign events. One useful technique is to sample newspapers for these references and see what percentage are factual American references. The results of this sampling suggest that the pistol scarcity claim is seriously wrong.

The word "pistol" appears in several accounts of foreign actions[128] and what appear to be works of fiction.[129] Of the first 20 newspapers that appeared when searching for "pistol," 5 contained foreign or fictional accounts involving pistols. The rest were factual accounts (usually of murder trials) in America. If this percentage applies equally to all 12,216 matches in the 1836–1847 newspapers, pistols appear in American news accounts 9,162 times—a startling number for an item that was, according to Bellesiles and Haag (who builds her book on Bellesiles's claims), without a civilian market before 1848. Here are a few examples:

The trial of Singleton Mercer for the murder of Mahlon Hutchinson Heberton commenced to-day. The prisoner stands indicted for shooting Heberton with a *pistol* ball on board of the John Fitch boat, on the night of the 10th of February last.[130] [emphasis added]

In the murder trial of William R. Elliott in the District of Columbia:

> Witness was sitting in a buggy near Mr. Nailor's stable, with his back towards the avenue, when he heard the report of a *pistol*. He immediately turned round, and saw a man down. He jumped out of the buggy and ran over. By the time he had got half way, some one had raised the wounded man up, and he saw blood on his breast. About that time, the man who fired had run. There was a great combat going on between him and another person. They had worked themselves almost across the street. It appeared as if the prisoner was rather backing when he was firing, and the other appeared to be stooping and dodging; witness could not tell for what.[131] [emphasis added]

A pistol figures prominently in the 1842 hatchet murder trial of John C. Colt, the brother of Samuel Colt, inventor of the revolver.[132] That he had his brother's product is never considered unusual or surprising in the published accounts.

Both Bellesiles and Haag present false descriptions of Samuel Colt's part in the trial to malign his character. They claim, based on secondary sources, and contrary to readily available primary sources, that Samuel Colt's expert testimony about the sound level from his revolver was an attempt to market his gun, rather than to give evidence that his brother had not *shot* the deceased.[133] (There had been some uncertainty about the murder weapon.)

Here is a report of a New York City murder trial:

> I am a clerk in the Police Office; I was present when Mr. Emeric was brought into court, on a charge of shooting Mr. Grousset. The *pistol* now shown appears to be the same that was placed in my hands, as being the one which had been used by Mr. Emeric.[134] [emphasis added]

Here is another murder trial:

> Witness took a *pistol* out of the pantaloons pocket of deceased, as well as several other things; did not examine the *pistol* to see if it was charged; his coat was taken off before witness got there; saw no knife or dirk.[135] [emphasis added]

In the same issue is the trial of John T. West:

> Said that he snapped the *pistol* in his pocket, but the lock caught in the lining, or he would have shot F. then; the reason for snapping

the *pistol* in his pocket was because he couldn't get it out, F. having hold of his hand.[136] [emphasis added]

And here is another:

Jesse Cady, who was in the reading room of the Carlton House when the *pistol* was fired, made the same statement that was published in the Herald in the morning after the murder, in which he said he thought he saw the glimpse of something or somebody turn the corner of Leonard and Elm streets, as he rushed out of the barroom; but whether it was a man, a woman, or a horse, he could not positively assert.[137] [emphasis added]

Another indicator of a civilian market for pistols is the story of an attempted suicide:

Tuesday evening a gentlemanly looking man, about 32 years of age, went into the shop of Mr. Moses, a pawnbroker, in Grand-street, in a state of considerable agitation, with some symptoms of having indulged too freely in the bottle, and asked for a *pistol*. Mr. Aaron (the assistant of the pawnbroker) asked what particular kind he wanted to purchase? He replied, "one that would do execution." This being rather a vague reply, a number of *pistols* were shown him, when he selected one, the price of which was $3. He then inquired if they were furnished with bullets, and expressed a wish to have one that would fit the barrel of the *pistol* he had bought. Mr. Moses, surprised at such questions, stepped forward and told the gentleman that pawnbrokers did not deal in such articles; he was also induced to ask, from the strange manner of the prisoner, for what purpose he was about to purchase the *pistol*: "I'll tell you at once," said the gentleman, "I want to blow my brains out; I have nothing to do; nothing to amuse me—no business, no news, in short I am dying of ennui piecemeal, and I am tired of the dull monotony of my stupid existence; can't you get me a bullet cast that will suit this *pistol*?"[138] [emphasis added]

The pawnbroker sent a messenger to the police, who hospitalized the pistol buyer.

Here is another murder in New York City:

The next witness sworn, was John Barton a waiter in the City Hotel. I heard the report of the *pistol*, and went up stairs about a moment afterwards, and when I came up to the parties, I saw three gentlemen all on the floor together; the ladies were I should say, all trying to get the two gentlemen off the prisoner, I saw a dagger in the hand of one the gentlemen, but I don't know who it was, by the head of Mr. Wilson, the prisoner; I begged of him not to stab him; the one I mean who was kneeling by the head of the accused, he told me to get out of the way or he would stab me, or stick me. I don't know which; I was kneeling down trying to get the two gentlemen that were down with him, off; when I got up, I saw Mr. Jennings and Mr. Smith standing by my side; they begged of them to loose their hold of Alexander, but they declined doing so, saying that if they did, he would arise soon as they let go of him; the *pistol* was finally taken from Alexander Wilson by one of his cousins—I don't know which.[139]

Some accounts report that pistol carrying was falling in some regions during this period, such as Florida, which is hardly an indication of a lack of a civilian market:

In former times it was requisite for the safety of an individual to carry—his Bowie knife and *pistols*; now the reverse is the case, and a more peaceable and quiet people cannot be met with.[140]

There was an altercation between Duff Green, editor of the *New York Herald*, and various federal officials in 1836. Green described some violent threats he received in which those threatening him drew pistols, as did Green.[141] William S. Moore shot at a member of the U.S. House of Representatives in 1844 with a pistol.[142]

When 1830s clergyman and abolitionist newspaper editor Elijah P. Lovejoy and his friends defended his printing press in Alton, Illinois, with pistols, the mob of "respectable gentlemen" of Alton murdered Lovejoy. Lovejoy died with a pistol in his hand.[143] Contemporary accounts gave no indication that a pistol was an unusual item to own.

Other abolitionists regarded pistols as common. Kentucky abolitionist Cassius Clay was keenly aware of the effects of mob violence against abolitionists:

We say, that when *society fails to protect us*, we are authorized by the laws of God and nature to defend ourselves; based upon *the right*, "the pistol and Bowie knife" are to us as sacred as the gown and the pulpit; and the Omnipresent God of battles is our hope and trust for victorious vindication. "Moral power" is much; with great, good, true-souled men, it is stronger than the bayonet! But with the cowardly and debased it is an "unknown God." Experience teaches us, common sense teaches us, instinct teaches us, *religion* teaches us, that it loses none of its force by being backed with "cold steel and the flashing blade," "the pistol and the Bowie knife."[144] [emphasis in original]

Near Natchez, Captain Crosly "drew a Bowie knife, and made a pass at the throat of the passenger," but without causing any injury. Crosly ordered the passenger to leave the boat; he retrieved a pistol from his cabin and accidentally shot the passenger.[145]

Thomas Cather, an Ulster Scot traveler to America in the 1830s, gives this account: "Everyone goes armed with dagger, [Bowie] knife, or pistols, and sometimes with all three, and in a society where the passions are so little under control it is not to be wondered . . . that murderous affrays should so often take place in the streets." British naval officer and novelist Frederick Maryatt describes America in 1837: "The majority of the editors of the newspapers in America are constantly practicing with the pistol, that they may be ready when called upon, and are most of them very good shots."[146]

In 1831, Arkansas territorial governor Pope argued that the willingness of juries to reduce murder to manslaughter encouraged killing: "Men should be brought to bridle their passions when life is at stake, and no excuse for shedding blood should be received but that of *absolute necessity*. The distinction between murder and manslaughter should be abolished in all cases where a dirk, pistol or other deadly weapon is used, except in cases of *self-defense*" [emphasis in original].[147]

Dueling oaths (requiring those wishing to hold public office to swear an oath that they had not participated in a duel) were a topic of debate at the Kentucky Constitutional Convention of 1849. One delegate argued that dueling was the lesser evil. While only 31 years old, he lamented of his boyhood friends,

Some twelve or fourteen have perished in violent affrays in the streets, and I have never known one who fell in fair and honorable duel. And why is this? It is because a thousand opportunities exist of effecting a reconciliation between parties where a challenge has passed and a duel is proposed, and the difficulty by the interference of friends may be adjusted; but in the murderous street fight

the parties excited with passion, heed no one, and arming themselves, go forth in the thoroughfares and the by-ways, and there in
a bloody affray, to the terror of every passer-by, settle their quarrel
with the knife and the *pistol*.[148] [emphasis added]

Frederick Law Olmsted described a not completely concealed Colt
revolver on a Kentucky railroad in 1853. This suggests that concealed carrying of pistols was at least common less than five years
after 1848:

> In the cars in Kentucky a modest young man was walking through
> with the hand[le] of a Colt out of his pocket-skirt behind. It made
> some laugh & a gentleman with us called out, "You'll lose your
> Colt, Sir." The man turned and after a moment joined the laugh and
> pushed the handle into the pocket.
>
> John said, "There might be danger in laughing at him." "Oh
> no," replied our companion, evidently supposing him serious,
> "he would not mind a laugh." "It's the best place to carry your
> pistol, after all," said he. "It's less in your way than anywhere
> else." . . .
>
> "Are pistols generally carried here?"
>
> "Yes, very generally."
>
> Allison said *commonly*, but he thought not generally.[149] [empha-
> sis in original]

Kentucky, Louisiana, Indiana, Alabama, Georgia, Virginia, and Arkansas
all passed laws between 1813 and 1840 prohibiting the carrying of concealed pistols (among other deadly weapons),[150] when there was apparently "little market beyond the officers in the army and navy."[151]

Newspaper ads offered pistols for sale and repair of pistols. There are
travel accounts and newspaper accounts in large numbers that demonstrate that handguns were commonly carried in at least some parts of
the United States, and the presence of handguns is *never* presented as
a surprise. Whether handguns were as common as rifles or muskets is
certainly an arguable point. The necessarily fragmentary evidence suggests that, like today, they were less common than long guns. The claim
that they enjoyed "little market beyond the officers in the army and
navy" is clearly incorrect. Haag's and Bellesiles's claims of a scarcity
of gun murders in antebellum America, discussed on page ix, is clearly
incorrect.

The sources from the Early Republic provide persuasive evidence that firearms and hunting were the norm—not the exception. While not all of these accounts reveal evidence of "gun culture," it is hard to read Audubon's or Carlton's accounts (with a whole chapter devoted to rifle marksmanship in Carlton) and pretend American gun culture was a later development.[152]

CHAPTER 7

Gun Manufacturing in the Early Republic, 1783–1846

W as gun manufacturing a new activity for Americans in the Early Republic as the revisionists claim? Felicia Deyrup is not the only historian who has studied arms manufacturing in the Early Republic and come to much different conclusions than the revisionists. Bishop describes the state of the iron and steel industry in Massachusetts in 1798. In Plymouth and Bristol Counties, there were many steel mills, forges, and associated industries, including the production of consumer products. Bishop lists "fire-arms," along with nails, spades, shovels, saws, and scythes, among the items that "were made in large quantities."[1]

Bishop's description of 1791 Pittsburgh reports that, of 130 families, there were 37 families engaged in some form of manufacturing, of which 2 were gunsmiths.[2] About 1.5 percent of the families in what was still a frontier community were therefore making their living as gunsmiths, apparently making guns. Cuming lists two gunsmiths in 1807 Pittsburgh.[3] Fearon includes a table of "manufactories in and near the city of Pittsburgh, in the State of Pennsylvania, in the year 1817," listing 14 men employed as "Gun-smiths, and bridlebit-makers," with a yearly value of $13,800.[4]

The most complete Early Republic statement of firearms manufacturing comes from the 1810 manufacturing census. Inconsistencies in the data clearly demonstrate that this survey was haphazard and incomplete. As an example, Massachusetts manufactured 19,095 guns classified as "other," but listed no gun manufactories and no gunsmiths. Only 9 of the 17 states are listed as having made any guns at all, and there is no firearms manufacturing listed in any of the 5 territories or the District of Columbia. Only Maryland, South Carolina, and the territories of Orleans and Louisiana reported any gunsmiths. Despite the 1807 and 1817 data from Fearon and Cuming for Pittsburgh showing a growing community of gunsmiths there, there are *no* gunsmiths listed in Pennsylvania. New York, at the time one of the great manufacturing states of the union, showed no gun manufacturing or gunsmithing at all. Even with these clearly incomplete records, however, there were 117 "Gun manufactories" in the United States; 37 gunsmiths (a severe undercount, based on Fearon and Cuming's reports for 1807 and 1817 for Pittsburgh alone); and 42,853 firearms manufactured.[5]

It is always hazardous to make comparisons between such different times as 1810 and the present. Firearms manufactured in 1810 were far less precise than modern weapons, and they had shorter useful lifetimes as well. During this period, "it was assumed that a musket would have a life of 12 years in the regular service or 10 years if in use by State militia."[6] Nonetheless, it is intriguing to compare 1810 production rates per capita with modern production rates.

The *minimum* 1810 U.S. production rate was 592 guns per 100,000 people. By comparison, in 1969, U.S. production and importation of firearms was 2,605 guns per 100,000 people.[7] To add to the impressiveness of this per capita gun manufacturing rate, in 1969, the United States had an army that approached 1 percent of the total population, and it was actively at war in Vietnam, where guns were being used up and lost; by comparison, in the 1820s, the U.S. Army "fluctuated between 5,500 and 5,700 until the end of the 1820s"[8] out of a population of 13,000,000[9]— or 0.04 percent. Despite a far larger military, with an active war consuming small arms, when small arms had much longer lifetimes, the United States manufactured *no* more than 4.5 times as many small arms per capita in 1969 as it did in 1810. The 1810 manufacturing census is unquestionably incomplete in a way that the 1969 manufacturing records are not; it is likely that the *actual* number of guns manufactured in 1810 would raise the per capita rate close to 1969 levels.

Whisker gives the details of several small gunmakers based on the 1820 U.S. Census of Industry. Because the 1810 U.S. Census of Manufactures included only firms grossing more than $500 a year, or employing more than one person, it provides a false impression of the number of gunsmiths making guns in America, tending to underreport the one-man gunmaker. We know of at least one illiterate Virginia gunsmith, Joseph Shelton, who made guns for at least three decades, starting in 1820, but who appeared only in the 1820 Census of Industry.[10] It seems inevitable that many other small gunmakers are also missing from the censuses, but this in no way indicates that they were not making guns. Considering that new guns often sold for as little as $10, a gunmaker who made a few dozen guns a year without any employees would simply not show up in the Census of Manufactures—even if every gunmaker that was supposed to be counted actually was.

Whisker also claims that

> Cottage industry gunsmiths supplied the militia needs of most states well through the War of 1812. Many Civil War militia regiments were armed with sniper and common weapons made by individual gunsmiths in their small shops. . . . Despite the growth of large industrial facilities for the manufacture of arms in the post Civil War era, the cottage industry remained a primary source of weapons until well after 1870.[11]

The Henry gunmaking business has left us a pile of documents establishing that they were a substantial gun manufacturer in the Early Republic, with many pages of such items as a November 10, 1819, ledger that shows $23,359.75 in assets and a balanced amount in cash and notes held by two banks, J. Joseph Henry, and in cash. There is a July 8, 1813, order from the State of Maryland for 1,000 muskets at $12.25 each, to be delivered in six weeks, "and will continue to take one thousand stand of muskets every six weeks till the order shall become terminated of which three weeks notice shall be given."[12] There are many pages of such documents demonstrating that the Henry's firm was very busy filling orders for thousands of guns during this period.[13]

These were firms that were large enough that they were required to report their activities, yet they were still small enough to leave few traces in other official documents. Samuel Baum of Columbia County, Pennsylvania, reported that in the year ending June 30, 1820, he employed two workers, had a $550 capital investment, and made guns valued at $1,200. John Bayles of Georgia employed three journeymen gunsmiths during that same period. Joseph Shelton of Lewis County, Virginia, employed two men and made guns valued at $520. He also made gun repairs that he valued at $150.

There are many other similar examples that Whisker reports of small operations that made a small number of guns, and it would appear that there were many such gunmakers in America in 1820.[14] Otho Sheets of Frankford, Virginia, employed three men and had made 90 firearms in the year previous to the census date, "each valued at $18."[15] Whisker describes how the counties of Lancaster and Berks, Pennsylvania, specialized in the manufacturing of gun barrels from the time of the Revolutionary War onward, with these barrels found on guns "made in Ohio, Kentucky, New York, Indiana, Illinois, and elsewhere." Daniel Cryscher was one of these specialists in the making of gun barrels. Some surviving records show that he made barrels to order for gunsmiths in other counties, and one transaction in 1830 involves an order for 15 gun barrels, with Cryscher offering 10 more if wanted.[16]

Gun manufacturing was a well-established craft and even an industry before the Revolution, and it remained a substantial craft and industry after the Revolution. To claim otherwise requires destroying a vast number of documents from the period.

CHAPTER 8

Federal Government Gun Contractors in the Early Republic, 1783–1846

Perhaps the most amazing revisionist claim is that there was so little gunmaking capacity in the United States after the Revolution that the federal government had to strongly encourage the manufacturing of guns for military use—often without success.[1] Without question, the federal government strongly encouraged the development of a new way of making guns that moved it from a craft to an industry. The reasons were very different from the revisionist claim. The consequences were a vigorous contract system with the private sector for making guns for the federal military establishment.

Bellesiles's examination of gunsmithing in the Early Republic is heavily focused on the manufacturers who worked under contract to supply arms to the U.S. government. This is not surprising; the most detailed records in early American history tend to be governmental. Had Bellesiles's goal been to write a history of government arms making, this would have been a very useful strategy to take. In so doing, however, he gives the impression that government arms manufacturing was almost the entire gun industry in the United States—and this was *not* the case.

Bellesiles's focus on federal arms contracts was driven by the assumption that there was no significant civilian market for guns in the Early Republic. This is an example of circular reasoning: assuming no private demand for guns means you only look at governmental contracts.

Because governments are among the best keepers of records, reliance on official records tends to overstate the importance of government contracts relative to the private sector.

Firms that grew up around federal gun contracts, starting in the 1790s, have high visibility in records for the same reason that a large textile mill with hundreds of workers is more visible than hundreds of individual weavers working at home. Bellesiles, with his focus on government contracts, consequently only saw these large firms.

Others who have examined the gunmaking business in the Early Republic have come to very different conclusions than the revisionists. Deyrup explains that "until the emergence of the federal contract system in 1798," gun manufacturing was primarily a handcraft in America. This does not mean that there were few guns manufactured in America. Rather, there were many small gunmakers, perhaps a gunsmith working by himself or with a journeyman gunsmith and a few apprentices. The system relied on masters and apprentices sworn to secrecy about the craft. Arms making was often a family tradition, "occasionally remaining in one family for several generations."[2]

Another area where the traditional American gun industry was substantially different from the new, larger, and more sophisticated gun manufacturing system that developed under U.S. government contracts is the nature of the workers. The Springfield Armory made use of the apprentice system, but unlike the traditional gunmaking industry of America, it almost immediately focused on the use of unskilled machine operators. When, in 1825, a father asked the superintendent of the Springfield Armory about apprenticing his son there to learn the gunsmith's trade, he was encouraged to apprentice his son to an individual tradesman, as he would more likely learn all the skills required to become a gunsmith by doing so. Springfield Armory was already well on its way toward specialization and division of labor.[3]

After describing how rising international tensions led Congress to establish national armories at Springfield, Massachusetts, and Harpers Ferry, Virginia, to build guns, Bellesiles claims, "Congress knew from the start that American gunmakers could not collectively produce in a reasonable period the fourteen thousand arms they hoped to buy."[4] Even with subsidies and encouragement, according to Bellesiles, the companies that chose to make guns for the United States were nearly incompetent to do so. "Nonetheless, American gunmakers had troubles producing their seven thousand muskets." According to Bellesiles, this was because there was effectively no expertise or interest in the making of guns in America.[5]

Other historians recognize the problems associated with government contracts as a source of information and are considerably more careful about the conclusions that can be drawn from *only* using governmental sources. Deyrup's detailed examination of the Connecticut Valley arms manufacturing industry acknowledges that she knew of other records of arms manufacturers of the period, but these were unavailable, and the early records of the predecessor firms of Winchester and Smith & Wesson had been destroyed and were therefore also unavailable.[6]

Deyrup's study was therefore "based in large part upon the records of the federal Armory at Springfield, Mass." This is not surprising; the government's armories have a very detailed set of records, "kept with a preciseness and detail uncommon in early American enterprise, and unique as far as New England arms manufacture is concerned." Deyrup observes that before 1800, few businesses, aside from moneylenders and merchandisers, kept detailed records. Consequently, "little is known of the details of arms making in the Connecticut River Valley in the late eighteenth century."[7]

In the Early Republic, Bellesiles does admit that some guns were manufactured in the United States, mostly at government arsenals, but he downplays the number of both makers and guns made.

Also interesting are Bellesiles's claims about the inability of private gun manufacturers to build to government contracts and how differently less ideological historians report the same facts. After reporting that Congress decided to supply all the arms of the militia, Bellesiles claims that "Congress ordered the purchase of seven thousand muskets. Over the next two years, the government was able to purchase only 480 'rifle guns.'"[8]

M. L. Brown gives a very different description of the 1792 contract:

In 1792 Congress, further alarmed by increasing British and Spanish activity along the vast frontier, raised a battalion of riflemen consisting of four companies each comprised of 82 privates which were to be armed with the American rifle. . . .

The contract rifles . . . were purchased from Pennsylvania riflesmiths between September 12, 1792, and May 5, 1793, at an average cost of $10.00 per stand.[9]

A total of 436 rifles were produced and delivered in less than nine months[10] to arm 328 soldiers. The limitation was not that private industry could not supply enough rifles, as Bellesiles's use of "only" seems to imply, but that the government was only buying enough *rifles* for four companies of riflemen.

Concerning the 7,000 muskets that Bellesiles represents as being ordered by Congress at the same time as the rifles in 1792, Deyrup cites the same source (Hicks's *Notes on United States Ordnance*) but reports that the order was in 1794 and that the government successfully bought 2,000 rifles that same year.[11] Examination of Bellesiles's and Deyrup's common source shows that, once again, Bellesiles has "misread" his source. The muskets were ordered in 1794, not in 1792. According to Hicks, the 7,000 muskets were ordered from abroad, "there not being any source of domestic supply of muskets at that time." Rifles were available from domestic manufacturers, and they continued to meet the relatively low volume of rifles for the army and for supply to friendly Indians until 1810. Hartzler gives examples of the federal government contracting with small gunsmiths for rifles intended for distribution to friendly Indians as late as 1811.[12]

While Bellesiles describes Congress as "ordering" 7,000 muskets from Britain and suggests that 480 rifles delivered by American makers represented some sort of failure to make guns quickly, Bellesiles buried in the endnote that it was five years before the muskets ordered from Britain were delivered. After a scathing criticism of the slowness of American rifle makers, it is misleading to hide the slowness of the British musket makers in the endnote.[13]

While the federal government continued to buy small quantities of rifles from established gunsmiths, it developed a combination of a contract system and national armories at Springfield, Massachusetts, and Harpers Ferry, Virginia, for making muskets. The contract system with private firms was complex and involved substantial advances and subsidies to the makers. Why did the government make use of this contract and national armories system instead of purchasing muskets and pistols on the open market, as they did with rifles? Bellesiles portrays this as recognition that American gunmakers "could not collectively produce in a reasonable period the fourteen thousand arms [the federal government] hoped to buy."[14]

Deyrup gives another explanation that details how the government was able to order and receive 436 rifles in less than nine months and 2,000 more rifles during 1794 but preferred a contract system instead for muskets. The federal government was reluctant to purchase large numbers of muskets over which they had no quality control and only limited opportunity to inspect the guns during production. The contract system, as well as government production of muskets, provided an opportunity for the government to have more control over the production process.[15]

How many guns did private contractors make for the government? The question is of some importance, as Bellesiles makes the argument that the poor quality and quantity of arms delivered by these contractors reflected the infant state of gunmaking in the Early Republic. Unfortunately, the quality of the data for the number of arms manufactured by contractors for the federal government is mixed—or perhaps the quality of the research done by those who have attempted to retrieve this information is mixed. Those who have taken the time to dig through the records have often been more gun enthusiasts or professional soldiers than historians, and one must wonder whether the seemingly contradictory numbers reflect errors or differing measurement periods.

Col. Arcadi Gluckman's seemingly authoritative, but insufficiently sourced, history of U.S. military long arms reports that Congress authorized contracts in 1798 for 30,000 stands of arms, but that the Ordnance Department actually contracted for 40,200 stands divided among 27 contractors. It appears that only 21 of the contractors actually delivered arms through June 10, 1801, for a total of 14,032. At least one of these contractors—the only one known to the average American today, Eli Whitney—delivered none.

Gluckman's total of arms delivered, 14,032, is a little higher than the sum of the individual contractors he lists, 13,234.[16] (The complete list is in appendix B.) Another source tells us that a report of firearms received "to the 1st of January 1803" showed a total of 24,136 muskets, rifles, and pistols manufactured by at least 35 different contract manufacturers.[17]

Concerning the 1808 musket contract, there are more discrepancies among the various sources. One source reports that a total of 31,030 muskets were delivered by 19 different private gunmakers under government contract between 1808 and October 1812,[18] providing yet another discrepancy with Gluckman's totals. Hartzler, generally quite careful in his citations, reports that Maryland gunsmiths Nicholas White, Thomas Crabb, Jacob Metzger, and Christopher Barnhizle delivered 548 muskets out of their contract for 1,000,[19] again, substantially higher than Gluckman's data.

If Bellesiles's conclusions concerning the failure of federal musket contractors is the result of trusting one set of sources over another, it would be very easy to sympathize with his situation, but detailed analysis shows more serious problems.

Bellesiles criticizes the firms that contracted to make muskets in 1798 as evidence that there was no real knowledge of how to make guns in the United States:

> The government's continuing financial support of private gunmak-
> ers flew in the face of results. Just under 1000 had been delivered
> by September 30, 1800, the date on which the government was
> supposed to have received the forty thousand muskets commis-
> sioned from twenty-seven gunmakers.[20]

Bellesiles's endnote cites Hicks, *Notes on U.S. Ordnance*, 1:42–43. There is *nothing* at 1:42–43 that relates to the 1798 contracts—it is all 1812 contracts and later. There is a discussion of the 1798 contracts on pages 1:19–23, but the only table that shows delivery counts reports that 2,646 muskets had been received as of September 26, 1801—not 1800—and this appears to only be a count of arms received by one set of govern-ment inspectors, as Gluckman reports that arms delivered by contractors through June 10, 1801, totaled 14,032 stands.[21]

Nor is there anything in Hicks that indicates that all the muskets were to be delivered by September 30, 1800. The only contract date in Hicks's discussion is a copy of the contract between the partnership of Nicho-las White, Thomas Crabb, Jacob Metzger, and Christopher Barnhizle of Frederick Town, Maryland—and that specifies that all of the muskets were to be delivered no later than March 1800.[22]

Bellesiles claims that "many gun factories turned out to be flash-in-the-pan operations, taking advantage of government contracts and then vanishing."[23] Bellesiles's endnote reads as follows:

> For instance, twelve Massachusetts gunmakers failed to fulfill their
> government contracts: Silas Allen of Shrewsbury; Asher Bartlett,
> Henry Osborne, and Caswell & Dodge of Springfield; Thomas
> French, Adam Kinsley, and Rudolph & Charles S. Leonard of
> Canton; Rufus Perkins of Bridgewater; Alvin Pratt, Elijah and Asa
> Waters, and Luke Wood of Sutton; Lemuel Pomeroy of Pittsfield.[24]

Bellesiles is still using the same source, Hicks, 1:42–43, and, again, those are not the right pages for the 1798 contract; that list of names is *not* on those pages. The correct pages for the 1798 contract say absolutely noth-ing about the failure of these contractors to fulfill their contracts.[25] These names and failures to fulfill their contracts would be correct for the 1808 contract, discussed at Hicks, 1:32–33; but the dates are of course much different than Bellesiles says, and the statement about "under one thousand had been delivered" does not fit any date in the table of musket deliveries for the 1808 contract.[26]

Bellesiles goes on to tell us that Eli Whitney did not complete his contracted 10,000 muskets until "late in 1809, nine years behind schedule. The other twenty-six gunmakers produced just two thousand muskets—twenty-eight thousand (93 percent) short of their goal—only one of them fulfilling his contract with the government, and that five years late."[27]

Bellesiles has confused two different contracts and two different sets of contractors. Whitney's muskets for the 1798 contract were indeed delivered nine years late (in January 1809, not "late in 1809"),[28] but the other 1798 contractors had delivered at least 13,234 muskets by January 1, 1803[29]—not "just two thousand muskets," as Bellesiles claims. Furthermore, as detailed in appendix B, at least three of the contractors for 1798 had either completed or overfilled their contracts by January 1, 1803: Nathan and Henry Cobb (100%); Huntington, Livingston, Bellows, and Stone (122%); and Amos Stillman & Co. (105%). One other contractor was close: Allen, Grant, and Bernard delivered 93 percent of their contracted amount. Bellesiles's source, whatever it was, confused the deliveries by contractors under the 1808 contract, which, of course, were still in process when Whitney completed his late deliveries for the 1798 contract.

Worse than the confused citations and the confusion of the 1798 and 1808 contract deliveries is his characterization of these 12 musket makers as "flash-in-the-pan operations," which makes them sound like they were set up to get the contract and then went bankrupt. Henry Osborne appears to have been in the gunmaking business until at least 1821. Adam Kinsley had delivered muskets for the 1798 contract. Rufus Perkins was in business from 1799 through 1812. Asa Waters had been a gunmaker as early as 1776, and he delivered muskets as part of the 1818 and 1823 contracts.[30]

Furthermore, the statement "failed to fulfill their government contracts" really means that they did not deliver the full number of muskets specified in the contracts—not that they failed to deliver guns. The characterization of "delivered just a few guns and then abandoned the business" is also misleading. Appendix B shows the number of guns contracted and the number delivered as of October 7, 1812, for the 1808 contract.

Only three of the contractors could with any accuracy be said to have "delivered just a few guns and then abandoned the business": Rufus

Perkins; Wheeler & Morrison; and Sweet, Jenks & Sons. Concerning Wheeler & Morrison, however, a more accurate statement is that Wheeler abandoned his partner Morrison by dying in 1809, and I suppose in that sense could be considered to have "abandoned the business." Sweet, Jenks & Sons is an interesting case because Jenks & Sons had a completely separate musket contract as well, and they certainly did not abandon *that* contract, as they fought a continuing battle for compensation as late as 1820—and that battle is a reminder that the problem of making muskets was *not* a deficiency of gunmaking skills in America, as Bellesiles claims.

The firm of Jenks & Sons of Providence, Rhode Island, contracted in October 1808 to make 4,000 Model 1808 muskets at the rate of 800 per year. In an era before blueprints and written specifications, the government supplied a pattern musket, which the contractor was supposed to disassemble and use to produce tooling, in much the same way that paper dress patterns are used today.

The pattern musket supplied by the government to Jenks & Sons was defective, and these defects were not discovered until well into the manufacturing process. When Jenks sought reimbursement for the substantial expenses involved in correcting these problems, the federal government refused. Though Jenks & Sons made a number of poor decisions during the process, it is clear that the primary reason that Jenks & Sons failed to complete its 1808 contract was not an inability to make guns, but a series of management mistakes by both the government and the contractor.

At least 1,000 of the contracted 4,000 muskets were delivered to the federal government and determined to be "of good quality" by the superintendent of Springfield Armory. The muskets rejected by the federal government's arms inspector were sold—at a higher price than the government paid—for export. It is not clear that all of these arms were actually defective; it appears that many of Jenks & Sons rejected arms were completely functional, but out of specification, unlike some of the other contractors in this period.[31]

Hicks reproduces a letter from Callender Irvine, the commissary general, to Secretary of War John Armstrong dated April 5, 1813, in which Irvine explains some of the problems that the contractors were having in filling their contracts:

> Those Contracts were founded on imperfect Muskets as Standards, and at prices for which it was impossible to have made good Muskets so that if the Contracts are complied with strictly by

individuals, the Government will be saddled with so many defective Arms of which description there are enough already in store near this City.[32]

Irvine then went on to blame his predecessor, Tench Coxe, for having made contracts that produced a large pile of guns only suited for scrap.[33]

Bellesiles portrays the failure of the federal contractors to fulfill their contracts as indicative of a fundamental lack of knowledge of gun manufacturing in America, claiming that Eli Whitney "recognized the basic problem with large-scale arms production in the United States; there were not enough trained gunsmiths."[34] But what Whitney was attempting to do was to create a division of labor that allowed interchangeable gun parts to be made by less-skilled workers. Whitney never really made this idea work. The problem was not a lack of trained gunsmiths, but an inability to develop the technology that would allow him to *not* hire trained gunsmiths.

A letter from Col. Decius Wadsworth of the Ordnance Office to Secretary of War John Armstrong, dated June 6, 1814, reproduced in Gluckman, gives a bit more detail about the problems that confronted not only Whitney but the other contractors as well. It also explains why the government was so tolerant of late and incomplete deliveries, quite different from the one that Bellesiles suggests: that the government let the contractors take terrible advantage of it. Irvine's letter gives a very different picture than Bellesiles's description of Whitney's muskets as "dreadful," and it also explains why some (but only some) contractors delivered just a few guns, or went bankrupt:[35]

Most of the individuals of small property who engaged in these contracts were absolutely ruined thereby, and the difficulties were so much greater than had been apprehended, it proved in general losing business to the concerned. Mr. Whitney having never before engaged in such a business, and *not having workmen brought up to the trade, was under the necessity of executing various parts of the work adapted to the inexperience of his hands, and calculated to obviate the necessity of employing men alone who had been bred to the trade. . . .*

It may not be amiss to state that I think *his arms as good, if not superior, to those which have in general been made anywhere else in the United States, not excepting those which have been made at the public armories.*[36] (emphasis added)

Other manufacturers, while not trying to lead the technology as aggressively as Whitney, were attempting to transform a traditional, small-scale handcraft industry—gunmaking—into a large factory system. "Contractors were forced into division of labor and the invention of machine tools, which, though of incalculable benefit to the industry, delayed them in filling their contracts."[37] As we will see in chapter 10, American officials were attempting to create an entirely new system of manufacturing, not just buying guns.

Bellesiles also portrays the failure of contract manufacturers as government largesse without any acknowledgment of the unusual circumstances under which the contract manufacturers operated, claiming that "it never seemed to occur to any contemporary that gun manufacturing should be left to the vagaries of the free market, perhaps because they all knew that the public was not sufficiently interested in guns."[38]

Everything about the government contracts, however, was an attempt to defeat a free market. Contractors were not allowed to use imported parts because that would defeat the government's goal—creation of a large-scale U.S. factory system for making military weapons. The government was very selective about who received arms contracts, excluding those who had gunsmithing experience, but not property. The government's goal seems to have been to make recovery of damages for nonperformance easier. Government contractors were also usually prohibited from doing business with any other customers, leading to serious problems when a contract had been fulfilled but a new one had not yet been granted.[39]

Perhaps the hardest problem to understand in an age when accountants calculate manufacturing costs to fractions of a penny is that cost accounting was still in its infancy. The contractors—and the government—were still learning how to deal with overhead, depreciation of tools, and distinguishing investments in the factory from investments in the land on which the factory was built.

The Henry gun manufacturing firm's records provide examples of this increasing sophistication in accounting. Each year in the 1830s, different items are added to the expenses used to calculate net profit: interest in 1831; freight and fire insurance in 1835 and value of inventory; and on January 1, 1837, inventory no longer includes just manufactured goods but also the estimated value of all production tools and assets. An 1815 estimate of costs for Henry's Boulton Rifle Works lists parts costing as little as $0.03. By 1817, they are including the depreciation of grindstones, coal for forging, and wood for annealing the steel as expenses. They also used spreadsheets to calculate costs and prices for guns.[40]

It appears that along with the surprises and delays associated with pioneering large-scale gun manufacturing in the United States, the government contractors in the period 1798–1830 were building muskets for an average cost of $12.88. Yet, from 1807 to 1810, the price the government paid contractors was $10.75. Many of the early contractors lost money on every musket delivered—and that some went out of business is therefore no great surprise.

Even the government's own Springfield Armory, a model of success to Bellesiles, figured its production costs in the early years as high as $16.48 per musket, and usually exceeding $13.00 each.[41] Springfield Armory's success in making guns was consistent with the $300 hammer horror stories of modern Department of Defense contractors. This also explains why, as Bellesiles smugly notes, a number of contractors asked to be let out of their federal contracts.[42] If contracts were money-losing propositions, the temptation to manufacture for the more lucrative private sector would have been very strong.

The government's musket contractors are probably no more typical of gun manufacturing in the Early Republic than defense industries in the late 20th century were typical of private-sector manufacturing companies. By focusing attention on the emerging large government contract firearms factories, Bellesiles completely missed the decentralized and still largely handcraft civilian gunmaking business in America.

To argue as the revisionists do that the American gun industry was so weak as to be unable to make guns because of a lack of knowledge requires willful misreading of official documents and a sizeable secondary literature.

CHAPTER 9

State Militia Gun Contractors in the Early Republic, 1783–1846

In addition to the dichotomy between contractors to the federal government and gunmakers who produced for the private sector, Bellesiles largely missed the substantial industry that made guns under *state* contracts. Let's start with Pennsylvania militia contracts. Along with Thomas and John Ketland's November 15, 1797, contract with Pennsylvania to make 10,000 firearms in Britain (voided by the British government), there were a number of contracts with American gunsmiths as well, totaling 11,200, 19,000, or 19,200 guns, depending on whose version you believe. (The details of the contractors and the contracts can be found in appendix B.) At least some of these arms were made, and Holt provides photographs of surviving muskets, some with government proof marks produced under these contracts by Lether & Co., William Henry, Melchior Baker, Owen Evans, and John Miles.[1]

Other muskets made for the Pennsylvania militia have survived as well, including one (based on markings inside the gunlock) believed to have been made by Adam Angstadt. Another surviving musket was made by a Joseph Miles (perhaps John Miles's brother, or the result of misreading the maker's mark). An 1814 Pennsylvania militia contract for 200 rifles is represented by two surviving examples, one made by Henry Deringer and another by George Tyron.[2]

How many other Pennsylvania militia contracts were there? The records are somewhat scattered. For instance, we know of a January 2, 1815, contract with Joseph G. Chambers of Washington County to make 25 "Swivel Guns" of a proprietary design and the "alteration of five hundred muskets belonging to the State."[3]

Other silent survivors tell us of contracts for which the paperwork has not surfaced. Lindsay lists a surviving pistol signed "Land & Read Boston" that was made for the Massachusetts militia, apparently in the middle 1820s to 1830s.[4] How many other gunsmiths made guns for state militias, for which neither guns nor contracts have come to light? We do not know, and it would be presumptuous to guess.

Virginia also armed its militia through a combination of private contracts and a state gun factory, and Bellesiles does describe Virginia's attempt to arm its militia with standardized weapons. There is a near-complete disconnect between what Bellesiles's sources say and what Bellesiles says that they say. The entire paragraph to be dissected below from *Arming America* has a single footnote. The source Bellesiles lists is Giles Cromwell's marvelously detailed history of the Virginia Manufactory of Arms:

> The shortage of gunmakers in the early republic is clearly illustrated in the history of Virginia's effort to establish an armory. In 1797 Governor James Wood informed the legislature that his government had searched the state to find anyone who could make arms for the militia, without success.[5]

Bellesiles's source for this claim, Cromwell's book, tells a somewhat different story:

> At the junction of the Rivanna and Fluvanna Rivers, the Point of Fork Arsenal centered around the storing of munitions and repairing arms, and a small force of artificers was maintained there from 1781 to 1801. Furthermore, scattered throughout the mountain and valley regions were many individual rifle makers who advanced their skills by making exceptionally fine rifles.[6]

Bellesiles further describes how Governor Wood of Virginia sought to obtain more arms for the state militia: "Wood therefore contracted to purchase four thousand stands of arms from England and another four thousand muskets from the Globe Mills in Pennsylvania. The latter source made just 925 arms over the next five years and then went bankrupt."[7]

Cromwell's account matches this, in part, but then describes how after McCormick went into bankruptcy, his foreman, James Haslett, finished another 50 arms, bringing the total up to 975. Then Cromwell describes how John Miles Sr. completed the original 4,000 musket contract and made 250 pairs of pistols for Virginia. George Wheeler of Culpeper County also made at least 1,000 muskets for Virginia, and James Haslett completed another contract for 600 muskets.[8]

In addition, Virginia also contracted with a number of gunsmiths to make 2,145 rifles in the years 1809–1819—and Cromwell makes the point that these contracts were "generally limited . . . to residents of Virginia." (Cromwell's appendix B.8 lists the 20 Virginia contract rifle makers and the number of guns completed and delivered.)[9]

By leaving out these other contracts for muskets and rifles, Bellesiles misleads the reader into thinking that gunmakers were so scarce that when Virginia's one private American contractor went bankrupt, Virginia was left in the lurch and was forced to start a state gun factory for this reason: "It was at this point that the Virginia government agreed with a plan that John Clarke had been promoting for several years to build an armory in Virginia to make guns for state use."[10]

Cromwell discusses Clarke's involvement, and at no point does Cromwell suggest that the armory was Clarke's idea—quite the opposite. The sequence as described by Cromwell was that the Virginia government came up with the idea. After discussing the "mammoth task" and "special and selected skills" that would be required, Cromwell states, "By whatever methods employed, however, the Executive ultimately chose John Clarke of Powhatan County." There is no indication in Cromwell that Clarke's involvement predates Virginia's decision to go into the gunmaking business.[11] Maybe there is evidence out there somewhere, but Bellesiles does not cite it. And what Bellesiles does cite—Cromwell—indicates just the opposite.

Bellesiles continues: "In creating the Virginia Manufactory of Arms, Clarke found it necessary to buy all his tools in England."[12] Cromwell agrees that Clarke bought all his tools in England, but not for the reason that Bellesiles implies—that there was not much of a gun industry in America. "Clarke favored purchasing such implements as vises, anvils, bellows, and files from Europe, where he believed better terms could be arranged. He felt that there were no tool manufacturers large enough in the United States to meet the requirements of the armory."[13] At the time, England was also the center for manufacturing in the Western world.

The armory was a large-scale gun manufacturing operation, much like the federal government's arsenals at Harpers Ferry, Virginia, and Springfield, Massachusetts, and the number of tools required was quite large. But the inability of American toolmakers to produce enough gunmaking tools is not an indication that there was not a large American gunmaking industry—many of whom doubtless also purchased their tools from England. It is only an indication that the tools for making guns were not made in America in sufficient quantities.

Bellesiles goes on to claim that Clarke "quickly discovered that there were only a few gunsmiths in Virginia and they all did exclusively repair work."[14] Cromwell does mention that Virginia was short of "skilled artificers," but he then goes on to explain the problems that Clarke was having, and in terms that do not fit Bellesiles's characterization:

> The various gunsmiths in the different sections of the state were restricted primarily to limited repair work and in some instances to rifle making itself, and while some of these rifle makers would eventually seek employment in the armory, in most instances they were financially better off remaining in their own independent shops.
>
> Consequently, Clarke defended his travels by saying that had he remained in Richmond and advertised for gunsmiths most probably he would have acquired the most indifferent workmen who were unable to find employment at other works.[15]

So the problem was not that Virginia lacked gunsmiths, but that the terms that Clarke was prepared to offer would not attract the better Virginia gunmakers, who made a decent income from their own shops. Somehow, this does not sound like a scarcity of gunsmiths, nor a shortage of demand for their products.

Bellesiles also claims that "Clarke ended up hiring sixty-eight workers, all of them from outside Virginia and a dozen brought over from Ireland."[16] The reason that Cromwell gives for hiring outside of Virginia is very different from Bellesiles's claims about a scarcity of gunsmiths in Virginia. "Clarke had found during his travels that the lowest wages were paid in Massachusetts and Rhode Island; so he concentrated on hiring people in those areas."[17] Hartzler quotes a letter from Clarke in full that confirms that he "found the wages of such men lower in Massachusetts and Rhode Island than in any other of the States. I therefore engaged in those states all the workmen of the desired description I could find, and on my return back again to the works I first visited [in Philadelphia], the workmen were induced to fall in their prices."[18]

Concerning those "dozen brought over from Ireland," Cromwell's account does not match Bellesiles's representation of it. According to Cromwell, "He was also successful in hiring artificers from Pennsylvania, where they had previously been employed by Haslett, and of the nineteen workmen who came to Richmond from this source, the majority were originally natives of Ireland."[19] Clarke's letter reproduced in Hartzler is also clear on this: of the gunsmiths that Clarke hired in Philadelphia, the "greater number of these men are natives of Ireland," but they were not "brought over" from Ireland to work in the Virginia Manufactory of Arms.[20]

Bellesiles's claim is that gunsmiths were so scarce that Clarke had to bring over a "dozen" from Ireland to work at the Virginia Manufactory of Arms. This is simply not so; they were already at work in Pennsylvania when Clarke hired them.

Bellesiles continues:

> For the rest of its brief history, this need to find skilled gunsmiths prevented the armory from ever producing many arms. Virginia's was the only state armory in antebellum America, averaging 2,130 muskets per year, or twenty-six guns per worker.[21]

What Bellesiles does not tell you, however, is that the manufactory made a lot more than muskets—and had he read beyond the 55 pages that he cited (or just flipped through the rest of the book, looking at the pictures and chapter titles), he would have known that. Significantly, the reason Cromwell gives for why Virginia shut down its manufactory in 1821 does not match Bellesiles's claims about a factory that had problems "producing many arms"; it almost directly contradicts it. Cromwell describes an important factor:

> By 1821 the armory had produced enough small arms to equip most of the state's militia, for from the beginning of operations in 1802 until its closing in 1821, the Virginia Manufactory of Arms had produced approximately 58,428 muskets and bayonets, 2,093 rifles, 10,309 swords, and 4,252 pistols for a total of 75,082 small arms. . . . The annual federal quota of new firearms began arriving regularly in the state by 1820. Thus the armory was slowly outgrowing its reason for existence.[22]

Concerning the shortage of gunsmiths impairing their operations, it is worthwhile to examine Cromwell's appendix D. It is a 14-page list of gunsmiths who had worked at the manufactory during its less than 20-year period of operation. This does not sound like a serious shortage of gunsmiths!

Bellesiles's claims about the reliance of American gunmakers on imported gunlocks also collapses. From the very beginning, *all* the muskets made at the manufactory had lock plates stamped with its name. The spare parts collection in an inventory completed after the manufactory closed reveals that lock plates and sears (both fundamental parts of a gunlock) were made there. It does not appear that the manufactory imported gunlocks. An examination of the list of suppliers to the manufactory for the years 1798–1809 reveals no gunlocks. The only complete subassembly of guns listed among the suppliers are gunstocks.[23]

How many other guns were made for state militias by private gunmakers? We really do not know. But we do know that revisionists seem to have a serious problem with reading their sources, and their mistakes are all in favor of the revisionists' highly peculiar interpretation of the history of American gunmaking.

CHAPTER 10

How the American Gun Culture Changed the World, 1800–Present

The American firearms industry, both private contractors and government arsenals, played an important role in creating the world in which we now live. Machine tools and modern manufacturing techniques created what we in the First World rely on today for our comfortable industrial civilization. This part is generally unknown by most of the beneficiaries of this technology.

Almost everything we own or use on a daily basis is either directly the child of an engine lathe or mill (the two most common machine tools), or was produced from a mold that was created with these tools, or the mold was created from a model produced by these tools. Most of the products that we use that are astonishingly inexpensive are the consequences of interchangeable parts, which require machine tools to make, and mass production. Specialization of labor, where unskilled or semiskilled laborers each produce only one part or perform one step toward a final product, allows mass production, which is a by-product of interchangeable parts and machine tools.

Interchangeable parts *require* machine tools, but mass production only *benefits* from interchangeable parts and machine tools; it does not require either. The Royal Navy made use of mass production for ship pulley blocks for some years without it spreading into British industry; it was only well after reimportation of the technique from America that it spread. While interchangeability of parts sometimes resulted from the Royal Navy's pulley block mass production techniques, "it was coincidental and was not turned to account."[1]

These innovations were so successfully perfected and adopted in the United States that "for many years it was known in Europe as the 'American System' of manufacture." There is some question as to how generally this expression was used. It does appear in at least one 19th-century account, but by an American.[2]

What provoked American leadership in manufacturing? Interchangeable parts for gunmaking appears to have been tried unsuccessfully by the French,[3] and the Royal Navy was a leader in mass production. Modern machine tools are largely American inventions or refinements of English inventions.

One explanation for why all these ideas and techniques became "the American system" is that wages were always higher in America than in Europe. As an example, colonial Massachusetts governor John Winthrop gives an amusing account of a laborer who exchanged his labor for one of a farmer's oxen. When the laborer proposed to continue this arrangement, the farmer asked what would happen when he ran out of oxen. "The servant replied, you shall then serve me, and so you may have your cattle again." In the margin, Winthrop describes the laborer as "insolent."[4]

The availability of land meant that agricultural workers were tempted to strike out on their own instead of laboring for others. Laborers were thus scarce and expensive. The investment of both capital and intellect to make machines to take the place of craft operatives was more imperative in America than Europe due to the relatively high cost of labor.[5]

When Chauncey Jerome started to make clocks by these methods and shipped them to Britain for sale, they were confiscated because their stated price was so low that British Customs confiscated them for being "clearly undervalued by English standards" (what we would call "dumping" today). British Customs could not imagine how clocks could be so cheap. But it reimbursed Jerome at the "undervalued" invoice price, giving Jerome an immediate sale without any additional selling costs. The second shipment was similarly confiscated at the "undervalued" invoice price. This was such a good deal for Jerome that he sent a larger third shipment, at which point British Customs had either figured out that they were *not* undervalued or they wanted out of the clock wholesaling business.[6]

British needs for improved firearms manufacturing during the Crimean War and the startling examples of U.S. manufacturers at the Crystal Palace exhibition in 1854 led Parliament to send a commission to America to learn more about how Americans manufactured.[7]

British engineers working on improving governmental gunmaking were given a demonstration of the new system. "Major Ripley ordered ten guns of the manufacture of ten years, from 1843 to 1853, to be stripped, and the parts mixed and reassembled promiscuously, which was successfully done." The engineers reported what they had found, and the result was that the British government equipped "a new Government rifle-making plant at Enfield with no less than 157 American machine tools including 74 milling machines."

While the advantages of the American System were obvious to those British engineers, they "had little or no general effect on European production methods for 50 years or more." An example of this is that in 1908, Cadillac "won the British Dewar automobile prize. Three Cadillacs were given a test drive, taken apart and disassembled, their parts mixed up and reassembled, and subjected to another test drive, which they passed handily—and the British still found it amazing."[8] Having helped my father rebuild a 1960s Triumph car transmission, I have personal experience with how late the notion of "interchangeable parts" bore fruit in Britain.

Machine tools, interchangeable parts, mass production, and specialization of labor are all individual inventions, but there is a strong synergy between them. Interchangeable parts require manufactured components that are nearly identical in dimension. Machine tools are required to produce parts of high precision. Once both are available, mass production using less skilled labor to operate specialized machines becomes practical.

Mass production leads to great wealth, and much of that wealth can and often does end up in the hands of the workers. In 1914, Henry Ford's mass production of cars led him to astound the car industry by paying workers $5 per day when the prevailing wage was $2 to $3 a day. The high wages improved worker productivity and reduced absenteeism.[9] Ford's motivation was not to make his workers happy but to make himself rich.

Ford was also a leader in another way. "Ford's policy for employing African Americans resembled that of other industrialists for several years." Blacks "largely held janitorial or menial positions. This changed in 1919 when Ford's policies took a radical turn as he began employing larger and larger numbers of African Americans for positions throughout his Detroit-area factories. He soon became the largest employer of blacks in the auto industry." Ford not only employed blacks on the assembly lines but in white-collar and supervisory jobs, with blacks even supervising entirely white crews. Rather than passively hiring blacks, Ford sent buses "into Detroit's black neighborhoods to recruit workers."[10]

The great textile factories of Lowell, Massachusetts, in the 19th century used mass production and equipment made by machine tools. The conditions of the workers greatly impressed Charles Dickens when he visited in 1840. He described the young women who had flocked to factory work from the comparative misery of farm life:

> These girls, as I have said, were all well dressed: and that phrase necessarily includes extreme cleanliness. They had serviceable bonnets, good warm cloaks, and shawls; and were not above clogs and pattens [overshoes]. Moreover, there were places in the mill in which they could deposit these things without injury: and there were conveniences for washing. They were healthy in appearance, many of them remarkably so, and had the manners and deportment of young women: not of degraded beasts of burden.[11]

Dickens goes on to comment favorably on their living conditions and the company's care for these young ladies, while carefully avoiding a comparison to the working and living conditions of their British counterparts; he clearly thought his description spoke for itself.[12]

Mass production in the gun business seems to have raised wages as well. In 1854, Dickens described Colt's revolver manufacturing plant in London: "The girls here earn from two to three shillings per day; the boys the same. The men get from three to eight shillings per day of ten hours; while one or two, being quick, clever, and reliable, are paid regularly twelve shillings per day."[13] Eight shillings per day would be 48 shillings, or £2, 8 shillings per week; 3 shillings per day would be £1, 6 shillings per week. That same year, Norfolk mental hospital attendants' weekly wages ranged from 7 shillings and 8 pence to 10 shillings. Farm laborers earned 9 to 11 shillings per week. London wages were higher than rural areas because of the higher cost of living; omnibus conductors received 4 shillings per day while often working more than 20 hours per day. An average laborer's wage "was between 20 and 30 shillings a week in London."[14] Colt's workers were thus paid at least twice as well as the average London laborer.

Colt showed considerable concern for his U.S. workers as well. His Connecticut factory had a worker housing development, Coltsville. Colt also introduced the 10-hour workday and the lunch hour. Presumably, these were not driven solely by paternalistic concern. He also provided a "clubhouse to discourage after-hours carousing." Haven and Belden's *History of the Colt Revolver* (1940) compares the poor conditions of industrial production elsewhere to Colt's factory: "Colt's men worked in steam-heated, gas-lighted, artificially ventilated rooms with sixteen foot ceilings and running water, for the highest pay in the country for the class of work they did, provided with up-to-date homes."[15]

Mass production in the ammunition industry seems to have had similar benefits. Pamela Haag's hostile history of the gun industry describes how Russia's Grand Duke Alexei Alexandrovich toured the Bridgeport, Connecticut, plant that made ammunition for his country in 1871 and was "shocked by the matter of how working girls could afford silk dresses."[16]

Interchangeable Parts

That the gun industry not only made use of but also became the source of interchangeable parts has long been recognized. Joseph Roe's *English and American Tool Makers* (1916) explains:

> The interchangeable system was developed by gun makers. It is commercially applicable chiefly to articles of a high grade, made in large numbers, and in which interchangeability is desirable. Of the typical articles, such as firearms, bicycles, typewriters, sewing machines, and the like, now produced by the interchangeable system, guns and pistols are the only ones which antedate the system itself.[17]

To Roe's 1916 list we can now add automobiles, consumer electronics, pens, and nearly every other product of our industrial civilization.

There had been European attempts at interchangeable gun parts in 1717, 1785, and 1806, but none had been successful in changing the world. Thomas Jefferson met with French inventor Honoré Le Blanc while he was the ambassador to France:

> Supposing it might be useful to the United States, I went to the workman; he presented me the parts of fifty locks taken to pieces, and arranged in compartments. I put several together myself, taking pieces at hazard as they came to hand, and they fitted in the most perfect manner. The advantages of this, when arms need repair, are evident.[18]

Jefferson attempted to bring Le Blanc to America;[19] it may well be that this experience made him a sympathetic ear when Eli Whitney promised this same system.

Interchangeability of parts was largely the result of continuing efforts by the U.S. military to gain advantages in the repair of arms. This was a long-term project that required 30 years to come to fruition. Eli Whitney, having lost a fortune in fruitless efforts to enforce his cotton gin patents, next turned to gunmaking with the goal of mass production using unskilled labor. He promised the U.S. government when he contracted to make muskets in 1812 that he would make parts interchangeable: "as much like each other as the successive impressions of a copper-plate engraving."

Some sources claim that Whitney demonstrated this to the secretary of war with 10 piles of parts, which he assembled at random into 10 muskets. A letter from President Thomas Jefferson to James Monroe in 1801 appears to report such a demonstration; perhaps this was hearsay: "He has invented molds and machines for making all the pieces of his locks so exactly equal, that take 100 locks to pieces and mingle their parts and the hundred locks may be put together as well by taking the first pieces which come to hand."[20]

By 1808, one of Whitney's competitors, Simeon North, had adopted the mass production model "by confining a workman to one particular limb of the pistol." North's 1813 government contract to make 20,000 pistols required interchangeability of parts. Both Whitney and North attempted interchangeability; Whitney has traditionally been credited as the originator for having spread this idea to the federal armories at Springfield, Massachusetts, and Harpers Ferry, then in Virginia.

Both Whitney and North probably played a part in the development of interchangeable parts, but there is considerable evidence that Captain John H. Hall better deserves the honor; Whitney's methods were fast, but a bit short of true interchangeability. An 1827 report "testifies that 100 Hall rifles, made in 1824, were stripped and the metal parts mixed and remounted on 100 new stocks, the parts all coming together well. . . . The joint of the breech-block was so fitted that a sheet of paper would slide loosely in the joint, but two sheets would stick."[21]

To be fair to Whitney and North, the definition of interchangeability was a moving target. An 1882 report observed that

uniformity in gun-work was then, as now, a comparative term; but then it meant within a thirty-second of an inch or more, where now it means within half a thousandth of an inch. Then interchangeability may have signified a great deal of filing and fitting, and [an] uneven joint when fitted, where now it signifies slipping in a piece, turning a screw-driver, and having a close, even fit.[22]

An additional struggle of interchangeability is that many steel parts of the gunlock had to be hardened for final use. Once hardened, they were no longer readily milled. The usual practice before interchangeability was to assemble and fit the parts while soft and mark them so that, after hardening, matching but not interchangeable parts could be reassembled. To harden them before assembly required the parts to be interchangeable in the "soft" state and therefore interchangeable after hardening.[23]

Interchangeability also required ways to verify that parts were made to the specified dimensions. "Limit-gauges, or, as they are called, go-in and not-go-in gauges, are in common use; that is, a set of two close gauges, one of which will receive a piece which will not go into the other, thus establishing a limit of accuracy both for openings and for exterior outlines."[24]

The result of the 1851 Crystal Palace exhibition in London, which showed the capabilities of American gun manufacturing, was a dramatic expansion of sales of both American guns to the world's militaries and of American gun manufacturing tools.[25]

By the time Samuel Colt began manufacturing revolvers, the idea of interchangeability had completely permeated the American gun industry. When Colt restarted his revolver manufacturing company in 1846 to make guns for the Mexican-American War, he rented space from Eli Whitney Jr. in Whitneyville, Connecticut. When Colt opened his own manufacturing plant, he hired Eli Whitney Jr. to assist him in creating a factory that used interchangeable parts and mass production. One consequence was that no gun was unique: "the parts of any particular model could replace those of any other. . . . Hand work was practically eliminated and automatic and semiautomatic machinery substituted." Most skilled craftsmen were replaced by unskilled workers, increasing profits.[26]

Something of the importance of these early beginnings to modern industry can be found in this family tree: George S. Lincoln & Co. built a type of milling machine known as a Lincoln miller for Colt. Two of the Lincoln Company's men went on to found Pratt & Whitney, today a manufacturer of jet engines. When Smith & Wesson went into the revolver business in 1857, there were similar connections. Smith had worked at Whitney's firm.[27]

Machine Tools

Machine tools is an area in which the average person is profoundly ignorant. I confess that I was among them as a young man. Now I own some of these machine tools for a manufacturing business. Two machine tools are fundamental to modern industrial civilization: the engine lathe and the milling machine.

The engine lathe, an English invention adopted and improved in America, as the name suggests, was originally developed for the making of steam engines. Before the engine lathe, steam engine cylinders and pistons were seldom perfectly round. Watt's early efforts at making his steam engine were a constant struggle to keep the piston tight to the cylinder walls, wrapping the piston, in his words, with "cork, oiled rags, tow, old hats, paper, and other things, but still there were open spaces left, sufficient to let the air in and the steam out."[28] An engine lathe places a cutting tool against either an exterior surface (for the piston) or interior surface (for the interior walls of the cylinder) while the metal workpiece (the item being machined) rotates. As the workpiece turns, the cutting tool is moved the length of the workpiece. After each pass, the cutting tool moves inward (for pistons) or outward (for cylinders) by a small amount, often measured in thousandths of an inch. Each rotation of the workpiece makes a perfect circle, cutting off another layer of metal. (If you are having trouble visualizing a thousandth of an inch: a sheet of photocopier paper is typically three-thousandths of an inch thick.)

Once consistent and accurate screw threads were available, it was very easy to move the cutting tool a few thousandths of an inch at a time, producing perfectly round objects. (Using a 20-threads-per-inch thread, common in Imperial unit machine tools, one revolution of the screw moves the cutting tool 0.050 inches.) Marking the handwheel on the end of the lead screw in 50 divisions allows 0.001-inch movement per division.

Even before computer controls became common, there were lathes capable of ten-millionths of an inch accuracy. While valuable machine tools, lathes were largely the work of English inventors.[29]

Milling machines are distinctly and clearly American, although dependent on the consistent and regular screw threads made possible by English inventor Henry Maudslay's invention of the screw-cutting lathe sometime before 1800.[30] A milling machine uses a cutting tool that can be moved with the same precision as a lathe. There are two categories of milling machines: horizontal and vertical, depending on the direction the cutting tool moves. Horizontal mills predate the vertical mill. Vertical mills have the advantage that they can mill both the top and sides of a workpiece without moving the workpiece.

In a horizontal mill, a cutting tool is positioned on a shaft driven by the power source (often water power at the start of the 19th century, but usually an electric motor or steam engine by the end of the century); the workpiece is securely held on the table and fed through the cutting tool. The table holding the workpiece can be moved with high precision on all three axes while cutting.[31]

The milling machine's origins remain obscure because of the loss of records and the trade secrecy common to early American gun manufacturers. While Eli Whitney has long been given the honor of "milling machine inventor," more recent research suggests that Whitney was only one of several parallel developers. Some historians give more credit to the clock and textile industry for the development of machine tools.[32]

What is the origin of the milling machine? The traditional method of making parts of a standard shape and size, such as a gunlock sideplate, involved placing the part against a pattern and filing the edges of the part until it matched to the pattern.[33] The earliest mills appear to have used cutters that were more like rotary files, used for removing small pieces of metal, rather than a modern milling cutter that rips off large chunks of metal at a time.[34] (For this reason, modern milling cutters are available both in roughing and finishing forms. The roughing mills excavate large blocks of metal; finishing mills cut off smaller pieces and leave a smoother surface.) A detailed technical history of the multiplicity of improvements to the milling machine can be found in Woodbury's *History of the Milling Machine* (1960).

Also invented in 1818 was Blanchard's "gun-stocking" lathe. This tool works much like a three-dimensional version of a modern key duplicating machine. One "reading" tool follows the shape of a model gunstock. Fixed at the same relative position on the stock blank is the cutting tool. The reading tool follows the model's surface while the model rotates and moves end to end; the cutting tool removes wood on the blank to match, producing standardized stocks to fit standardized metal parts.[35]

The machine tools originally developed for gun manufacturing were soon used for mass production of clocks and sewing machines. Grinding machines (for precisely grinding flat surfaces) soon developed as a second generation of machine tools from these new uses.[36] In much the same way, the American firm of Brown & Sharpe's gear cutting machinery and gear standards developed from gun manufacturing machine tools and were soon used throughout Western industry.[37]

Mass Production

Once interchangeable parts became practical, the highly skilled gun-smith became less important. Each machine operator had a part to play, but that part did not require years of experience. Indeed, Eli Whitney preferred to hire inexperienced workers over experienced gunsmiths. As previously mentioned, in 1825, Springfield Armory's superintendent discouraged a father from apprenticing his son there because the specialization of tasks meant that the son would not become a gunsmith but only a semiskilled machine operator.

A panegyric to Colt published in 1866, explaining the advantages of division of labor, pointed out, along with the many efficiencies articulated in Adam Smith's *Wealth of Nations* (1776), that there was yet another: a job for everyone, regardless of skill level. "One man is too ignorant to manage a machine for stocking, but he can oil that machine, or at least sweep away its chips, a service for which two men are paid each a dollar a day."[38]

The mass production system created a vast consumer society by putting many formerly expensive luxury goods within the reach of ordinary people. Division and specialization of labor, each worker doing one task, was not an American invention, but firearms manufacturers like Simeon North, Eli Whitney, and Samuel Colt certainly contributed to its widespread adoption.[39] As discussed above, at the same time, the firearms industry distributed previously unimaginable wages to those who had formerly been the poor.

American gun culture, by creating a strong demand for firearms, along with federal and state contracts, created a vigorous and inventive gun manufacturing industry that can truly be said to have created much of the modern industrial world.

CHAPTER 11

The Myth of 19th-Century Gun Marketing

In the last two decades, two remarkable claims have been made by the revisionists: (1) that there was little civilian interest in guns until governmental surplus gun sales after both the Mexican-American War and the Civil War and (2) only very effective marketing by the early mass production gun manufacturers created a demand that had hitherto been lacking. As discussed at the beginning of this book, Bellesiles simply denied that guns were common in America and claimed that there was no civilian demand for handguns before 1848, when the Colt revolver was effectively marketed, creating demand that had not previously existed. More recently, Pamela Haag's *The Gunning of America* (2015) argues that "the creation, discovery, invention, and reinvention of gun markets—the visible hand of the gun industrialist at work—was a recurrent, bedrock project of the gun business."[1] Haag's focus is on Colt's and Winchester's supposed marketing of firearms to create a previously nonexistent demand for firearms.

There are two interesting questions that this claim raises:

1. How do you create demand for a product when there was no previous demand?
2. Does the evidence support this claim?

Creating Demand for a New Product

In 1985, Coca-Cola introduced New Coke, a reformulation of their flagship product, and discontinued the old formula. This became known as "the biggest marketing blunder of all time." Here was an established company selling a modest change to an existing product with a large existing market, where the new product was inexpensive; involved no new technology to use (e.g., new straws or can openers); and represented no life-threatening risk relative to the old product. But consumers vigorously rejected the new formula. Coca-Cola eventually brought back the old formula as Classic Coca-Cola and eventually discontinued New Coke.[2]

The IBM PCjr, introduced in 1983, is another example of an aggressively marketed product by a well-established company that failed. The IBM PCjr was a low-priced version of the very successful IBM PC, but consumers simply would not buy them. IBM had 100,000 to 300,000 of them in warehouses that were so unsellable that, in desperation, IBM offered them as a premium to schools ordering five or more IBM PCs.[3] Here was an existing market, although admittedly a new one in the 1980s: personal computers. For several generations, IBM had been the brand that came to mind when you said "computer," and it had found itself in the position of having to give away PCjrs to empty its warehouses.

Ford's introduction of the Edsel is another example of an established firm with a well-known name failing to create demand for a new product in a large existing market, at what should have been a perfect time: 1950s America, when the car reigned supreme.[4]

In all three examples, companies with good reputations and well-known brand names were attempting to persuade buyers to purchase products in existing market segments where there were no technological barriers to new adoption, no cost differential between the new and old products (at least for Coca-Cola, and cheaper for the PCjr), and no obvious safety concerns that might discourage purchase of the new product. Yet, these three are all examples of how, with modern marketing expertise, America's largest corporations utterly failed to create consumer demand for new products.

Colt and Winchester were both unknown companies. In both cases, they were selling products that involved new technologies that might or might not work, potentially leaving customers with complex pieces of nonfunctional machinery. Replacing known lower technology solutions (single-shot pistols and single-shot rifles) with something new that *might* be an inadequate replacement for self-defense is a risk-taking decision. Yet, Colt and Winchester somehow managed to persuade large numbers of Americans to take that risk for a product that revisionists claim they neither wanted nor needed.

Did They Create New Demand?

A previous book by this author[5] and the pistols subsection starting on page 106 provide many examples that show that there was widespread manufacture, possession, and use of pistols in America before 1848. This demolishes both Bellesiles's and Haag's claims that there was no civilian demand for pistols before 1848 and that only clever marketing by Colt and Winchester created demand for guns.

Concerning Bellesiles's claim about firearms marketing creating a demand and Haag's subsequent embellishment of that claim, it is worthwhile to examine Haag's sources, which include both Samuel Colt's letters and the business records of Colt's Patent Firearms Company.

Among the pieces of evidence cited by Haag in defense of her claim that firearms makers had to create a demand for their product is "a letter book in the archives of Colt's Patent Fire-Arms Manufacturing Company [that] reveals detailed, fractious bickering over how many guns the dealers should be expected to 'push.'"[6] She points to page 174 of the Allies letter book.[7] (Colt used the term "Allies" to refer to distributors or wholesalers of Colt products.) An examination of those pages reveals how Haag's failure to read in context has led her astray from the facts.

The reference to "push" is the following:

> We fail to see that the "facts" warrant the closing sentence of the letter therefore do not concede all that is set forth in reference to the "Line." But as we do not propose at present to discust [sic] the merits and *push* of the Allies on the goods covered by the agreement, we rest. [emphasis added][8]

This is the closing sentence of the letter to which this was a response:

> It is hoped that you will readily accede [sic] to our request, when the fact is conceded that the Line upon which we have the Discount, is not only smaller—but also, that notwithstanding our best efforts the sale of this class of Arms has decreased.[9]

Colt's desire for its distributors to "push" its product is clearly referring to one *particular* product line whose sales were decreasing. As a result, the distributors were asking for a better profit margin.

Examination of other correspondence between Colt and its distributors and from Colt during this period suggests that there was no need to "push" the products:

> [Proposed contract] would meet the unanimous consent of the allies & in the long run be more advantageous to the Colt Pat. Fire Arms Co- The quantity should be 150 to 175 per month at the outside assorted viz. 22 cal [125]. 32 cal [30] 38 cal [5] 41 cal [15] with privilege of taking more of the larger or less of the smallest if demand required it.[10]

The bracketed numbers were quantities of each revolver caliber requested per month.

A January 24, 1874, letter from Colt to the Allies shows that the quantities of revolvers under discussion, and the hard-nosed pricing from Colt, does not suggest a problem selling Colt revolvers:

> For we have between 4 & 5 thousand Pistols on hand and in the works. The price named to the Allies (5.25 less 8%) is the lowest price we shall quote for them. We have 1486 New Pocket BL [breech loading] Rim Fire and 408 do [ditto] do [ditto] pistols that we will sell to the Allies at 5.00 Each net 60 days.[11]

A June 29, 1874, letter from the Allies to Colt reads, "Please accept this order from each of the subscribers for two hundred OM [Old Model] 7 Shot Revolvers at $2.99 each, weekly for one year."[12] Three Allies signed the letter, so this was an order for 31,200 revolvers a year. On August 22, 1874, Colt confirmed an order from the Allies for "Ten Thousand (10000) new model 7 shot Pistols to be delivered within Twelve months from Sept 1st/74 at the net price of Five Dollars and Thirty five cents (5.35) each. The first delivery of 1000 Pistols to be made in November 1874."[13]

A December 30, 1874, letter to Colt ordered "Five thousand (5000) of the new 30 cal Revolvers."[14] A December 29, 1874, letter asks, "How many new Pk't [Pocket] 4 1/2 to 6 1/2 [inch barrel length] Rev[olvers] have you all told including finished pistols & those that can be produced from parts on hand, if not over 2,000 we might be induced to take them with 1/2 to 2/3 altered to metallic ctgs [cartridges] (at a price) & the balance at less the cost of altering." The use of "induced" suggests a willingness to buy if Colt gives them a bargain. This is a sign of distributor "pull," not manufacturer "push."

The following sentence demonstrates that demand for handguns was not limited to Colt's products:

> We are of the opinion that it will be necessary for you to reduce the price of your new 38 & 41 [caliber] Rev[olvers] for they move very slow since the reduction of Allen and other manufacturers of 38 & 41 [caliber] Revolvers, being 40 to 50/ [cents?] higher in price.[15]

This was Colt's response:

> The stock of new Pocket that we have on hand and the works cannot exceed 2000 Pistols of these about 1500 are finished. The remainder are in the works, of those on hand their [*sic*] are about an equal quantity of 4 1/2, 5 1/2 and 6 1/2 inch [barrel length]. By altering them into Breech Loaders we could make them all 4 1/2 inch [barrel length] if desired. We will let the "Allies," have them as they are (C&B [cap and ball]) at 4.00 ea. net or we will alter them into Breech Loaders at 5.50 ea. net.[16]

On January 5, 1875, the Allies agreed to the "new Pkt [Pocket] Revolvers on hand & in your works & which will not exceed Two thousand (2000) Revolvers."[17]

What Haag describes as "fractious" correspondence is really just business negotiation, such as this February 9, 1875, letter to Colt:

> We the undersigned agree to purchase jointly from the Colts Pt [Patent] Fire Arms [illegible] Co. Fifteen hundred (1500) new 38 cal[iber] and one thousand (1000) new 41 cal[iber] Revolvers, provided that the said Co. reduce the price of said Revolvers one dollar each & allow a similar reduction on the stock in the hands of the undersigned.[18]

Later sentences agree to "increase the above purchase to Thirty five hundred (3500) of above named Revolvers assorted prior to January 1st 1876, said Co. are to make a further allowance of Fifty cents that is one dollar & fifty cents on each of said Thirty five hundred (3500) Revolvers purchased, including the stock in the hands of the undersigned." Another sentence involves a similar price break for 5,000 revolvers.[19]

By April, the demand was apparently high enough for the Allies to request 4,000 "Army Revolvers of 45 caliber center Fire solid frames & of either finish" to be delivered in 1875.[20] Similar orders appear throughout 1875 (7500 "army Revolvers" in .44 caliber)[21] as well as a request for 42,000 (model and caliber unspecified) at $2.99 each.[22] Another order is for 3,000 revolvers.[23] Business must have been good. The same day they sent another order for "the additional Two thousand (2000) Army Revolvers 45 cal[iber]."[24]

Even if one ignores the immediate context of the "push" on page 174 of the letter book, as Haag apparently did, the sheer volume of orders from the Allies and the recognition that competing revolvers were forcing price cuts on Colt products demolish Haag's claim that the demand for Colt's revolvers required any sort of marketing "push."

Also of interest in the January 24, 1874, letter is a willingness to give the Allies a market opportunity that Colt today reserves for itself: "By referring to our agreement with the Allies we find that we have no right or authority to offer the Police pistols on any other conditions, consequently have decided that we will not disturb the current arrangement during its existence."[25]

A letter Samuel Colt wrote in 1852 concerning establishment of his London gunmaking factory reads, "The demand for arms here is unabat[ed] & I am doubling up my facillates [sic] to make them for this market."[26] In 1849, Colt produced the 1849 .31-caliber pocket pistol, which eventually sold 325,000 units.[27] All of these indicate, contrary to Haag's claims, that there was a thriving civilian market for handguns only four years after Colt opened his Hartford factory.

Haag also tells us that "Colt had sent an agent named Eaton out to California to tap into the gold-rush market in 1853, but he found the market saturated. The new crop of settlers was more interested in agriculture than gold, and they had little need for guns."[28] Her source for this is William B. Edwards's *The Story of Colt's Revolver*,[29] a popular book without footnotes or any indication of the source for this claim.[30] The previous two pages in Edwards's book fail to match Haag's misrepresentation of it. Colt's agent started a business in California in 1851. By 1853, he had sold pistols totaling $70,979.37. In 1854, Eaton ceased operations because of declining demand for pistols; indeed, as Haag says, farmers had become the dominant immigrants to California.[31] But Colt had not sent Eaton to sell guns in 1853, and sales were obviously substantial for the years 1851–1853.

How much demand for pistols was there in Gold Rush California? Ads from Gold Rush California newspapers placed by retailers suggest it was substantial. J. A. McCrea advertised Colt's revolvers (and Warner's revolvers) in the January 1, 1853, Sacramento *Daily Union*. Perhaps he was mistaken about there being demand for them. But then why did he run this same ad in the same paper 199 times in 1853 and 281 times in 1854?[32] If there were no demand for the pistols, why would he continue advertising them? Perhaps he did not realize his mistake on the first several hundred ads.

This confusion was apparently endemic. A December 7, 1852, *Daily Alta California* ad offered 10 "cases Colt's pistols."[33] How many to a case? At *least* one. And there are 16 repeats of that ad in 1852.[34] In the 1850s, there are 1,231 advertisements in California newspapers for "Colt's pistols."[35] There are 483 ads for the singular "revolver,"[36] 1,283 ads for "revolvers,"[37] and 4,317 for "pistols," which of course includes "Colt's pistols."[38]

There are two possibilities here:

1. Merchants continued to advertise products for sale in a "market saturated" with guns. If advertising were cheap, this might make sense. The Sacramento *Placer Times* charged $4 for 10 lines of a column and $2 for every "subsequent insertion,"[39] which in 1850 was not a trivial amount. This would seem a discouragement to advertising unsellable goods.
2. Demand in California was strong for pistols.

More evidence of a gun culture in this period in California comes from ads inviting patrons to "shooting galleries" (as shooting ranges were then called). Shooting gallery ads appear many times.[40]

A search for "shooting" in gold rush newspapers finds 1,838 matches, some of which do not refer to guns but are small flaws in reading images of old documents that have been introduced by modern optical character recognition (OCR) technology on old, very small text and are actually "sheeting."[41] But some are "shooting," such as an ad from Backus & Harrison, apparently a wholesaler by the quantities of goods sold ("2,000 lbs of bacon, 20 cases anchovies, 10,000 lbs. of sweet potatoes"), who offered "36 fancy shooting coats."[42]

Searching articles instead of ads found 2,885 matches, a few of which are metaphorical ("grass shooting up on the prairies"). But most are of this form: "John Southworth was arrested for firing a pistol at his partner with intent to kill." "A Case of Shooting at San Francisco" describes a suicide by a merchant in financial trouble. "Another Affray at the Humboldt" concerns a pistol shooting. Another account reports on two shootings in one day (at least one described as with a "revolver") at a gambling establishment. An account of court proceedings in San Francisco reports on a fist fight that escalated: "Lilly said that Kay struck at him, and that thereupon he (Lilly) presented a pistol and would have killed Kay had not his pistol missed fire." "Shooting at Stockton" involves a pistol shooting at a faro table. Another quarrel in a gambling establishment at Nevada City describes "the issue was, the 'gent' betting, pulled out one of 'Colt's best,' and without shooting the right one, wounded three others."[43] All of these incidents are from the first seven months of 1850.

J. D. Borthwick's *Three Years in Calafornia* [sic] (1857) describes how San Francisco was awash in places of entertainment with signs that announced "No weapons admitted." While Borthwick thought little of the entertainments available, he did describe why it was nonetheless worth going:

> If only to watch the company arrive, and to see the practical enforcement of the weapon clause in the announcements. Several doorkeepers were in attendance, to whom each man as he entered delivered up his knife or his *pistol*, receiving a check for it, just as one does for his cane or umbrella at the door of a picture-gallery. Most men draw a *pistol* from behind their back, and very often a knife along with it; some carried their bowie-knife down the back of their neck, or in their breast; demure, pious-looking men, in white neckcloths, lifted up the bottom of their waistcoat, and revealed the butt of a *revolver*; others, after having already disgorged a *pistol*, pulled up the leg of their trousers, and abstracted a huge bowie-knife from their boot; and there were men, terrible fellows, no doubt, but who were more likely to frighten themselves than any one else, who produced a *revolver* from each trouser-pocket, and a bowie-knife from their belt. If any man declared that he had no weapon, the statement was so incredible that he had to submit to be searched; an operation which was performed by the doorkeepers, who, I observed, were occasionally rewarded for their diligence by the discovery of a pistol secreted in some unusual part of the dress.[44] [emphasis added]

Rifles appear repeatedly in 1850–1859 California newspapers: 3,953 matches, including ads for the "Sharp's Patent Rifles." Sometimes these are articles in which rifles play a part, such as this account of horse thieves:

The Spaniard on the opposite side of the table then rose, and fired a revolver at Mr. Clark, missing him. Mr. B.F. Moore then came in, and the Spaniard fired at him, but missed. He then took up a rifle and fired, at about five inches' distance, blowing off the top of the Spaniard's head.[45]

Haag's claim of Colt's sales difficulties not only misrepresent her unscholarly source; the other evidence demonstrates that there was a strong and vigorous gun culture already in existence in California before and after 1853.

By comparison to Pamela Haag's largely false claims about Colt's efforts to create demand, Haag's efforts concerning Winchester are largely empty. Instead, Haag engages in guilt by innuendo, observing that Winchester helped form the Ammunition Manufacturers Association in 1883, a cartel that "by modern standards would be illegal," but was legal then, to prevent competition,[46] which might have lowered prices. If the goal was to create a gun culture, driving up prices would reduce demand—not at all compatible with her claim. She tars Winchester as a merchant of death, pointing out their sometimes knowingly shipping guns to revolutionaries in the Third World, but fails to tie this to creating an American gun culture.[47] At no point does she claim intentional manipulation of consumer tastes or preferences by Winchester.

Haag does unintentionally show that the gun market was substantial when she explains that Sears, then an up-and-coming mail order firm, offered "pages and pages of guns" at the start of the 20th century, and she expresses her amazement that "Sears also offered the take-down shotgun . . . as a premium for customers who spent over $300. Strange as it is today to imagine a gun was an added bonus, tossed in for buying a sewing machine or shoes."[48] Clearly, Sears recognized that this would be an attractive premium to its customers, showing how little Haag understands of American culture, then or now. Haag demolishes her own argument about Winchester trying to create a bigger market by describing how Sears attempted to get around Winchester's minimum retail prices by surreptitiously buying guns from Winchester dealers after Winchester refused to directly sell to Sears.[49] If the goal was to create a gun culture, selling vast quantities through America's largest retailer at low prices would make sense; cutting off their supply to drive up prices would not.

Haag later argues that Winchester employed gun "missionaries" and Remington hired "business getters" for the purpose of creating demand, but her examples demonstrate that the goal was to promote their brands over competitors.[50] She also devotes several pages to a discussion of the emerging sportsman's disdain for "market hunters" (hunters who did so to sell game to others as food). Her only point relevant to gun culture was that there were, then as today, several gun cultures in America.[51] This digression is irrelevant to her claim.

Haag also ties Winchester's growth to the development of the dime novel Wild West literature. There is no dispute that this literature was largely fictional, with descriptions of gunfights exaggerated, if not completely false; however, her research is clearly deficient. "Other characters—Buffalo Bill, Billy the Kid, Belle Star, Calamity Jane, and the California bandit Murietta, contrived out of whole cloth—would follow the same path—from lowbrow fiction into highbrow historical fact." It appears that "contrived out of whole cloth" refers only to Murietta, because Haag elsewhere acknowledges the historicity of Buffalo Bill and Calamity Jane. Juan Murietta's historicity is hardly "contrived out of whole cloth"; there are quite literally tens of thousands of books about him.[52]

Discussing the post–Civil War period concerning Winchester's expansion, Haag asserts that "the gun today is mired in political fetishization, but the Second Amendment was a slumbering giant during the years of the gun's most intense diffusion."[53] She cites Adam Winkler's *Gunfight* for this claim, which only lists some Colonial era limits on militia duty, while ignoring the enormous "right to keep and bear arms" jurisprudence in state and federal supreme courts in the antebellum and postbellum period.[54] Clearly, Haag has only a limited knowledge of this subject and has done no serious research.

Haag quotes the Indian agent for the Ute Indians expressing his outrage that traders were selling modern guns (like Winchesters) to them, "which they know will be used to destroy the lives of innocent white citizens."[55] While irrelevant to Haag's claim about gun culture creation, it does show the carelessness of her research. Examining her source shows a more complex situation. The agent explains:

> Previous to the late Ute outbreak the Indians were amply supplied with Winchester and Spencer rifles and fixed [metallic cartridge ammunition] obtained from traders outside of their reservation. Game was abundant on or near their reserve, and for some time the Utes had been making sales of peltries [furs] to a large amount, and were thus enabled to provide themselves with such arms and ammunition as they desired.[56]

The agent's upset with the traders was that they had failed to identify that increased purchases indicated the Utes were preparing to go to war against whites.

An additional possible reason for the agent's ire is that Indian agents often made substantial wealth above and beyond their salaries through corrupt trading:

> Reformers reserved their harshest language for the Indian agents. Since agents were ordinarily responsible for approving trading licenses, they were seen as the root of much corruption. A Minnesotan reported: "It is believed that the trader is, in all cases, a partner of the Agent. He is usually a near relative."

The temptation for Indian agents to become corrupt were enormous; according to one adviser to President Lincoln, a corrupt agent could make a fortune in four years, equivalent to the president's salary.[57] Other sources report that "supplying goods to the reservations provided a multimillion dollar opportunity for fraud and corruption."[58] While there is no way to determine whether the Indian agent to the Utes quoted by the Secretary of the Interior had corrupt dealings relevant to the question of firearms, it should at least be recognized that he might have had motivations other than his official duties.

Haag also repeatedly makes false statements, which seem intended to provoke emotional, irrational reactions. Throughout her book, Haag incorrectly uses the word "semiautomatic" to refer to guns that are not: "The family name, which became the rifle name, eventually stood for the genus, becoming a synonym for repeating, *semiautomatic* rifles" [emphasis added]; "As the *semiautomatic* ancestor of automatic machine guns, the Henry performed 'a terrible work of death'" [emphasis added]; and "Winchester had emerged the preeminent name for *semiautomatic* rifles" [emphasis added].[59]

But the Henry and Winchester rifles were *not* semiautomatic rifles. "The semi-automatic rifle—that is, the military rifle fitted with self-loading mechanism but fired by the trigger shot for shot"[60]—does not describe the Henry or Winchester rifles, which must be reloaded by operation of the operating lever.[61] Because Haag describes the Winchester mechanism and how it works,[62] this is clearly not ignorance, but perhaps an attempt to transfer some of the horror she associates with modern semiautomatic weapons to guns in the historical period she is examining. This is especially problematic because the proper term "repeater" or "repeating" appears in several places in her book.[63]

Regardless of Haag's motivation, her repeated use of the incorrect terms casts serious doubt on either her level of research or her honesty. It would be similar to referring to the role of "airplanes" for reconnaissance in the Franco-Prussian War of 1870–1871 instead of the more accurate "balloons."

At one point, Haag makes the claim that Winchester rifles developed a will of their own. "Speed (not power) and accuracy from a distance were the mechanical soul of all Winchesters. With each design advance, the volition of the rifle became more volitional." "Small, mortal operations of armed conflict occurred through the technological ingenuity of the mechanical hand, and the confrontation became less intimate or physically immediate. The gun 'did' more of the motions and actions of the killing."[64] Here is another example: "Instead, people and animals were shot faster, at greater distances, with a more mechanically volitional weapon."[65]

"Volition" refers to "making a choice." [66] Was Winchester making the earliest intelligent robotic gun? No. Haag clearly believes that the finger does not pull the trigger; the trigger pulls the finger. Again, human agency has been replaced by gun agency. History is not about feeling better; facts are an impartial interpretation of them.

The claim that the first mass production gunmakers created a demand for a previously unwanted product runs both contrary to the overwhelming evidence of a large and vibrant gun culture in the Colonial, Revolutionary, and Early Republic periods, and fails examination of its own claims.

CHAPTER 12

Postbellum Gun Culture, 1865–1930

Even the revisionists agree that America was a gun culture from the Civil War onward. Searching the Library of Congress's *Chronicling America* database of newspapers for references to guns for the years 1865–1924 returns 778,653 matches, or 13,197 per year.[1] Some matches are startling indicators of how widely the gun culture spread: "Fall Skirt Will Have Pistol Pockets."[2] Others are non-gun references, such as the character Pistol in reviews of Shakespeare's *The Merry Wives of Windsor*.[3] Of the first 20 pages, pistol as a gun is present in 19. Overwhelmingly, these articles concern criminal misuses of pistols, or suicides, which certainly demonstrates a widespread ownership of them. There are sporting use references as well.[4]

The broader search for "pistol," "handgun," "rifle," "revolver," or "shotgun" returns 2,105,091 pages, or 27,905 per year.[5] Of the first 20 pages, 3 are about firearms competition, 2 are gun ads, 3 are news reports of crimes involving guns, 1 is an article about "An Outline of History as Told by Firearms," 1 is a cartoon making fun of the hazard of being a gun salesman, 1 is fiction, 3 announce sporting exhibitions, 1 describes the federal government's promotion of civilian marksmanship, 2 are articles about gun designer John M. Browning, 4 contain sporting uses, and 1 article criticizes "Pistols as the Most Dangerous and Least Useful Sort of Firearms" while praising rifles and shotguns for their hunting use. (Some pages have articles in more than one category.) It is hard to look at these articles as anything but evidence of a widespread gun culture in postbellum America, much of it focused on hunting and other sporting uses.

Another indicator of the extent of gun culture in this period is the case law in the state courts related to the regulation of firearms discussed on page 162. While many of these cases involve attempts to regulate firearm ownership or carrying, the need for such a swarm of decisions strongly demonstrates that guns were widely owned.

Competition

The disappointing marksmanship of Union soldiers during the Civil War led several New York National Guard officers to start the National Rifle Association of America in 1871, although for many years, it was primarily a New York State organization. This was in conscious emulation of the National Rifle Association of Great Britain, to promote marksmanship for national defense purposes. Its first president was the Civil War general Ambrose Burnside. Throughout its first 40 years, NRA presidents were overwhelmingly National Guard officers and retired U.S. Army generals. Adoption of the National Rifle Association of Great Britain's "target and scoring standards" soon created an international competition environment.[6]

Despite the marksmanship concerns that led to the NRA's formation, American competitors soon dominated the international competitions. The Irish Rifle Association, an affiliate of the National Rifle Association of Great Britain and the winner of their most recent competition, challenged one of the National Rifle Association of America affiliates to a match in which the Americans, a small and still not very practiced group, narrowly defeated the Irish Rifle Association and, in subsequent years, teams from other British Empire nations.[7]

Attempts to reduce New York State spending by New York's governor, and his belief that there would never be another war even in the lifetime of his children, soon impaired New York National Guard participation in NRA-sponsored competitions, causing the NRA to go moribund. All its files spent 1892–1900 in storage.[8]

In 1900, at the height of the Spanish-American War, the NRA arose from its filing cabinet crypt. With President (and Spanish-American War veteran) Teddy Roosevelt's encouragement, Congress created the National Board for the Promotion of Rifle Practice, to improve both military and civilian marksmanship. Roosevelt remained active in promoting the NRA for many years. Subsequent federal involvement in firearm competition sport included the sale of surplus military firearms and ammunition to NRA-affiliated clubs, a practice that continues today. Public schools from high school through college organized rifle teams with encouragement and assistance from the federal government and the NRA (in those years, a quasi-governmental entity).[9] The Boy Scouts, originally established in Britain to improve competence in the wild after the disastrous Boer War, soon took up marksmanship under the NRA's encouragement.[10]

Police officers, almost as remote from marksmanship training as the Civil War's Union soldiers, began to compete in NRA-sponsored events in the 1920s.[11] During World War I, the NRA became a source of civilian marksmanship trainers for the U.S. Army.[12]

Black Gun Culture: Putting Holes in the Robes and Hoods

One often surprising aspect of American gun culture is the black tradition of firearms. From the Colonial period through the Jim Crow era, statutes either openly prohibited or severely limited gun ownership by both free and slave blacks; in more recent times, governments continued these limitations through unlimited discretion on the part of license-granting officials.[13] Before the Civil War, black leaders encouraged blacks in the North to be armed against "kidnappers" making use of the Fugitive Slave Act of 1850. Frederick Douglass asserted, "The True Remedy for the Fugitive Slave Bill . . . a good revolver, a steady hand, and a determination to shoot down any man attempting to kidnap."[14] Runaway slaves and those engaged in leading them north, such as Harriet Tubman, made use of firearms.[15]

During Reconstruction, immediately following the Civil War, freedmen made extensive use of firearms to preserve their newfound liberty from the Ku Klux Klan and other terrorist groups.[16]

After the end of Reconstruction, lynchings and other forms of mob violence caused the prominent journalist Ida B. Wells to argue that "the Winchester Rifle deserves a place of honor in every Black home."[17] She also bought a pistol. At about the same time, W. E. B. Du Bois, the intellectual leader of black Americans for a generation, reported that his classmates at the black Fisk University in Nashville were habitually armed.[18] What evidence exists suggests that black ownership of firearms in the South, despite repeated efforts to limit it, was widespread for both hunting and self-defense.[19] Something of the flavor of Southern motivations can be found in discussions of the Mailing of Firearms Act, which prohibited shipping concealable firearms through the U.S. Post Office. It was debated in several Congresses before its passage in 1927. A sponsor

of that bill in 1925 was Sen. Shields (D-Tenn.), who explained the need
for this law because of the high murder rate in Memphis, Tennessee:

> Fifty-three negroes killed by negroes. Only seven negroes killed
> [by] whites. Only two whites killed by negroes—one a white bur-
> glar and the other assassinated by negro bandits. . . .
>
> Here we have laid bare the principal cause for the high murder
> rate in Memphis—the carrying by colored people of a concealed
> deadly weapon, most often a pistol. Can we not cope with this
> situation?[20]

Prohibiting mail order shipping of handguns was supposed to make it
easier to enforce state laws regulating handgun ownership—of which
the focus was apparently blacks.

North Carolina's 1919 law requiring a permit to purchase a pistol
may have been similarly driven by concern about the presence of a black
gun culture. Enforcement of the existing law requiring a license to carry
concealed handguns shows evidence of racial bias. Some newspaper
reports of criminal court dockets overwhelmingly identify defendants
on this charge as black.[21]

Newspaper accounts of the effects of the new law, while denying that
the law discriminated based on race, suggest that it was perceived as
having a racial effect: "While other sections have recently been subjected
to race riots in more or less violent degrees, North Carolina generally
and Wilmington in particular has so far been free from any race trouble
whatever."[22] In addition, the requirement that a pistol purchaser must be
of "good moral character" suggests a racist purpose.

A few years earlier, the Alabama Constitutional Convention of 1901
disenfranchised those convicted of "any crime . . . involving moral tur-
pitude." This provision in the Alabama Constitution of 1901 came out
of a convention called for the purpose of disfranchising blacks,[23] and
this provision "disfranchised approximately ten times as many blacks as
whites. This disparate effect persists today."[24] The similarity in language
suggests a similar intent.

There are other examples of remarkable honesty from the state
supreme courts on this subject, of which the finest is probably Florida
Supreme Court Justice Buford's concurring opinion in *Watson v. Stone*
(1941) discussing the Jim Crow era origins of the concealed weapon
license law. A conviction for carrying a handgun without a permit was
overturned because the handgun was in the glove compartment of a car:

I know something of the history of this legislation. The original Act of 1893 was passed when there was a great influx of negro laborers in this State drawn here for the purpose of working in turpentine and lumber camps. The same condition existed when the Act was amended in 1901 and the Act was passed for the purpose of disarming the negro laborers and to thereby reduce the unlawful homicides that were prevalent in turpentine and saw-mill camps and to give the white citizens in sparsely settled areas a better feeling of security. The statute was never intended to be applied to the white population and in practice has never been so applied.[25]

Some have argued that the development of gun culture in the post-bellum 19th century and 20th century "facilitate[ed] the formation of a masculine identity."[26] This was doubtlessly true, as a man unable to protect his home, wife, and children would not then, or even now, be regarded as terribly manly. Ida B. Wells argued that "the more the Afro-American yields and cringes and begs, the more he is insulted, outraged and lynched."[27]

Gangster Gun Culture

The gangster culture that Prohibition created is certainly an example of a criminal gun subculture, one that expressed itself in the use of the Thompson submachine gun. This, plus the rise of interstate criminals such as John Dillinger, led to passage of the National Firearms Act of 1934. This law was originally intended to license and tax handguns as well as concealable semiautomatic and automatic weapons, such as submachine guns, but not rifle-caliber machine guns. In response to substantial public criticism, handgun regulation was removed from the law, and rifle-caliber machine guns were added,[28] suggesting widespread ownership of handguns.

The attorney general and the assistant attorney general, in arguing for the law, admitted that a general prohibition or licensing of firearms, even machine guns, exceeded the federal government's authority; they could achieve the same net result by taxing firearms in interstate commerce and requiring proof of payment of the tax, analogous to the federal government's licensing of drugs.[29]

CHAPTER 13

Modern Gun Culture, 1930–Present

American gun culture, primarily associated with hunting and competition, persisted well into the 1960s as a generally accepted part of American life. Evidence includes published book reviews and articles concerning competition shooting.[1] Col. Charles Askins Jr.'s *The Art of Handgun Shooting* was listed in the *Journal of Health, Physical Education, Recreation* under "New Books Received,"[2] which also detailed how to establish secondary school rifle clubs and how to obtain free ammunition and guns from the U.S. government.[3] The National Rifle Association, in cooperation with the federal government (because of the perceived national defense reasons), continued its earlier involvement in secondary school rifle competitions. Some descriptions of this may shock modern urban elites. "Rifle marksmanship was virtually unknown in most secondary schools across the nation, but had become a thriving sport in some locales, especially New York City and Washington, D.C."[4] Pistol and revolver matches were part of the "Havalanta Games" in 1950, in which Havana citizens competed against Atlanta residents.[5] As an example of how mainstream firearms ownership was, *Life* magazine, a mass circulation publication, had a full-page ad for Browning firearms, including the high-capacity semiautomatic Hi Power 9mm pistol.[6]

Gun Ownership

Gun ownership would seem an obvious way of measuring the gun culture. But measuring gun ownership in America is harder than it appears because there is no national requirement for gun licensing or registration. Of course, even when state laws require it, such records are necessarily incomplete; ex-felons, illegal immigrants, and a few other categories are prohibited under both federal and state laws from gun ownership. In addition, there are many otherwise law-abiding persons who would prefer that the government remain ignorant of their gun ownership. The reason for such privacy concerns can be best explained by Stephen Halbrook's comprehensive book on how the Nazis used both preexisting Weimar Republic and their own gun control laws to disarm Jews and political opponents before reducing them to ash.[7] Charles E. Cobb Jr.'s memoir *This Nonviolent Stuff'll Get You Killed: How Guns Made the Civil Rights Movement Possible* shows how gun restrictions in the South were used to attack the civil rights movement through intimidation and murder.[8]

Gun Background Checks

The National Instant Criminal Background Check System (NICS) was created by the Brady Handgun Violence Prevention Act of 1993. It requires federally licensed firearms dealers to run a background check for all firearms purchases, new or used. As such, it provides a fairly reliable measure of gun purchases. However the 0.58 percent of applicants that are refused purchase permission because they are prohibited from ownership must be subtracted,[9] as well as background checks performed by states who use NICS when issuing or renewing gun licenses, which for May 2014 were about 35 percent of NICS checks.[10] Because firearms dealers may sell more than one gun at the same time with the same background check, and private transfers are lawful in most states, the NICS counts, even with those adjustments, are probably a low measure of firearms sold. Since NICS began operation in November 1998, it has performed 257,495,166 checks,[11] or an average of almost 13 million per year (for both purchases and gun licenses)—a pretty good measure of the size of American gun culture.

Another measure of the size of American gun culture is contained in a recent U.S. Court of Appeals for the Fourth Circuit decision:

> We think it is beyond dispute from the record before us, which contains much of the same evidence cited in the aforementioned decisions, that law-abiding citizens commonly possess semi-automatic rifles such as the AR-15. Between 1990 and 2012, more than 8 million AR- and AK-platform semi-automatic rifles alone were

manufactured in or imported into the United States. . . . In 2012, semi-automatic sporting rifles accounted for twenty percent of all retail firearms sales. . . . For perspective, we note that in 2012, the number of AR- and AK-style weapons manufactured and imported into the United States was more than double the number of Ford F-150 trucks sold, the most commonly sold vehicle in the United States.[12]

If a category of guns regularly castigated in the news media is more popular than America's best-selling pickup, there must be a substantial gun culture.

Surveys

Surveys of gun ownership reveal that it is widespread. According to the Pew Research Center, households admitting ownership of at least one gun are 37 percent of the population; the highest percentages of gun ownership are white, male, over 30, married, rural, living in the South and Midwest, with at least some college education.[13] The primary reason stated for gun ownership is protection (48%), followed by hunting (32%).[14]

While not a perfect match for gun ownership, public opinion surveys concerning the right to keep and bear arms are pretty clearly an indicator of public perceptions of gun ownership and thus America's gun subcultures. The Pew Research Group's polling on the question, "What do you think is more important—to protect the right of Americans to own guns, OR to control gun ownership?" from December 1993 through December 2014 showed a shift from a large minority on the gun rights side (34%) to a majority (52%).[15]

Rasmussen Reports is a national opinion-gathering organization; one survey asked whether respondents would "feel safer living in a neighborhood where nobody was allowed to own a gun over one where they could have a gun for their own protection": 68 percent preferred the neighborhood where they could have a gun.[16]

What makes this so curious is the Gallup surveys showing declining rates of gun ownership. In answer to the question, "Do you have a gun in your home?" Gallup's answers fell from 49 percent in 1961 to 39 percent in 2016.[17]

Changing opinions about banning handguns are another indication of a growing gun culture: 60 percent supported a handgun ban in July 1959, compared to 23 percent in October 2016. Curiously, in light of the Pew polling about gun rights, Gallup found in its 2016 poll that 55 percent support stricter laws concerning the sale of guns (although this is much below the 78 percent level in the early 1990s).[18]

Other measures suggest widespread support or at least acquiescence to the gun culture. Pew's 2016 survey asked about bans on high-capacity magazines and "assault-style weapons." Despite several decades of mass murders largely and inaccurately perceived as committed with such weapons,[19] only 54 percent supported such bans.[20] Yet, in 2016, Gallup found only 34 percent supported such bans.[21] Regardless of which is correct (and the enormous disparity on this question raises serious questions about the validity of the polling methods), the gun culture includes a substantial part of American society.

Some surveys seem to indicate declining gun ownership. The National Opinion Research Center's General Social Survey reports a decline in gun ownership from 47.0 percent in 1973 to 31.0 percent in 2014. Although the percentage refusing to answer the question rose from 1.0 percent to 3.2 percent during that period, this is not enough to explain the difference between the 39 percent gun ownership reported in the 2016 Gallup survey and the 31.0 percent in the 2014 NORC poll.[22]

It seems likely that some significant fraction of Americans is not honestly answering such questions from a stranger on the phone. Because gun ownership in some parts of the United States is licensed or otherwise regulated, some owners may be reluctant to admit a violation of the law. Gun control laws have undergone great change in some states and localities in recent years, so respondents may be uncertain whether guns that they acquired lawfully in the past remain lawful today.

There may also be genuine ignorance by some of those surveyed about the presence of guns in the house. When attending my father-in-law's third wedding, as I was walking out the door, I asked him whether he had bought a gun since we had last discussed it. He responded by telling me about two handguns he had purchased; his bride, with whom he had been living for six months, was utterly surprised.

Current Gun Subcultures

In the 1960s, American society began to fragment, leading to the death of widely read "mainstream" non-news publications, such as *Life* and *Saturday Evening Post*. Unsurprisingly, American gun culture also fragmented.

Hunters

As discussed in previous chapters, hunting has always been a substantial part of American culture, for subsistence and for entertainment. To people who have grown up in urban environments, hunting may seem extraordinarily foreign. Growing up in Los Angeles, I knew no one who hunted, nor were my perceptions of hunters very high.

After moving to a rural part of Northern California, I had neighbors who hunted. I found that many loved the outdoors and wilderness so deeply that if they had grown up in a big city, I am sure they would have been Sierra Club members. The stalking and killing of wildlife was in many respects incidental to their desire to be in the wild.

The 2011 census of hunting and fishing found 13.7 million hunters in the United States engaged for 282 million days. (Hunting included not only firearms but also bowhunters.) They spent $14.3 billion on hunting. Unsurprisingly, a majority (52%) of hunters engaged in target shooting in preparation for hunting.[23]

Contrary to the stereotype of hunters as poorly educated rednecks, the largest household income category of hunters was $75,000 to $99,999 per year (9%). A startling 5 percent of hunters had household incomes exceeding $150,000 per year, and 27 percent had four or more years of college. Compared to the 2006 census, the percentage of the population that hunts has increased by 9 percent.[24]

There are many magazines devoted to hunting, some specific to gun hunting, some to bowhunting, and some that could be either but are primarily gun-oriented: *Petersen's Hunting*, circulation 202,833;[25] *Gun Dog*, 41,669;[26] *North American Whitetail*, 133,289;[27] *Wildfowl*, 41,378;[28] and *Field & Stream*, 1,000,000.[29]

Competition Shooters

Firearms culture has always had a target-shooting element. This is unsurprising. The hunting culture involves killing an animal; the more quickly it dies, the less it suffers, and the less effort a hunter has to spend chasing his prey. Marksmanship is therefore a useful skill. Military, police, and civilian self-defense applications also put a premium on hitting your target.

Until the 1950s, police, military, and civilian pistol competition involved one-handed slow shooting at targets. This was left over from the days of cavalry officers dismounting and shooting one-handed while holding reins with the other hand. It was completely unsuited to either 20th-century warfare or police needs.

In the 1950s, Col. Jeff Cooper (USMC, Ret.) started a new form of competition better suited to modern needs; it involved moving targets and moving competitors. Initially known as the Southwest Pistol League, it was later renamed the International Practical Shooting Confederation (IPSC). Initially, this appealed to police officers, for whom there was a real-world applicability. It is now a global form of sport present in "Australia, Central and South America, Europe, and Southern Africa" and 90 different countries. The sport emphasizes "accuracy, power, and speed"; making every bullet hit the intended target; using handguns in calibers powerful enough to be realistic for self-defense; and balancing hitting targets against quick shooting. The International Defensive Pistol Association (IDPA) is a similar organization, except that it limits competition to standard off-the-shelf pistols, while IPSC pistols are often highly customized "race guns."[30]

The Single Action Shooting Society is the sanctioning body for Cowboy Action Shooting:

> [A] multi-faceted shooting sport in which contestants compete with firearms typical of those used in the taming of the Old West: single action revolvers, pistol caliber lever action rifles, and old time shotguns. The shooting competition is staged in a unique, characterized, "Old West" style. It is a timed sport in which shooters compete for prestige on a course of different shooting stages. Currently, SASS has 30,000 members.[31]

The Civilian Marksmanship Program (CMP) is the granddaddy of firearms target shooting. Originally established in 1903 as a division of the Department of Defense to create a cadre of skilled marksmen in the event of war, it is funded by the sale of surplus U.S. Army firearms to members. It organizes shooting competitions across the United States, culminating in the annual Camp Perry rifle matches. These competitions use both the World War II–era M1 Garand and AR-15s (the semiautomatic version of the Vietnam-era M16). The Camp Perry matches in 2016 included 4,667 competitors; CMP's Talladega range was used by "17,497 shooters and 1,819 spectators in FY16." "The CMP sanctioned more than 2,274 matches for approximately 23,934 competitors in 2016."[32]

The National Muzzle Loading Rifle Association sanctions matches with muzzleloading rifles.[33] Membership numbers are unavailable.

The International Metal Silhouette Association has matches shooting at metal silhouettes of animals. This is a long-time sport that has become more humane since World War II: "Initially live farm animals were used as targets, but since around 1948 the targets have been metal silhouettes of chickens, pigs, turkeys and rams, that are set at various distances."[34]

The parallel International Handgun Metal Silhouette Association does the same with handguns. It was started in 1976, but membership numbers are unavailable.[35]

Concealed Carriers

Until the 1980s, permits to carry concealed weapons were in nearly all states issued at the discretion of a police chief, sheriff, or judge. At one time, this was primarily a method for prohibiting blacks, Hispanics, Chinese, and other "undesirables" from carrying concealed weapons,[36] but by the 1970s, the abuse potential was obvious enough that permits became increasingly difficult for most citizens to obtain, although bribery seems to have remained an important part of the qualification process in some jurisdictions.[37] Following Washington State's lead in 1961, and especially Florida's 1987 law, most American states have since adopted "shall issue" statutes that clearly define who may be denied a license and who must be issued a license.[38]

There are currently 14.5 million concealed carry permits in the United States, or 6.06 percent of the U.S. population. Eight states have followed Vermont's lead and allow all persons not prohibited from gun ownership to carry guns concealed without a license. Two other states only require concealed carry licenses for nonresidents.[39]

The dramatic expansion of concealed weapon licenses availability is believed to be a major part of the dramatic expansion of gun ownership by females.

Gun Collectors

For some, it is difficult to understand gun collecting; why allow gun ownership so that a few eccentrics can collect instruments of death? Gun collectors are usually far more deeply interested in history, technology, and design esthetics than in shooting guns. Most collectible guns are either too old or too fragile to shoot, or too valuable to risk damaging. Nonetheless, gun collectors are a part of the gun culture and are often shockingly affluent. In many respects, gun collectors are similar to those who collect stamps, coins, or art.

There are a number of gun collector magazines aimed primarily at affluent collectors, such as *Arms Heritage* magazine, with a circulation of 3,000 monthly, and *Man at Arms Magazine for the Gun and Sword Collector*, with a circulation of 45,000 copies a month.[40]

The federal government even has a Federal Firearms License (FFL) for collectors of "curios and relics" that allows collectors to transfer such firearms interstate without going through the conventional background check system. There are currently 56,493 such licenses.[41] Collectors who make their purchases intrastate or through FFLs do not need these licenses and may prefer avoiding the license fee and record-keeping requirements of the gun collector license.

Gun Culture Magazines

There are many general interest gun magazines with large circulations, such as *Guns & Ammo* (circulation 386,190); *Rifle Shooter* (60,487); *Handguns* (122,886); *Shooting Times* (164,448), and *Firearms News* (85,650).[42] The National Rifle Association sends one of its three magazines to each of its 5 million plus members. *America's First Freedom* is primarily focused on the political struggle over gun ownership. *American Hunter*, as the title suggests, is about hunting. *American Rifleman* is primarily competition, historical, and technical in nature.

Victim Groups

Many groups have identified themselves (often with good reason) as likely to be victimized, and for them, gun ownership became a path toward self-defense.

Blacks

Throughout the civil rights movement, willingness to use deadly force in defense of both leadership and field workers was common.[43] Don B. Kates, a civil rights movement activist and close friend of mine, describes the situation:

> I found that the possession of firearms for self-defense was almost universally endorsed by the black community, for it could not depend on police protection from the KKK. . . . Everyone remembered an incident several years before, in which the state's Klansmen attempted to break up a civil rights meeting and were routed by return gunfire.[44]

National surveys show lower rates of black gun ownership (18.1%) compared to whites (39.0%), perhaps in part because gun ownership is correlated with income (18.2% ownership for all races with household incomes below $25,000 per annum, versus 44.0% for incomes above $90,000).[45] Another reason might be because blacks were prohibited from gun ownership for so long. Why would past disarmament affect the present?

"Sport owners of guns were . . . more likely to have parents who owned guns."[46] Several generations of gun ownership among whites may have a mirror image among blacks who do not own guns because several generations followed a parental model derived from past legal obstacles to black ownership. Interestingly, surveys conducted at the neighborhood level in Detroit find comparable levels of gun ownership by whites and blacks.[47] Another factor that may influence responses is that a felony conviction, even decades earlier, is a firearms disqualifier, and 25 percent of blacks are ex-felons, compared to 6 percent of whites.[48] While ex-felons are prohibited from gun ownership, it seems unlikely that all obey the law, and wariness of honestly answering the question might explain much of the apparent gun ownership racial disparity.

The National African-American Gun Association has 24 affiliated black gun clubs, with more than 18,000 members.[49] The election of President Trump in 2016 appears to have increased black interest in and purchase of firearms, out of concern about attacks by what is perceived as an increased tolerance of racism.[50]

Indians
The Ku Klux Klan (KKK) was not hostile just to blacks; in 1958, Robeson County, North Carolina, KKK leaders organized a rally in opposition to the Lumbee Indians after a campaign of cross burning and threats. In response, Lumbee Indians massed, armed, across from the rally.[51] In the ensuing chaos, hundreds of shots were fired; only two people, one a reporter and the other a bystander, were slightly injured by gunfire.[52] The result was that the KKK never again held a rally in Robeson County.[53]

Women
Largely in apparent response to concerns about assault, gun ownership among women is rising, with "a 60% increase in women target shooters from 2001–2013."[54] One-fifth of gun purchases are by women.[55] Surveys of gun ownership find that while only 12 percent of women report gun ownership, 30 percent report that they live in a home with a gun.[56] In

addition to defensive purposes, women hunters are becoming more common: "3.3 million women hunted in 2013, up 85 percent from 2001."[57]

A number of female-oriented gun groups exist to encourage and support women interested in guns. There is Second Amendment Women,[58] and the Well Armed Woman (349 chapters, "almost 11,000 members") started in January 2012.[59]

LGBTs

Pink Pistols was established in the 2000s to encourage LGBTs to arm themselves for self-defense against those inclined to vent their hostility on members of the LGBT community, and to do so with maximum publicity as a deterrent to attack. It has 45 chapters nationwide. Membership numbers seem to be unavailable.[60]

Survivalists and "Preppers"

Starting in the 1970s, at the heights of the Cold War, the survivalist movement developed. It was focused on preparing for the risk of nuclear war, but it was also concerned about survival preparation for civil collapse and natural disasters (earthquakes, floods, tsunamis). This preparation for the loss of essential government services and civil order, as well as the pejorative association of political and common criminals self-identifying as "survivalists," has caused many to prefer the term "prepper." The concern about the collapse of police protection along with the rest of civilization makes preppers a part of the gun culture, both for anticipated self-defense and subsistence hunting.

While some may see this as a form of redneck delusional thinking, the last few years have brought many of the nation's wealthiest citizens to the movement. Describing why Steve Huffman, the CEO of tech company Reddit, recently had laser eye surgery, a *New Yorker* article explains that Huffman was concerned that "if the world ends—and not even if the world ends, but if we have trouble," glasses or contact lens might not be available, even on a long-term basis. The article gives many examples of what is a widespread movement among Silicon Valley executives, with gun ownership prominently mentioned by most. Hollywood stars and other wealthy Americans are doing likewise. The Survival Condo Project, based in a retired Atlas missile silo, starts at $1.5 million—hardly Jethro and Bubba's price range.[61]

There seems to be no precise number for how many preppers there are, but the American Preppers Network "claims 52,000 members." And *Survival Blog*, run by James Wesley, Rawles (he insists on the comma), has 320,000 readers a week,"[62] many of whom are doubtless repeat visitors and some who are not even remotely preppers. Not every prepper necessarily owns a gun, but if you keep years of freeze-dried food stored against The End Of The World As We Know It (TEOTWAWKI: a very popular acronym in these circles), it seems unlikely that you are not going to defend the stockpile you believe you will need for your family to survive.

Criminals

The preppers may be disconcerting to many, but they are generally not a threat to others. Many are so far isolated from what they consider a doomed society that they are not a hazard to others. But the criminal gun culture is a source of concern to nearly all Americans. Firearms are the cause of death in 71.4 percent of murders and non-negligent manslaughters.[63] There is a distinct gun subculture concentrated in relatively few urban areas. This is why 53.4 percent of murderers are black,[64] as well as 53.0 percent of the victims.[65] More significantly, the victims tend to be from the same criminal class as the killers. In Milwaukee, Newark, Baltimore, and Philadelphia, a majority (sometimes as much as 91%) of murder victims, like those charged with their murders, have lengthy criminal histories.[66] At least in part, widespread gun ownership in the criminal gun subculture is probably both a response to perceived powerlessness from growing up in a ghetto, where opportunities for advancement seem remote, as well as the necessary ownership of deadly weapons for robbery and defending drug-selling territories.

As disagreeable as this subculture is to law-abiding gun owners, it is a genuine gun subculture in modern America and the target of much public policy concerning gun regulation.

Revolutionaries

In the 1960s, a number of groups fancied themselves revolutionaries preparing to overthrow the U.S. government to achieve a more just society. The Black Panthers especially emphasized their right to be armed against what they perceived as brutal, racist police officers. In this, they were hardly innovators. Malcolm X, their predecessor in black militancy, reminded his followers that the Second Amendment guaranteed a right to keep and bear arms. The Black Panthers armed themselves, ostensibly for defense against an oppressive system of urban repression. Their founders, however, were violent criminals before they became darlings of liberal Americans.[67] The concern about felons overthrowing the federal government, discussed on page 5, was more likely aimed at the Black Panthers than nonpolitical criminals.

At least one of their prominent leaders, Eldridge Cleaver, having made a dramatic journey from socialist revolutionary to conservative Republican patriot, admitted that he and other Black Panthers had been actively ambushing Oakland police officers, not simply defending themselves.[68]

To protest a bill under consideration by the California legislature that would have prohibited open carry of firearms in cities (as the Black Panthers were doing in Oakland), "two dozen armed Negroes entered the State Capitol at noon today and 10 made their way to the back of the Assembly Chamber before they were disarmed and marched away by the state police." Their weapons (including "pistols, rifles, at least one sawed-off shotgun") were returned to them after they were escorted from the building. The bill, which became California Penal Code § 12031, almost certainly benefited from the Panthers' actions. Governor Ronald Reagan was on the steps of the statehouse at the time the Panthers were escorted from the building: "Reagan also said it was a 'ridiculous way to solve problems that have to be solved among people of good will.' He added he was against 'even the implied threat weapons might be directed against fellow Americans.'"[69]

The Black Panthers had a skill for publicity, but political astuteness was never one of their strong points. By the time the bill reached the state senate, on July 27, 1967, the U.S. Army had been sent into Detroit to restore order, and rioting had broken out in dozens of American cities. In the context of these threats to public safety, the surprise is not that the law in question was passed, but that there were legislators prepared to argue against it; the final vote in the state senate was 29–7.

While some proponents of the bill argued that it would have no effect on anyone with a gun for a "lawful reason," such as hunting or target shooting, several conservative Republicans (unlike Governor Reagan) disagreed. State senator John G. Schmitz argued, "It would destroy the Second Amendment to the Constitution—the right to bear arms," and "The right of self-defense is not an unlawful reason." But surprisingly enough, Schmitz also referred to what was going on in Detroit as, "A revolution, not a riot."[70]

While the Black Panthers certainly had blood on their hands, they were sometimes the victims of FBI-encouraged killings by police under circumstances where deadly force was of questionable need.[71]

The Black Panthers were not the only revolutionary groups to take up the gun and form their own gun subculture. The Weather Underground spinoff of Students for a Democratic Society engaged in bank robberies that killed innocents in addition to their indiscriminate use of explosives.[72]

If not for their murder victims, and Patty Hearst, who they kidnapped, abused, and brainwashed into joining their cause, the Symbionese Liberation Army might have been mistaken for a parody of a revolutionary group. But the bullets started flying, and people died.[73]

Revolutionary violence with guns was hardly a monopoly of traditional socialists. In the 1970s and 1980s, a variety of groups espoused violence against what they perceived as a conspiratorial, out-of-control federal government. In some cases, they were traditional white supremacists with new labels and ideological justifications.[74] In other cases, they were ideologically and politically naïve anarchists, often driven by horror at the abuses of governmental power at Ruby Ridge, Idaho, and Waco, Texas. To people with limited political and economic power, rebellion against a system that seemed to ignore their concerns, the prospect of a violent confrontation at the end of a gun seemed the only logical answer.

Mentally Ill Mass Murderers

Mass murderers using guns are a tiny fraction of all murders in the United States: only about 1 percent of all murders.[75] And of the 328 mass murders in USA Today's database of post-2006 incidents, 24.3 percent did not involve shooting: 11.8 percent were stabbings, 8.8 percent were arson; and a surprising 6.4 percent were blunt force mass murders.[76] The highly publicized nature of the mass shooting murders and their use for promotion of various gun prohibition laws make them a tiny but politically significant gun subculture.

This subculture appears to be of relatively recent origin. With the singular exception of Charles Whitman's 1966 sniper attack at the University of Texas in Austin, "the first highly publicized mass shooting of its type in the United States,"[77] these crimes seem to have suddenly become part of the American cultural landscape in the 1980s.

The reason may not be immediately obvious. In the 1960s and 1970s, well-intentioned efforts to reform the involuntary mental hospital commitment laws freed large numbers of psychotics from mental hospitals and made it very difficult to hospitalize persons who were a danger to themselves or others. The result was that many were now free to wander the streets and live in cardboard boxes, on steam grates, and in public parks. Many of the gun mass murderers have in retrospect turned out to be "as mad as hatters," often with severe paranoid delusions and hallucinations.[78]

Web Site Gun Buyers

Even though interstate gun sales and transfers are strongly regulated by the federal government, a number of Web sites exist whose purpose and effects are often misrepresented: www.gunbroker.com, www.armslist. com, and gunsamerica.com. These sites provide a way for private sellers and Federal Firearms Licensees (FFLs) to advertise guns and accessories for sale nationally. All interstate firearm transfers take place through local Federal Firearms Licensees, who perform all required federal and state background checks. Intrastate sales are subject to state laws, much like a gun advertised through a newspaper classified ad.

Historical Reenactors

While the Mountain Men and Cowboy Shooting organizations have a substantial historical focus, various historical reenactor organizations are definitely part of gun culture. Civil War reenactors have re-creations of period firearms and cannon that are fired with blank rounds at these events. The numbers of reenactors seem to be falling, with about 30,000 estimated in 2011.[79] Less well-known and smaller in numbers are reenactors of World War II,[80] World War I,[81] the Mexican-American War,[82] the War of 1812,[83] and the Revolutionary War.[84]

Epilogue

American Gun Culture: Transformative and Still Kicking

Revisionists claim that American gun culture, gun manufacturing, and hunting do not date to the Constitutional era. They also claim that widespread gun violence is a surprisingly modern development because guns of all types, and especially handguns, were rare before 1848. Their motivation is to argue that the Second Amendment's guarantee of a "right to keep and bear arms" was not understood by the Framers of the Constitution as an individual right.

As previous chapters have demonstrated, America's gun culture is as old as America. Gun ownership in the Colonial period was nearly universal because militia laws required every able-bodied white man to be a member of the militia and to arm himself and often his sons and indentured servants for that obligation. Gun ownership was also widespread because hunting was a common pastime for both subsistence and recreation. Gun ownership, gun manufacturing, hunting, handgun ownership, and, tragically, gun violence remained prevalent in the Constitutional and Early Republic periods.

American gun culture was not a post–Mexican-American War creation of the first mass production gun manufacturers using clever marketing to sell guns to people who neither wanted nor needed them. Those manufacturers were successful because they were tapping into an existing interest and demand for guns.

The American gun manufacturing industry (with encouragement from the federal government) created our modern industrial civilization through the synergistic development of mass production, machine tools, and interchangeable parts.

American gun culture, despite the elites' contempt for it, persists and has even grown in recent years.

APPENDIX A

Gunsmiths in Early America

At http://claytoncramer.com/gunsmiths/AFM.xlsx, I have combined information from a variety of sources of varying quality in a Microsoft Excel spreadsheet. I may update it as I find new gunsmiths. Different tabs in the spreadsheet provide information on the gunsmiths and sources. The sources that are collections of early American gunsmiths are less likely to consistently provide proper citations. In a few cases, these are works produced by well-intentioned gun collectors who are, unfortunately, amateurs when it comes to history. While the information contained therein is interesting, not obviously wrong, and probably quite useful for gun collectors, I have not used these as sources.[1]

Other books produced by gun collectors, however, have turned out to be quite useful because they were created with attention to sources and citations. I have generally found that when I was able to verify these books against scholarly works and primary sources, such as city directories and government records, they were accurate. If a source is listed in this appendix with only an author's name or title abbreviation, the source is an alphabetical list of gunsmiths or gunmakers, and a page number seemed superfluous.

Several of the sources, however, either conform to proper standards of citation, such as Hartzler's *Arms Makers of Maryland* (with the maddening exception of using dates instead of volume numbers for references to *Archives of Maryland*), Demeritt's *Maine Made Guns and Their Makers,* and Achtermier's *Rhode Island Arms Makers & Gunsmiths*

1643–1883, or are somewhat unconventional in their citation style but clearly researched with high standards, such as Kauffman's *Early American Gunsmiths*.

Every gunsmith's entry is identified as to the specific document or set of documents from which the information came: a tax list, a state census, a deed, a business directory, or a secondary source.

Excluded from this list are all gunsmiths or gunmakers with no known dates of operation. This, unfortunately, excludes a large number of gunsmiths known only from their surviving guns and about whom we can only guess as to their years of operation. This list of gunsmiths should be regarded as a fraction of the gunsmiths that actually operated in early America—perhaps a small fraction.

Some of the compilers of early gunsmiths list a variety of sources that document the existence of a gunsmith, but only some of the sources clearly indicate that the person was a gunsmith. In those cases, I have used only the range of years during which the person was identified as a gunsmith in the documents listed by the compiler. In some cases, this probably understates their actual years of operation.

Many gunsmiths are known by only a single reference. Consequently, this list certainly understates the years in which many of these gunsmiths operated. It is also a certainty that many gunsmiths came and went out of business without ever leaving a trace. A number of regional lists of gunsmiths that were available were not consulted because of exhaustion on the part of the researcher.

Attempts to sample the data and draw conclusions about the number of gunsmiths present in the United States as a whole are doomed to inaccuracy. At least some of the gunsmiths in this list come from either explicitly regional books, such as *The Gunsmiths of Manhattan 1625–1900*, or from books written by authors who have worked disproportionately in particular regions, such as Henry J. Kauffman.

In cases where two different sources give slightly different names for a gunsmith in roughly the same years and location and the name is not common, I have combined them into a single gunsmith. As an example, two different sources list what is almost certainly the same gunsmith. In one source he is Joseph Mullen, a gunsmith in Salem, North Carolina, in 1774. In the other, a Joseph Muller is listed in Salem, North Carolina, during the Revolution.

Where the gap of time between two different sources is dramatic, such that it is unlikely that the two gunsmiths could be one and the same man (or in rare cases a woman), I have left them as two separate records, as they may be father and son or grandfather and grandson. If the names are common (e.g., John Moore) and there is no other basis for conclud-ing that these are only one man, I have generally left multiple entries in the list.

In several cases, the same gunsmith appears in two entries, in different locations, at different times. In a few of these cases, this is one gunsmith who moved. In other cases, the connection is uncertain. This may inflate the number of gunsmiths listed very slightly.

Examination of the family names in these lists shows, not surprisingly, a strong tendency for gunsmithing to run in families, and this is espe-cially apparent for the more unusual family names.

One source that adds a significant dose of imprecision is M. L. Brown's *Firearms in Colonial America*. Although a scholarly work, there is an appendix in which Brown lists gunsmiths who worked for the American Revolutionary cause. The number of names is astounding, and the list includes details of what sort of work they did: general gunsmith, musket maker, riflesmith. It was difficult to leave out such a large body of data. Unfortunately, there was nothing to indicate which exact years each of these gunsmiths operated. I have taken the liberty of using the dates 1775 to 1783 for those gunsmiths listed in Brown's list for which there is no other date information. If another source provides dates, I have limited that entry to those dates. Any entry that uses Brown 404–409, and only that source, should be regarded as approximate as to date.

A similar problem exists with Arcadi Gluckman's list of Committee of Safety musket makers. That list is dated 1775–1777, and while gener-ally consistent with other such lists (with a few interesting differences), it also suffers the problem that it does not sufficiently narrow down the operating dates. It does, however, narrow down the dates of those Committee of Safety musket makers from Brown's list. Any entry that uses Brown 404–409 *and* Gluckman 50–51, and only those two sources, should also be regarded as approximate as to date.

In a few cases, I found that Brown's information conflicted quite dra-matically as to location, and in those cases, I have given precedence to sources with more detailed statements of who worked as a gunsmith, where, and when. Thus, Emanuel Pincall is shown by Brown as a gun-smith in Pennsylvania during the Revolution. However, Kauffman's *Early American Gunsmiths* lists an Emanuel Pincall working as a gun-smith in 1777 Charleston, South Carolina. It being unlikely that there were two gunsmiths of such an unusual name working at the same time in America, I discarded the data from Brown's appendix for Pincall.

In a few cases, there are makers listed in Kauffman's *Early Ameri-can Gunsmiths* who were probably *capable* of making small arms, but whose listing indicates that they were in the business of making and selling cannon to the general public, such as Russel & Co.[2] These have been excluded. Those gunsmiths who made only stocks or whose descriptions suggested that they were entirely gun merchants have also been excluded. Similarly, those people whose involvement with gunmaking is ambiguous (and may have been procuring guns for governments), such as John Hanson Jr., have also been excluded.[3]

It is worth mentioning that while many of the gunsmiths in this list may have been individual craftsmen, working by themselves, we know that some had apprentices, and some were apprentices to others. In a few cases, we have gunsmiths for whom the individual name is the name on a contract, such as James Haslett. He made and delivered 600 muskets to Virginia over a period of six months.[4] We know that he could not have made all of these muskets himself, and one must conclude that there were many other gunsmiths working for Haslett during this time, but whose names are lost to history.

There are a number of large gun factories in the Early Republic period, such as the federal arsenal at Springfield, Massachusetts, and the Virginia Manufactory of Arms at Richmond, Virginia. In the case of the Manufactory of Arms, we have a detailed list of operatives involved in the making of guns, with detailed descriptions of their tasks—hundreds of them over a period of less than 20 years. Few of them, however, would be considered "gunsmiths" in the all-inclusive sense of the craftsmen in this list, and even fewer would be consider gunmakers, as most made only one small part of a gun. It is worth remembering, however, that leaving such factory operatives off the list tends to understate the number of workers involved in the manufacturing of guns in early America.

One decision that I made in compiling these lists was difficult. If someone was apprenticed to a gunsmith, explicitly to learn the gunsmith's trade, I have included him as a gunsmith. It is certainly true that at least some of these apprentices may have ended up in another profession after completing their apprenticeships. Others almost certainly died before their apprenticeships were over. But even apprentices were gunsmiths, either making parts of guns or repairing guns. Including apprentices gives a fuller picture of the number of Americans engaged in the day-to-day business of making or repairing guns. In a few cases, there are children bound as apprentices to gunsmiths at such a young age that I have not included them in this list, such as "John Connor aged three years old" who was bound to David Grass in 1805.[5]

If a gunsmith was apprenticed to a gunsmith known to have made guns during the period of the apprenticeship, the apprentice is listed as a maker, not a gunsmith, unless there is evidence that the apprentice did *not* make guns on the completion of his term.

APPENDIX B

Partial List of Government Arms Contracts

Pennsylvania Militia Contracts and Deliveries of 1797[1]

Contractor	Location	Contract Date	Quantity
Owen Evans	Evansburg, PA	1797/12/07	1,000
William Henry II	Nazareth	1797/12/13	2,000
Lether & Co.	York, PA	1798/04/11	1,200
Abraham Henry and John Graeff	Lancaster	1798/04/11	2,000
John Miles	Philadelphia	1798/09/03	2,000
John Fondersmith	Lancaster	1799/01/14	500
Melchior Baker and Albert Gallatin	Fayette County, PA	1799/02/05	2,000
John Miles	Philadelphia	1801/04/16	2,000
John Fondersmith	Lancaster	1801/04/16	500
Jacob Haeffer	Lancaster	1801/04/17	500
Henry DeHuff Jr.	Lancaster	1801/04/17	500
Peter Brong	Lancaster	1801/04/17	500
Jacob Dickert and Matthew Llewellyn	Lancaster	1801/04/17	1,000

(Continued)

Contractor	Location	Contract Date	Quantity
Conrad Welshanse, Jacob Doll, and Henry Pickell	York, PA	1801/04/17	1,000
John Jr. and Samuel Kerlin	Bucks Co.	1801/05/02	500
Edward and James Evans	Evansburg, PA	1801/05/02	1,000
Robert McCormick and Richard B. Johnston	Philadelphia	1801/05/04	1,000
John Jr. and Samuel Kerlin	Bucks Co.	1801/06/30	500
Total			19,700

Federal Musket Contract of 1798: Contracts and Deliveries through January 1, 1803[2]

Contractor	Contracted	Delivered	%
Allen, Grant, and Bernard	1,500	1,396	93%
Elijah Baggett	500	–	0%
Thomas Bicknell	2,000	1,300	65%
Elisha Brown	1,000	775	78%
Chipman, Crafts, Hooker, and Smith	1,000	575	58%
Alexander Clagett	1,000	433	43%
Joseph Clark	500	325	65%
Nathan and Henry Cobb	200	200	100%
Matthew and Nathan Elliott	500	235	47%
Owen Evans	1,000	–	0%
Richard Falley	1,000	750	75%
Daniel Gilbert	2,000	875	44%
William Henry II	500	252	50%
Huntington, Livingston, Bellows, and Stone	500	608	122%
Stephen Jenks and Hosea Humphries	1,500	1,050	70%
Adam Kinsley and James Perkins	2,000	1,550	78%

(Continued)

Contractor	Contracted	Delivered	%
Robert McCormick	3,000	–	0%
Jonathan Nichols Jr.	1,000	–	0%
Abijah Peck	1,000	775	78%
William Rhodes and William Tyler	2,000	950	48%
Mathias Shroyer	1,000	150	15%
Amos Stillman & Co.	500	525	105%
Thomas Townsey and Samuel Chipman	1,000	275	28%
Ard Welton	1,000	–	0%
Eli Williams	2,000	–	0%
White, Crabb, Metzger, and Barnhizle	1,000	235	24%
Eli Whitney	10,000	–	0%
Total	40,200	13,234	33%

Federal Musket Contract of 1808: Contracts and Deliveries through October 7, 1812[3]

Contractor	Contracted	Delivered	%
Joshua and Charles Barstow	2,500	1,625	65%
A. and P. Bartlett	2,500	1,500	60%
Oliver Bidwell	4,000	750	19%
I. I. and N. Brooke	4,000	1,257	31%
O. and E. Evans	4,000	1,960	49%
French, Blake, and Kinsley	4,000	2,175	54%
Daniel Gilbert	5,000	875	18%
Goetz and Westphall	2,500	1,019	41%
W. and I. I. Henry	10,000	4,246	42%
Stephen Jenks & Sons	4,000	2,300	58%
R. and C. Leonard	5,000	2,125	43%
John Miles Jr.	9,000	2,407	27%
Rufus Perkins	2,500	200	8%

(*Continued*)

Contractor	Contracted	Delivered	%
W. and H. Shannon	4,000	1,001	25%
Ethan Stillman	2,500	825	33%
Waters and Whitmore	5,000	3,000	60%
Wheeler and Morrison	2,500	125	5%
Winner, Nippes & Co.	9,000	3,900	43%
Sweet, Jenks & Sons	3,000	250	8%
Total	85,000	31,540	37%

APPENDIX C

Glossary

Flintlock

A firearm *flintlock* is a spring-loaded hammer that strikes a piece of flint against a piece of steel. The flying sparks ignite the powder in the pan, setting fire to the main gunpowder charge in the barrel. A hole leading into the barrel provides the path by which the burning gunpowder in the pan ignites the powder in the barrel. You use a *priming wire* to remove gunpowder ash from this hole.

Flintlocks appeared in the 16th century and had largely replaced matchlock guns in America by the mid-17th century.

Fowling Piece

A *fowling piece* is the ancestor of the modern shotgun, distinguished from a musket by generally being of smaller caliber, with shorter range, and primarily designed to fire shot for bringing down birds, although fowling pieces could fire lead balls as well.

Fusee, Fuzee, or Fusil

A *fusee, fuzee,* or *fusil* is a smaller and lighter form of the musket.

Gunlock

A *gunlock* refers to the lockwork mechanism of trigger and hammer (or cock) that fires the gun. The hammer carried the flint that sent sparks into the pan. Adding to the confusion, a gunlock was often simply called a *lock*, and many craftsmen who made gunlocks also worked as locksmiths, making or repairing locks for doors.

Matchlock

A *matchlock* used a slow-burning material known as *slow match*; when you pulled the trigger, the slow match dropped into the pan, igniting the primer powder. The fire from the primer would burn through a small hole into the barrel, ignite the main charge, and fire the lead ball out of the barrel. (Of course, if the powder in the pan failed to set off the main charge in the barrel, there was a flash of light and smoke—but no explosion—a "flash in the pan.")

Pistol

A *pistol* (spelled in an astonishing number of different ways in the Colonial period) was any weapon intended to be fired one-handed. (Adding to the complexity of reading documents of the time, a "pistole" was a coin often used in Colonial America, and merchants used "pistol" as an adjective to describe certain types of cloth.)

Proof Marks

When a gun is tested for safety at the end of manufacturing, it is loaded with a more powerful ammunition load than it is intended to ever fire. If the gun survives "proofing," a *proof mark* is stamped into the metal.

Revolver

The *revolver* has a single barrel and a cylinder that rotates, allowing multiple shots without reloading. Others had experimented with revolving cylinder weapons in the 19th century, but Samuel Colt perfected it in 1836.

Rifled Barrel

A *rifled barrel* (from which our word *rifle* comes) has several spiral grooves cut inside the barrel that spin a ball or bullet as it leaves the barrel. This spinning stabilizes the bullet so that a rifle is more accurate at long range than a musket.

Snaphance or Snaphaunce

One particular style of flintlock mechanism is known as a *snaphance*, which is sometimes claimed to be derived from Dutch words describing a hen dropping to the ground to peck at grain.

Wheellock

The *wheellock* works like a modern friction-type cigarette lighter, with a spinning piece of metal striking flint to light the powder in the pan. The wheellock made pistols practical because of their compactness and because you could carry such a weapon in your coat—no slow match setting fire to your pocket or smoke giving away that you were armed. Wheellocks appeared in the 16th century, and while already obsolete at the time the English settled the American colonies, they were still in use until the middle of the 17th century.

Notes

Preface

1. George Orwell, *Nineteen Eighty-Four* (New York: Alfred A. Knopf, 1992), 43.

2. Alexander Hewatt, *An Historical Account of the Rise and Progress of the Colonies of South Carolina and Georgia* (London: Alexander Donaldson, 1779), 2:60.

3. Michael A. Bellesiles, "The Origins of Gun Culture in the United States, 1760–1865," *Journal of American History* 83:2 (September 1996), 425–455.

4. Michael A. Bellesiles, *Arming America: The Origins of a National Gun Culture* (New York: Alfred A. Knopf, 2000), 73, 174, 212, 220–221, 301, 306, 322–325, 378.

5. See, e.g., "Take Another Look at Gun Rights History," *San Francisco Chronicle*, September 25, 2000: A22; Richard Slotkin, "The Fall into Guns," *Atlantic Monthly*, November 2000, at 114–118; Edmund S. Morgan, "In Love with Guns," *New York Review of Books*, October 19, 2000, http://www.nybooks.com/articles/2000/10/19/in-love-with-guns/ last accessed October 28, 2017; Garry Wills, "Spiking the Gun Myth," *New York Times*, September 10, 2000, http://www.nytimes.com/2000/09/10/books/spiking-the-gun-myth.html last accessed October 28, 2017.

6. James Lindgren, "Fall from Grace: Arming America and the Bellesiles Scandal," *Yale Law Journal* 111 (2002): 2195, 2200–2201, 2210.

7. Stanley N. Katz, Hanna H. Gray, and Laurel Thatcher Ulrich. "Report of the Investigative Committee in the Matter of Professor Michael Bellesiles," July 10, 2002: 12–15, 17–18.

8. Robert F. Worth, "Prize for Book Is Taken Back from Historian," *New York Times*, December 14, 2002, http://www.nytimes.com/2002/12/14 /business/prize-for-book-is-taken-back-from-historian.html.

9. Pamela Haag, *The Gunning of America: Business and the Making of American Gun Culture* (New York: Basic Books, 2015).

10. Haag, *Gunning of America*, 45–46.

Chapter 1

1. "Proceedings of the Virginia Assembly, 1619," August 2, 1619, in Lyon Gardiner Tyler, *Narratives of Early Virginia, 1606–1625* (New York: Charles Scribner's Sons, 1907; reprint, New York: Barnes & Noble, 1959), 273.

2. William Waller Hening, *The Statutes at Large; Being a Collection of All the Laws of Virginia, from the First Session of the Legislature, in the Year 1619* (New York: R. & W. & G. Bartow, 1823), 1:127.

3. Hening, *Statutes at Large*, 1:198.

4. Robert Beverley, *The History and Present State of Virginia*, ed. Louis B. Wright (Chapel Hill: University of North Carolina Press, 1947), 51.

5. Hening, *Statutes at Large*, 1:198; 5:19.

6. Hening, *Statutes at Large*, 1:401–402.

7. Hening, *Statutes at Large*, 2:304; Kathleen M. Brown, *Good Wives, Nasty Wenches, and Anxious Patriarchs: Gender, Race, and Power in Colonial Virginia* (Chapel Hill: University of North Carolina Press, 1996), 162.

8. Hening, *Statutes at Large*, 2:403.

9. Hening, *Statutes at Large*, 2:403; 3:13; 3:338; 5:17, 21; 6:116, 537.

10. Hening, *Statutes at Large*, 6:118; 7:94.

11. Hening, *Statutes at Large*, 8:125–126.

12. Hening, *Statutes at Large*, 1:226.

13. Hening, *Statutes at Large*, 3:451; Abbot Emerson Smith, *Colonists in Bondage: White Servitude and Convict Labor in America, 1607–1776* (Gloucester, MA: Peter Smith, 1965), 239; Farley Grubb, "The Statutory Regulation of Colonial Servitude: An Incomplete-Contract Approach," *Explorations in Economic History* 37 (January 2000):69, quotes a North Carolina statute of 1715 that allowed a master to choose between a suit or "a good well-fixed Gun" as part of freedom dues.

14. Hening, *Statutes at Large*, 2:481; Brown, *Good Wives*, 218–219.

15. Hening, *Statutes at Large*, 4:131.

16. Hening, *Statutes at Large*, 5:17. Indians and blacks to appear unarmed for muster reiterated in 1757 at Hening, *Statutes at Large*, 7:95.

17. 18 USC § 922(g) (2017).

18. 18 U.S.C. App. § 1201, quoted in *Lewis v. United States*, 445 U.S. 55, 68, n.6 (1980).

19. William Brigham, ed., *The Compact with the Charter and Laws of the Colony of New Plymouth* . . . (Boston: Dutton and Wentworth, 1836), 31, 44–45.

20. Brigham, *Compact with the Charter*, 84.

21. Brigham, *Compact with the Charter*, 70.

22. Brigham, *Compact with the Charter*, 115.

23. Brigham, *Compact with the Charter*, 74.

24. Nathaniel B. Shurtleff, *Records of the Governor and Company of the Massachusetts Bay in New England* (Boston: William White, 1853), 1:84.

25. Shurtleff, *Records of the Governor*, 1:93. These requirements are amplified and detailed on November 11, 1647 at Shurtleff, *Records of the Governor*, 2:222.

26. Shurtleff, *Records of the Governor*, 1:190.

27. Shurtleff, *Records of the Governor*, 1:85.

28. Shurtleff, *Records of the Governor*, 1:190.

29. Shurtleff, *Records of the Governor*, 1:210; 2:38.

30. Shurtleff, *Records of the Governor*, 1:125, 84, 85, 93; Joseph H. Smith, ed., *Colonial Justice in Western Massachusetts (1639–1702): The Pynchon Court Record, an Original Judges' Diary of the Administration of Justice in the Springfield Courts in the Massachusetts Bay Colony* (Cambridge, MA: Harvard University Press, 1961), 124.

31. Shurtleff, *Records of the Governor*, 2:124.

32. Shurtleff, *Records of the Governor*, 2:134. This requirement reiterated on November 11, 1647, at Shurtleff, *Records of the Governor*, 2:222.

33. Shurtleff, *Records of the Governor*, 2:118–119.

34. Shurtleff, *Records of the Governor*, 2:122; 1:34.

35. Shurtleff, *Records of the Governor*, 5:48–49.

36. Library of Congress, Printed Ephemera Collection; Portfolio 35, Folder 15b.

37. Shurtleff, *Records of the Governor*, 3:268.

38. Shurtleff, *Records of the Governor*, 3:397.

39. J. Hammond Trumbull, *The Public Records of the Colony of Connecticut, Prior to the Union with New Haven Colony* (Hartford, CT: Brown & Parsons, 1850), 1:3–4, 15–16. It is not clear when Connecticut required blacks and Indians to be part of the militia, but Trumbull, *Public Records of the Colony of Connecticut*, 1:349, records a May 17, 1660, order "that neither Indian nor negar servants shalbe required to traine, watch or ward"; Connecticut Colony, *Code of 1650, Being a Compilation of the Earliest Laws and Orders of the General Court of Connecticut* (Hartford, CT: Silas Andrus, 1822), 72–73.

40. Trumbull, *Public Records of the Colony of Connecticut*, 1:1, 2, 49, 182; Robert Slye was fined £10 for "exchanging a gunn with an Indian" with George Hubberd, John West, and Peter Blatchford "for the same," all were fined the same amount.

41. Trumbull, *Public Records of the Colony of Connecticut*, 1:95, 96.

42. Trumbull, *Public Records of the Colony of Connecticut*, 8:379–383.

43. Charles J. Hoadly, ed., *The Public Records of the Colony of Connecticut, Prior to the Union with New Haven Colony* (Hartford, CT: Brown & Parsons, 1850), 25–26, 96–97, 202, 122–123.

44. *Acts and Laws, Passed by the General Court or Assembly of the Province of New-Hampshire in New-England . . .* (1716), in *Early American Imprints, 1639–1800*, ed. Clifford K. Shipton (Worcester, MA: American Antiquarian Society, 1967; imprint 1985), 91–92.

45. *The Laws and Acts of the General Assembly of Her Majesties Province of Nova Caesarea or New-Jersey* (New York: W. Bradford, 1709), in *Early American Imprints, 1639–1800*, ed. Clifford K. Shipton (Worcester, MA: American Antiquarian Society, 1967; imprint 1412), 12–13.

46. John Russell Bartlett, ed., *Records of the Colony of Rhode Island and Providence Plantations, in New England* (Providence, RI: A. Crawford Greene and Brother, 1856), 1:79–80, 94.

47. Bartlett, *Records of the Colony of Rhode Island*, 1:224–234.

48. New York Colony, *The Colonial Laws of New York from the Year 1664 to the Revolution . . .* (Albany, NY: James B. Lyon, 1894), 1:49–50. Compare this to a 1655 militia law under Dutch rule exempting Jews from militia duty and obligating them to pay a special tax instead, because "first the disgust and unwillingness of these trainbands to be fellow soldiers with the aforesaid nation and to be on guard with them in the same guard house and on the other side, that the said nation was not admitted or counted among the citizens" in Amsterdam "nor (to our knowledge) in any city in Netherland."; *Proceedings of the Provincial*

Congress, in *Documents Relating to the Colonial History of the State of New York*, ed. Berthold Fernow (Albany, NY: Weed, Parsons & Co., 1887; reprint, New York: AMS Press, Inc., 1969), 12:96.

49. Delaware Colony, *Laws of the Government of New-Castle, Kent and Sussex upon Delaware* (Philadelphia: B. Franklin, 1741), 171–177. While the title page is clearly 1741, this must have been only for the first annual series, as the law was passed in 1742.

50. Delaware Colony, *Laws of the Government of New-Castle*, 171–177.

51. Delaware Colony, *Laws of the Government of New-Castle*, 171–177. See also a 1740 statute, Delaware Colony, *Laws of the Government of New-Castle*, 151, imposing similar requirements on the town of Lewes, which was apparently considered especially exposed to naval attack.

52. *A Relation of Maryland; Together with a Map of the Countrey* . . . (London: William Peasley, 1635), in *Narratives of Early Maryland: 1633–1684*, ed. Clayton Colman Hall (New York: Charles Scribner's Sons, 1910; reprint, New York: Barnes & Noble, 1959), 94; Matthew Page Andrews, *Tercentenary History of Maryland* (Chicago and Baltimore: S. J. Clarke Publishing Co., 1925), 1:150.

53. William Hand Browne, ed., *Archives of Maryland* (Baltimore: Maryland Historical Society, 1885), 1:77.

54. Browne, *Archives of Maryland*, 1:77.

55. Browne, *Archives of Maryland*, 1:77.

56. Browne, *Archives of Maryland*, 3:100–101.

57. Browne, *Archives of Maryland*, 3:103, 345.

58. Browne, *Archives of Maryland*, 1:103.

59. Browne, *Archives of Maryland*, 75:264; Abbot Emerson Smith, *Colonists in Bondage: White Servitude and Convict Labor in America, 1607–1776* (Gloucester, MA: Peter Smith, 1965), 239.

60. Browne, *Archives of Maryland*, 9:565. Also at 31:404 in 1760 and at 56:404 in 1761.

61. Browne, *Archives of Maryland*, 75:268.

62. Browne, *Archives of Maryland*, 52:450–451, contains a 1756 militia law that exempts "Papists, the Persons commonly called Neutralls, Servants, and Slaves." See instructions at 52:598 ordering that no soldier be enlisted "Roman Catholic or Deserter, knowing them to be such."

63. Joyce Lee Malcolm, *To Keep and Bear Arms: The Origins of an Anglo-American Right* (Cambridge, MA: Harvard University Press, 1994), 123. Britain and Ireland had different laws concerning the disarming of Catholics, with the Irish law somewhat more restrictive on the

possession of arms for self-defense. Malcolm compares 1 W. & M., ch. 15 (1689) with the Irish law 7 Will III c.5 (1695).

64. Joyce Lee Malcolm, "The Right of the People to Keep and Bear Arms: The Common Law Tradition," *Hastings Constitutional Law Quarterly* 10 (1983): 310.

65. Browne, *Archives of Maryland*, 25:288–289.

66. Browne, *Archives of Maryland*, 52:451–452, 454.

67. David J. McCord, *Statutes at Large of South Carolina* (Columbia, SC: A. S. Johnson, 1840), 7:397, 399–400, 404–405.

68. McCord, *Statutes at Large of South Carolina*, 7:417–419.

69. *Laws of North Carolina–1715*, ch. 25, in *The Earliest Printed Laws of North Carolina, 1669–1751*, ed. John D. Cushing (Wilmington, DE: Michael Glazier, Inc., 1977), 2:29–31; North Carolina Colony, *A Collection of all the Public Acts of Assembly, of the Province of North-Carolina: Now in Force and Use* . . . (Newbern, N.C.: James Davis, 1751), 215–216; John Hope Franklin, *The Free Negro in North Carolina, 1790–1860* (Chapel Hill: University of North Carolina Press, 1995), 101–102.

70. Allen D. Candler, comp., *The Colonial Records of the State of Georgia* (Atlanta, GA: Chas. P. Byrd, 1911), 19 (part 1):291, 296.

71. Candler, *Colonial Records of the State of Georgia*, 19(part 1):303. This statute contains many pages of highly detailed fines and provisions to handle every imaginable contingency.

72. Candler, *Colonial Records of the State of Georgia*, 19(part 1): 324–325.

73. Candler, *Colonial Records of the State of Georgia*, 19(part 1):137–140.

74. Candler, *Colonial Records of the State of Georgia*, 19(part 1):76–78.

75. A few scattered scraps that give some idea of the conflict between the governor and the legislature on passage of a mandatory militia law can be found at Pennsylvania Colony, *Pennsylvania Archives*, 4th series (Philadelphia: J. Severns & Co., et al., 1852–1935), 1:706–708; 2:441, 548, 555.

76. John Hammond, *Leah and Rachel, or, the Two Fruitfull Sisters Virginia and Mary-land* . . . (London: T. Mabb, 1656), in Hall, *Narratives of Early Maryland*, 285, 291.

77. Hening, *Statutes at Large*, 1:199; 2:96–97; 3:328, contains a minor revision of the 1699 law in 1705; Hening, *Statutes at Large*, 3:180.

78. Beverley, *History and Present State of Virginia*, 153, 309–311.

79. Hening, *Statutes at Large*, 8:592–593.

80. William Bradford, *Of Plymouth Plantation*, ed. Samuel Eliot Morrison (New York: Alfred A. Knopf, 2002), 276.

81. Audubon, *Delineations of American Scenery*, 57, 59–63; Dwight B. Heath, ed., *Mourt's Relation: A Journal of the Pilgrims at Plymouth* (Bedford, Mass.: Applewood Press, 1963), 88.

82. Heath, *Mourt's Relation*, 246.

83. Bradford, *Of Plymouth Plantation*, 111 n.7.

84. Heath, *Mourt's Relation*, 23–26, 43, 48.

85. Heath, *Mourt's Relation*, 82, 84, 86; Edward Winslow, *Good Newes from New England* (London: n.p., 1624; reprint, Bedford, MA: Applewood Books, n.d.), 34–35; Sydney V. James Jr., *Three Visitors to Early Plymouth* (Bedford, MA: Applewood Books, 1997), 79–80.

86. James, *Three Visitors to Early Plymouth*, 28–29.

87. Francis Higginson, *New England's Plantation or a Short and True Description of the Commodities and Discommodities of That Country: Written by a Reverend Divine Now There Resident* (London: Michael Sparke, 1630), quoted in http://www.winthropsociety.org/higgnsn1.htm.

88. J. Franklin Jameson, ed., *Johnson's Wonder-Working Providence: 1628–1651* (New York: Barnes & Noble, Inc., 1959), 175. Shurtleff, *Records of the Governor*, 1:211–212, gives the disarming orders.

89. Boston, MA., *Monthly Bulletin of the Statistics Department* (Boston: City of Boston Printing Department, 1912), 13:76–77.

90. [C.D.], "New England's Faction Discovered, 1690," in *Narratives of the Insurrections, 1675–1690*, ed. Charles M. Andrews (New York: C. Scribner & Sons, 1915; reprint, New York: Barnes & Noble, 1959), 261–262.

91. Hoadly, *Records of the Colony and Plantation of Connecticut*, 176–177.

92. Hoadly, *Records of the Colony and Plantation of Connecticut*, 176.

93. Hall, *Narratives of Early Maryland*, 80, 98.

94. George Alsop, *A Character of the Province of Mary-land . . .* (London: Peter Dring, 1666), in Hall, *Narratives of Early Maryland*, 345.

95. Alsop, *A Character of the Province of Mary-land*, 357.

96. Aubrey C. Land, *Colonial Maryland: A History* (Milwood, NY: KTO Press, 1981), 59–60, 74.

97. Browne, *Archives of Maryland*, 1:77, 103, 345.

98. Browne, *Archives of Maryland*, 3:255; 1:295–296. Also reiterated in 1654 at 1:351.

99. Browne, *Archives of Maryland*, 1:343–344; 7:51–52.

100. J. Thomas Scharf, *History of Western Maryland: Being a History of Frederick, Montgomery, Carroll, Washington, Allegany, and Garrett Counties from the Earliest Period to the Present Day* . . . (Philadelphia: L. H. Everts, 1882; reprint, Baltimore: Regional Publishing Co., 1968), 1:70–71.

101. Robert Horne, *A Brief Description of the Province of Carolina* . . . (London: n.p., 1666), in *Narratives of Early Carolina: 1650–1708*, ed. Alexander S. Salley Jr. (New York: Charles Scribner's Sons, 1911; reprint, New York: Barnes & Noble, 1959), 68–71.

102. Thomas Ashe, *Carolina, or a Description of the Present State of that Country* . . . (London: Mrs. Grover, 1682), in Salley, *Narratives of Early Carolina*, 150–151, 158. See also Thomas Newe, August 23, 1682, in Salley, *Narratives of Early Carolina*, 187, asking his father to send out 200 pounds of pigeon shot.

103. John Archdale, *A New Description of That Fertile and Pleasant Province of Carolina* . . . (London: John Wyat, 1707), in Salley, *Narratives of Early Carolina*, 289.

104. *Laws of North Carolina—1738*, ch. 10, in Cushing, *The Earliest Printed Laws of North Carolina*, 2:128.

105. William L. Saunders, ed., *The Colonial Records of North Carolina* (Raleigh, NC: Josephus Daniels, 1890; reprint, New York: AMS Press, Inc., 1968), 8:26 (hereinafter *Col.Rec.NC*).

106. William Penn, *Some Account of the Province of Pennsilvania in America* . . . (London: Benjamin Clark, 1681), in *Narratives of Early Pennsylvania, West New Jersey and Delaware, 1630–1707*, ed. Albert Cook Myers (New York: Barnes & Noble, 1959), 207, 211.

107. William Penn, *Letter from William Penn to the Committee of the Free Society of Traders* (London: Andrew Sowle, 1683), in Myers, *Narratives of Early Pennsylvania*, 228–229.

108. Pennsylvania Colony, *Pennsylvania Archives*, 4th series, 1:2, 116.

109. Gabriel Thomas, *An Historical and Geographical Account of the Province and Country of Pensilvania* . . . (London: A. Baldwin, 1698), in Myers, *Narratives of Early Pennsylvania*, 321–322.

110. Alexander Graydon, "A Philadelphia Boy's Sports," in Albert Bushnell Hart and Mabel Hill, *Camps and Firesides of the Revolution* (New York: Macmillan Co., 1937), 184.

111. Jasper Danckaerts, Barlett Burleigh James, and J. Franklin Jameson, eds., *Journal of Jasper Danckaerts: 1679–1680* (New York: Charles Scribner's Sons, 1913; reprint, New York: Barnes & Noble, 1959), 230.

112. Danckaerts, James, and Jameson, *Journal of Jasper Danckaerts*, 70.

113. Danckaerts, James, and Jameson, *Journal of Jasper Danckaerts*, 60, 92, 108.

114. Danckaerts, James, and Jameson, *Journal of Jasper Danckaerts*, 123.

115. Danckaerts, James, and Jameson, *Journal of Jasper Danckaerts*, 126.

116. Danckaerts, James, and Jameson, *Journal of Jasper Danckaerts*, 206–208.

117. Chris Tami, *New York City Wills* (Orem, UT: Ancestry, Inc., 1998–1999), http://www.ancestry.com under "New York City Wills," 1–11.

118. Joyce Hansen and Gary McGowan, *Breaking Ground, Breaking Silence: The Story of New York's African Burial Ground* (New York: Henry Holt and Co., 1998), 51.

119. New Jersey Colony, *Laws and Acts of the General Assembly of His Majesties Province of Nova Caesarea or New-Jersey . . .* (New York: William Bradford, 1722), 143–145.

120. Trumbull, *Public Records of the Colony of Connecticut*, 1:33, 50, 115.

121. David Humphreys, "Israel Putnam and the Wolf," in Hart and Hill, *Camps and Firesides of the Revolution*, 9–11.

122. The National Archives of the U.K. "Ledgers of Imports and Exports, America," CUST 16/1 83, 110, 171. In 1769: 229,545 pounds; 1770: 410,591; 1771: 390,558 pounds.

123. This calculation is necessarily imprecise, but it is based on statutes of the time that assumed 4 pounds of lead for every pound of gunpowder and a .75-caliber Brown Bess; Browne, *Archives of Maryland*, 1:77; Andrews, *Tercentenary History of Maryland*, 1:150; Hening, *Statutes at Large*, 5:17, 21. Many firearms in Colonial America were smaller caliber and consequently used less powder, increasing the number of shots that could have been fired. Edward E. Curtis, *The Organization of the British Army in the American Revolution* (New Haven, CT: Yale University Press, 1926; reprint, New York: AMS Press, 1969), 16n38, gives a somewhat lower weight for the bullets than my calculations based on the density of lead would suggest. This would, however, increase the number of shots that could be fired from the quantity of gunpowder involved.

124. Bellesiles, *Arming America*, 378.

125. Harold L. Peterson, *Arms and Armor in Colonial America* (Harrisburg, PA: Stackpole Co., 1956), 213–214. See Peterson, *Arms and Armor*, 202, 205, and 209, for photographs of American-made pistols of the Revolutionary period. See M. L. Brown, *Firearms in Colonial*

America (Washington, D.C.: Smithsonian Institution Press, 1980), 312, for photographs of American-made pistols that are believed to be from before the war. Frank Klay, *The Samuel E. Dyke Collection of Kentucky Pistols* (Highland Park, NJ: The Gun Room Press, 1972), 4–15, shows several surviving American-made pistols of the Colonial and Revolutionary periods. Felicia Johnson Deyrup, *Arms Makers of the Connecticut Valley: A Regional Study of the Economic Development of the Small Arms Industry, 1798–1870* (Menasha, WI: George Banta Publishing Co., 1948), 34, confirms that "few pistols were made here before the Revolution."

126. *Boston Gazette* issues with one or more ads offering pistols: May 30, 1720; November 17, 1741; December 8, 1741; February 2, 1742; May 11, 1742; May 18, 1742; May 25, 1742; July 13, 1742; August 10, 1742; August 24, 1742; August 31, 1742; [September 13?], 1742.

127. *Pennsylvania Gazette*, August 31, 1749.

128. *Pennsylvania Gazette*, December 28, 1774.

129. *Boston Gazette*, May 11, 1742, quoted in Henry J. Kauffman, *Early American Gunsmiths: 1650–1850* (New York: Bramhall House, 1952), 67.

130. George A. Stickels, "The William Smith Pistols Made by Medad Hills," *The Gun Report* (September 1979): 10–12.

131. *Wochtenlichter Pennsylvanische Staatsbote*, September 4, 1772, and September 14, 1773, translated and quoted in James B. Whisker, *The Gunsmith's Trade* (Lewiston, NY: Edwin Mellen Press, 1992), 159–160.

Chapter 2

1. Bellesiles, *Arming America*, 106.

2. Deyrup, *Arms Makers of the Connecticut Valley*, 34; Whisker, *The Gunsmith's Trade*, 5, also emphasizes that small shops built the entire gun.

3. Bellesiles, *Arming America*, 106.

4. Henry J. Kauffman, *Early American Ironware: Cast and Wrought* (New York: Weathervane Books, 1956), 111–113.

5. Kauffman, *Early American Ironware*, 113; Daniel D. Hartzler, *Arms Makers of Maryland* (York, PA: George Shumway, 1977), 45; Deyrup, *Arms Makers of the Connecticut Valley*, 33–34.

6. Kauffman, *Early American Ironware*, 107; *Staatsbote*, September 14, 1773, quoted in Kauffman, *Early American Ironware*, 25; Kauffman, *Early American Gunsmiths*, 24.

7. *New Hampshire Gazette*, July 17, 1767 quoted in Kauffman, *Early American Ironware*, 52.

8. Whisker, *The Gunsmith's Trade*, 145–163.

9. *York Recorder* (Yorktown, PA), May 2, 1800, quoted in Kauffman, *Early American Gunsmiths*, 61.

10. Kauffman, *Early American Ironware*, 52.

11. Pennsylvania Colony, *Pennsylvania Archives*, 3rd series, 14:153.

12. Pennsylvania Colony, *Pennsylvania Archives*, 14:202; Pennsylvania Colony, *Colonial Records of Pennsylvania* (Chicago: Library Resources, 1970), 10:550 (hereinafter *CRPA*); Peter Force, ed., *American Archives: Consisting of a Collection of Authentick Records, State Papers, Debates, and Letters and Other Notices Of Publick Affairs . . .* (1837–1853; reprint, New York: Johnson Reprint Co., 1972), 4th series, 6:1282 (hereinafter *AA*).

13. Sheila Bass, comp., *Buffalo, Erie County, New York Directory, 1832* (Provo, UT: Ancestry.com, 2001), http://search.ancestry.com/search/db.aspx?dbid=5484. Original data: *Buffalo, New York Directory, 1832* (Buffalo, N.Y.: L.P. Crary, 1832); Steven Jacobs, comp., *Boston City Directory, 1800* (Provo, UT: Ancestry.com, 2000). http://search.ancestry.com/search/db.aspx?dbid=4651. Original data: *Directory of Boston City Residents* (Boston: n.p., 1800); Steven Jacobs, comp., *Boston City Directory, 1805* (Provo, UT: Ancestry.com, 2000). Original data: *Directory of Boston City Residents* (Boston: n.p., 1805).

14. Bellesiles, *Arming America*, 109; *Federal Gazette*, September 21, 1791, quoted in Kauffman, *Early American Gunsmiths*, 14; *Lancaster Intelligencer and Weekly Advertiser*, September 23, 1801, quoted in Kauffman, *Early American Gunsmiths*, 13.

15. *Pittsburgh Gazette*, June 1, 1796, quoted in Whisker, *The Gunsmith's Trade*, 34.

16. John Bivins Jr., *Longrifles of North Carolina*, 2nd ed. (York, PA: George Shumway, 1988), 166–167; 143.

17. Whisker, *The Gunsmith's Trade*, 35.

18. *City Gazette and Daily Advertiser*, October 23, 1800, quoted in Kauffman, *Early American Gunsmiths*, 5.

19. *Maryland Journal and Baltimore Daily Advertiser*, April 15, 1777, quoted in Kauffman, *Early American Gunsmiths*, 57.

20. *Virginia Gazette* (Williamsburg). "A Horse Thief," November 29, 1776, in Tom Costa, ed., *Virginia Runaways: Runaway Slave Advertisements from 18th-Century Virginia Newspapers*, http://people.uvawise.edu/runaways. Accessed October 28, 2017.

21. Hartzler, *Arms Makers of Maryland*, 45, 49; Whisker, *The Gunsmith's Trade*, 31–32.

22. Whisker, *The Gunsmith's Trade*, 1–46.

23. Kauffman, *Early American Gunsmiths*, 24.

24. Theodore Dwight, *The Northern Traveller; Containing the Routes to Niagara, Quebec and the Springs* (New York: Wilder & Campbell, 1825), 2.

25. Joseph Willard, *Topographical and Historical Sketches of the Town of Lancaster, in the Commonwealth of Massachusetts* (Worcester, MA: Charles Griffin, 1826), 9.

26. John Lee Williams, *The Territory of Florida: Or Sketches of the Topography, Civil and Natural History* (New York: A.T. Goodrich, 1837), 121.

27. Dwight B. Demeritt Jr., *Maine Made Guns and Their Makers* (Hallowell, ME: Paul S. Plumer Jr., 1973), 3–11.

28. *The South Carolina Gazette*, December 15, 1737, quoted in Kauffman, *Early American Gunsmiths*, 67; Kauffman, *Early American Ironware*, 111; *The New York Journal or General Advertiser*, February 25 1773, quoted in Kauffman, *Early American Gunsmiths*, 2; Joseph H. Smith, ed., *Colonial Justice in Western Massachusetts (1639–1702): The Pynchon Court Record, an Original Judges' Diary of the Administration of Justice in the Springfield Courts in the Massachusetts Bay Colony* (Cambridge, MA: Harvard University Press, 1961); Boston, *Volume of Records Relating to the Early History of Boston, Containing Miscellaneous Papers* (Boston: Municipal Printing Office, 1900), 29:51–52; Ancestry.com (http://awt.ancestry.com/cgi-bin/sse.dll?ti=0&db=gedoth &f0=46760&f1=1948) lists a Daniel Nash, born in 1676, described as a "blacksmith" in his later years in the Springfield area, who was the grandson of Thomas Nash, the New Haven Colony armorer; *New York Mercury*, August 29, 1763.

29. Whisker, *The Gunsmith's Trade*, 104–111.

30. Fernow, *Documents Relating to the Colonial History of the State of New York*, 172; Kauffman, *Early American Gunsmiths*, 58, 63.

31. Kauffman, *Early American Gunsmiths*, 62.

32. Kauffman, *Early American Gunsmiths*, 63; George Washington, *The Diaries of George Washington*, ed. Donald Jackson (Charlottesville: University Press of Virginia, 1976), 1:130; 3:25; *Boston Gazette*, June 27, 1757, quoted in Kauffman, *Early American Gunsmiths*, 21.

33. Pennsylvania Archives, 2d ser., 13:347.

34. Commissary General of Subsistence, *Correspondence on the Subject of the Emigration of Indians* (Washington, D.C.: Duff Green, 1835), 2:372–373; 2:848.

35. Whisker, *The Gunsmith's Trade*, 14–15.

36. Hartzler, *Arms Makers of Maryland*, 169–192.

37. Hartzler, *Arms Makers of Maryland*, 238–244.

38. Kauffman, *Early American Gunsmiths*, 73.

39. Hartzler, *Arms Makers of Maryland*, 51, 212–216.

40. Arcadi Gluckman and L. D. Satterlee, *American Gun Makers*, 2nd ed. (Harrisburg, PA: Stackpole Co., 1953), 66–67, 143.

41. Bivins, *Longrifles of North Carolina*, 158.

42. Klay, *Samuel E. Dyke Collection*, 22–23, shows a pistol known to have been made by John Armstrong, and Merrill Lindsay, *The New England Gun: The First Two Hundred Years* (New Haven, CT: New Haven Colony Historical Society, 1975), 64, shows a pistol made by Matthew Sadd of Hartford, Connecticut, "in the middle 1700s."; Klay, *Samuel E. Dyke Collection*, 20–21, 24–27.

43. Fernow, *Documents Relating to the Colonial History of the State of New York*, 15:166–173.

44. Bank for Savings, *Fourth Report of the Bank for Savings in the City of New-York* (New York: Edwin B. Clayton, 1823), 5.

Chapter 3

1. Brown, *Firearms in Colonial America*, 151; also listed in Kauffman, *Early American Gunsmiths*.

2. Brown, *Firearms in Colonial America*, 151; Kauffman, *Early American Gunsmiths*; Museum of Early Southern Decorative Arts, *Index of Early Southern Artists and Artisans*, extract of gunsmiths, January 17, 2001.

3. Brown, *Firearms in Colonial America*, 149.

4. Brown, *Firearms in Colonial America*, 149.

5. Shurtleff, *Records of the Governor and Company*, 2:25. Similar orders appear at 2:222, relative to an expedition against the Indians.

6. Brown, *Firearms in Colonial America*, 149–150; Deyrup, *Arms Makers of the Connecticut Valley*, 33; Shurtleff, *Records of the Governor and Company*, 5:54.

7. Brown, *Firearms in Colonial America*, 150; Demeritt, *Maine Made Guns*, 2–3.

8. Demeritt, *Maine Made Guns*, 2–3.

9. Darrett B. Rutman, *Winthrop's Boston: A Portrait of a Puritan Town, 1630–1649* (New York: W. W. Norton & Co., Inc., 1965), 179; Brown, *Firearms in Colonial America*, 150.

10. Brown, *Firearms in Colonial America*, 150; Browne, *Archives of Maryland*, 7:336; "Claiborne vs. Clobery et als. In the High Court of Admiralty," *Maryland Historical Magazine* 28: 33, lists at least three gunsmiths who repaired guns on Kent Island.

Richard A. Randall Jr., "A Seventeenth-Century Account," *The American Arms Collector* (October 1958): 111–114, uses this same source to suggest that a fourth gunsmith may also have been so engaged. Randall also discusses the ambiguity as to whether guns were actually made there.

Browne, *Archives of Maryland*, 3:76, contains a description of the goods seized from Claiborne, including 10 guns; Hartzler, *Arms Makers of Maryland*, 21; Gabriel Thomas, *An Historical and Geographical Account of the Province and Country of Pensilvania and West-New-Jersey* (London: A. Baldwin, 1698), 32.

11. Browne, *Archives of Maryland*, 8:67.

12. Brown, *Firearms in Colonial America*, 150.

13. Harold B. Gill Jr., *The Gunsmith in Colonial Virginia* (Williamsburg, VA: Colonial Williamsburg Foundation, 1974), vii.

14. Gill, *Gunsmith in Colonial Virginia*, 76, 77, 82, 91, 96.

15. Gill, *Gunsmith in Colonial Virginia*, 70, 74, 75, 77, 79, 81–84, 87, 89, 91, 96, 99.

16. "George Washington to Robert Dinwiddie, October 11, 1755," in George Washington, *The Writings of George Washington from the Original Manuscript Sources, 1745–1799*, ed. John C. Fitzpatrick (Washington, D.C.: Government Printing Office, 1931–1944), 1:201.

17. Kauffman, *Early American Gunsmiths*, 67.

18. William Henry, the William Henry Papers at Historical Society of Pennsylvania, 1:7.

19. Henry, William Henry Papers, 2:18.

20. Henry, William Henry Papers, 2:20–21, 29.

21. Bellesiles, *Arming America*, 106.

22. Bellesiles, *Arming America*, 380.

23. Peterson, *Arms and Armor*, 179.

24. Michael H. Lewis, "An 18th Century 'American' Musket," *The Gun Report* (November 1997): 19. See also George C. Neuman, "Firearms of the American Revolution: Part I," *American Rifleman* (July 1967): 17; Peterson, *Arms and Armor*, 178–179, concerning the recycling of gun parts. Lindsay, *The New England Gun*, 42–52, shows several

surviving examples of these mix and match guns; Bivins, *Longrifles of North Carolina*, 9.

25. Lewis, "An 18th Century 'American' Musket," 18–19. Also see Lindsay, *The New England Gun*, 42–52, for examples of guns assembled from a combination of American stocks, furniture, and locks of European origin and, occasionally, an American-made barrel.

26. Herbert A. Applebaum, *Colonial Americans at Work* (Lanham, MD: University Press of America, 1996), 161.

27. Henry, William Henry Papers, 2:9.

28. See Browne, *Archives of Maryland*, 4:324–325, for the deposition concerning the making of the gunlock; 4:474 for a court order directing him to "fix the lock" (apparently a gunlock) of a plaintiff in a civil suit; 4:254, 260 for Dandy's 1644 arrest, conviction, and sentencing to death for murder (with a gun) of an Indian; 10:31–32 concerning Dandy's 1650 assault on one of his servants with a hammer; 3:98, 146, 187–188 contains the governor's pardon of Dandy, "Upon the petition of a Great part of the Colony," in exchange for becoming the public executioner for a period of some years. See 10:544 for Dandy's 1657 conviction and sentencing to death for the murder of Henry Gouge.

29. Browne, *Archives of Maryland*, 3:283.

30. *The New York Gazette Revived in the Weekly Post-Boy*, August 1, 1748, quoted in Kauffman, *Early American Gunsmiths*, 4.

31. *Boston Gazette*, April 13, 1756, quoted in Kauffman, *Early American Gunsmiths*, 20.

32. J. Leander Bishop, Edwin Troxell Freedly, and Edward Young, *A History of American Manufactures from 1608 to 1860* (Philadelphia: Edward Young & Co., 1864), 1:486–487; Deyrup, *Arms Makers of the Connecticut Valley*, 35.

33. The Saugus Iron Works was established in the 17th century at Saugus, Massachusetts, to smelt iron and make cast and wrought iron using ironworkers imported from Scotland and Ireland. Marsha L. Hamilton, *Social and Economic Networks in Early Massachusetts: Atlantic Connections* (University Park: Pennsylvania State University Press, 2009), 29–32.

34. Lindsay, *The New England Gun*, 3, 11.

35. Lindsay, *The New England Gun*, 3, 11, 25, 27, 31.

36. Lindsay, *The New England Gun*, 34, 38, 40, 52–55; Stickels, "The William Smith Pistols," 10–12.

37. Neuman, "Firearms of the American Revolution," 18; Peterson, *Arms and Armor*, 178–179; Lindsay, *The New England Gun*, 55–56.

38. Bivins, *Longrifles of North Carolina*, 170.

39. Klay, *Samuel E. Dyke Collection*, 4–9; Lindsay, *The New England Gun*, 64.

40. William L. Saunders, ed., *The Colonial Records of North Carolina* (Raleigh, NC: Josephus Daniels, 1890; reprint, New York: AMS Press, Inc., 1968), 5:479.

41. Chartered Insurance Institute, *Journal* (London: Charles & Edwin Layton, 2005), 7:171.

42. Massachusetts Provincial Congress, *The Journals of Each Provincial Congress of Massachusetts in 1774 and 1775* (Boston: Dutton and Wentworth, 1838), 63.

43. Massachusetts Provincial Congress, *The Journals of Each Provincial Congress*, 62–64, 103, 110.

44. Bishop, *History of American Manufactures*, 1:504, 538.

45. "William Grayson to George Washington, December 27, 1774," in Stanislaus Murray Hamilton, ed., *Letters to Washington and Accompanying Papers* (Boston and New York: Houghton, Mifflin & Co., 1902), 5:78–79.

46. Hamilton, "William Milnor to George Washington, November 29, 1774," 5:65–66.

47. *South Carolina & American General Gazette*, April 15, 1774, quoted in Kauffman, *Early American Gunsmiths*, 15; Kauffman, *Early American Gunsmiths*, 18.

48. Asa H. Waters, *Gun Making in Sutton and Millbury* (Worcester, MA: Lucius P. Goddard, 1878), 3–5; Deyrup, *Arms Makers of the Connecticut Valley*, 33.

49. Deyrup, *Arms Makers of the Connecticut Valley*, 35.

Chapter 4

1. Hartzler, *Arms Makers of Maryland*, 51.

2. Bellesiles, *Arming America*, 190.

3. Massachusetts Provincial Congress, *The Journals of Each Provincial Congress*, 291.

4. Massachusetts Provincial Congress, *Journals of Each Provincial Congress*, 540, 542, 548–549, 551–553. May 10, 1775: "Voted, That Nathan Cushing, Esq. Be desired forthwith to engage four armorers, for the service of this colony, and order them immediately to repair to the town of Cambridge, with their tools and other matters necessary for that purpose." May 12, 1775: "Voted, That Mr. Joseph Branch be, and he hereby is appointed, one of the armorers for the colony forces." May 15, 1775: "Voted, that Jonathan Blaisdel of Amesbury, be appointed

an armorer for the army. . . . Voted, That Thomas Austin, of Charlestown, be, and hereby is appointed an armorer for the army. Voted, That the above vote, appointing Mr. Thomas Austin one of the armorers for the army, be, and hereby is reconsidered." May 17, 1775: "Mr. William Beman, in Col. Fellows' regiment, is appointed by the committee to act as an armorer for the forces posted at Roxbury. . . . Voted, That Col. Fellows be directed to procure a shop and tools and every material necessary for an armorer, at Roxbury, to work immediately in the colony service." May 19, 1775: "Voted, That Mr. John Wood, of Roxbury, be, and hereby is appointed, an armorer for the army. Voted, That Mr. Dike, of Bridgewater, be, and he hereby is appointed, an armorer for the army."

5. Massachusetts Provincial Congress, *Journals of Each Provincial Congress*, 565.

6. Massachusetts Provincial Congress, *Journals of Each Provincial Congress*, 553.

7. Massachusetts Provincial Congress, *Journals of Each Provincial Congress*, 592.

8. Force, *American Archives*, 4th series, 3:360.

9. Frank Warren Coburn, *The Battle of April 19, 1775*, 2nd ed. (Lexington, MA: Frank Warren Coburn, 1922; reprint, Port Washington, NY: Kennikat Press, 1970), 18, 79; Kauffman, *Early American Gunsmiths*, 18.

10. Hoadly, *Public Records of the Colony of Connecticut*, 15:176; Force, 15:127, July 11, 1776, *American Archives*, 5th series, 1:244.

11. Jacob Baldwin paid £8:9:0 for repairing provincial firelocks, February 9, 1776, Pennsylvania Colony, *Colonial Records of Pennsylvania*, 10:480. A few days later, John Willis was paid £21:17:9 for repairing firelocks, February 13, 1776, Pennsylvania Colony, *Colonial Records of Pennsylvania*, 10:483. A few weeks later, Jacob Baldwin received another £4:12:0 for repair work, and a Thomas Palmer similarly received £25:19:0, March 4, 1776, Pennsylvania Colony, *Colonial Records of Pennsylvania*, 10:502. John Fox received £94:1:11 for repairing firelocks belonging to four different companies, March 14, 1776, Pennsylvania Colony, *Colonial Records of Pennsylvania*, 10:514. A Dr. Potts received £19:12:0 for repairing provincial arms, April 9, 1776, Pennsylvania Colony, *Colonial Records of Pennsylvania*, 10:537. John Handlyn received £22:16:0 for "repairing a number of Firelocks for Cap't Dorsey's Comp'y," July 30, 1776, Pennsylvania Colony, *Colonial Records of Pennsylvania*, 10:471. John Baker received £60 for "repairs done to Arms of Associators going into service." Force, *American Archives*, 5th series, 1:1319. "Baldwin & Tyler" received £28:13:9 for repairing arms,

August 23, 1776, Pennsylvania Colony, *Colonial Records of Pennsylvania*, 10:697. A John Tyler received £11:5:9 for repairing "a Number of Firelocks," February 1, 1776, *Minutes of the Supreme Executive Council of Pennsylvania* (Harrisburg, PA: Theo. Fenn & Co., 1852), 10:473. Ludwig Fohrer received £93:11:1 "for Firelocks, purchased of him . . . & for the repairs of sundry others," April 26, 1776, *Minutes of the Supreme Executive Council*, 10:550. Captain James Wilson received £3750 "to discharge bills for repairing arms" on December 12, 1780, perhaps representing several years of work. Wolfgang Haga also received £649:3:7 "for repairing arms" on August 12, 1779. One bill, a bit too omnibus to satisfy a modern accountant, "Paid sundry persons for arms and accoutrements, and for repairing and hauling arms, per account settled by Assembly, October 1778, £725:14:0"—a very sizeable sum, Pennsylvania Colony, *Pennsylvania Archives*, 3rd series, 6:358. This is doubtless a very incomplete list of gunsmiths for a fairly short period of time.

12. Pennsylvania Colony, *Pennsylvania Archives*, 3rd series, 6:376.

13. The Maryland Council of Safety paid John Youst (or Yost) £2:11:7 for gun repairs, and Samuel Messersmith £7:1:9 for mending muskets, March 8, 1776, Force, *American Archives*, 4th series, 5:1543; July 17, 1776, Force, *American Archives*, 5th series, 1:1338; Browne, *Archives of Maryland*, 11:214. Edward Timmons received six muskets on July 15, 1776, to be repaired; George Gordon received 12 muskets for repair, Browne, *Archives of Maryland*, 12:47. Timmons was given 18 more muskets a few days later, "to be repaired," and paid 22 shillings for it. Gordon was given another 24 muskets to repair and paid £5:6:6 for those repairs the following day, another 40 shillings on August 3, and £3 more on August 24. Shaw & Chisholme were paid £72:12:11 "for repairing and stocking guns" on August 17, 1776. Isaac Harris received £46:3:0 and £95:11:0 "for his services as Armourer," June 27, 1776, Browne, *Archives of Maryland*, 11:524; August 17, 1776, Force, *American Archives*, 5th series, 1:1354. Oliver Whiddon, who also made guns for Maryland, received £2:17:8 for repairing guns on August 30, 1776, Browne, *Archives of Maryland*, 12:248. Gordon and Whiddon, apparently collectively, received £10:8:11 for gun repairs on September 3, 1776, Browne, *Archives of Maryland*, 12:255. See March 13, 1776, Force, *American Archives*, 4th series, 5:1544, for some examples of these uninformative transaction records.

14. North Carolina Colony, *Colonial Records of North Carolina*, December 21, 1775, 10:354–355.

15. Force, *American Archives*, 4th series, April 19, 1776, 5:1330.

16. North Carolina Colony, *Colonial Records of North Carolina*, December 4, 1776, 10:952; Force, *American Archives*, 4th series, March 27, 1776, 5:1409–1410.

17. North Carolina Colony, *Colonial Records of North Carolina*, December 22, 1775, 10:358.

18. North Carolina Colony, *Colonial Records of North Carolina*, June 15, 1776, 10:631; North Carolina Colony, *Colonial Records of North Carolina*, 10:1002; North Carolina Colony, *Colonial Records of North Carolina*, December 23, 1776, 439.

19. "George Washington to Philip van Rensselaer, February 8, 1778," in Washington, *Writings of George Washington*, 10:431.

20. "George Washington to Henry Knox, November 30, 1780," in Washington, *Writings of George Washington*, 20:423–424.

21. Washington, *Writings of George Washington*, 20:423n34.

Chapter 5

1. Bishop, *A History of American Manufactures*, 1:572.

2. James C. Kelly and William C. Baker, *The Sword of the Lord and Gideon: A Catalogue of Historical Objects Related to the Battle of King's Mountain* (Boone, NC: Appalachian Consortium Press, 1980), 9, 21; Klay, *Samuel E. Dyke Collection*, 10–15; Michael H. Lewis, *The Gunsmiths of Manhattan 1625–1900: A Checklist of Tradesmen* (Alexandria Bay, NY: Museum Restoration Service, 1991), 6; Lindsay, *The New England Gun*, 52, 54, 56, 64.

3. Lindsay, *The New England Gun*, 82.

4. Bellesiles, *Arming America*, 178–179.

5. "John Penn to Thomas Person, February 14, 1776," in North Carolina Colony, *Colonial Records of North Carolina*, 10:455; Force, *American Archives*, 4th series, 5:83.

6. Frederick Mackenzie, *A British Fusilier in Revolutionary Boston*, ed. Allen French (Cambridge, MA: Harvard University Press, 1926), 31–32.

7. Pennsylvania Colony, *Colonial Records of Pennsylvania*, February 9, 1776, 10:481.

8. Ezra Ripley, *A History of the Fight at Concord on the 19th of April, 1775* (Concord, MA: Allen & Atwill, 1827), 20.

9. "Joseph Hewes to James Iredell, May 17, 1776," in North Carolina Colony, *Colonial Records of North Carolina*, 10:458. See "Joseph Hewes to Samuel Johnston, May 16, 1776," in North Carolina Colony, *Colonial Records of North Carolina*, 10:605, for another depressing

letter complaining about the problems of making or purchasing firearms and cannon, either in America or in Europe.

10. Gluckman and Satterlee, *American Gun Makers*, 60–61.

11. Pennsylvania Colony, *Colonial Records of Pennsylvania*, June 30, 1775, 10:230.

12. Pennsylvania Colony, *Colonial Records of Pennsylvania*, July 4, 1775, 10:233.

13. Force, *American Archives*, 4th series, January 17, 1776, 4:517.

14. Force, *American Archives*, 4th series, January 17, 1776, 4:517.

15. Force, *American Archives*, 4th series, January 17, 1776, 4:1576.

16. Bellesiles, *Arming America*, 184.

17. Pennsylvania Colony, *Colonial Records of Pennsylvania*, March 23, 1776, 10:523.

18. Pennsylvania Colony, *Minutes of the Supreme Executive Council of Pennsylvania*, 11:506; "Account of Expenditures for Arms & Military Accoutrements" ledger book in the William Henry Papers at the Historical Society of Pennsylvania.

19. Pennsylvania Colony, *Colonial Records of Pennsylvania*, July 21, 1775, 10:289; Pennsylvania Colony, *Colonial Records of Pennsylvania*, July 22, 1775, 10:290; Pennsylvania Colony, *Colonial Records of Pennsylvania*, 10:291, 648.

20. Pennsylvania Colony, *Colonial Records of Pennsylvania*, July 18, 1776, 10:650; Pennsylvania Colony, *Colonial Records of Pennsylvania*, July 21, 1775, 10:289; Pennsylvania Colony, *Colonial Records of Pennsylvania*, July 22, 1775, 10:290.

21. Whisker, *The Gunsmith's Trade*, 170–171; Pennsylvania Colony, *Colonial Records of Pennsylvania*, February 13, 1776, 10:484; Pennsylvania Colony, *Colonial Records of Pennsylvania*, April 20, 1776, 10:550; Force, *American Archives*, 4th series, February 27, 1776, 4:1577; Force, *American Archives*, 4th series, February 28, 1776, 4:1578.

22. Pennsylvania Colony, *Colonial Records of Pennsylvania*, August 24, 1775, 10:314; Pennsylvania Colony, *Minutes of the Supreme Executive Council of Pennsylvania*, March 26, 1776, 10:525; Pennsylvania Colony, *Colonial Records of Pennsylvania*, April 9, 1776, 10:536–537; Pennsylvania Colony, *Colonial Records of Pennsylvania*, July 19, 1776, 10:650.

23. Pennsylvania Colony, *Minutes of the Supreme Executive Council of Pennsylvania*, 10:357–358.

24. Force, *American Archives*, 4th series, September 26, 1775, 3:868; Pennsylvania Colony, *Minutes of the Supreme Executive Council of Pennsylvania*, February 14, 1776, 10:485.

25. Pennsylvania Colony, *Minutes of the Supreme Executive Council of Pennsylvania*, August 15, 1776, 10:687; Force, *American Archives*, 5th series, August 8, 1776, 1:1311.

26. Pennsylvania Colony, *Colonial Records of Pennsylvania*, July 24, 1776, 10:653.

27. Force, *American Archives*, 4th series, 3:1838.

28. "Letter from Joseph Hewes to Samuel Johnston," in North Carolina Colony, *Colonial Records of North Carolina*, November 9, 1775, 10:314.

29. "Joseph Hewes to Samuel Johnston," in North Carolina Colony, *Colonial Records of North Carolina*, February 13, 1776, 10:447.

30. Force, *American Archives*, 4th series, June 13, 1776, 6:1282.

31. Whisker, *The Gunsmith's Trade*, 224.

32. Pennsylvania Colony, *Pennsylvania Archives*, 1st series, 7:12.

33. Pennsylvania Colony, *Colonial Records of Pennsylvania*, March 4, 1776, 10:502; Force, *American Archives*, 4th series, 4:1567; Pennsylvania Colony, *Colonial Records of Pennsylvania*, February 6, 1776, 10:477; Pennsylvania Colony, *Colonial Records of Pennsylvania*, March 4, 1776, 10:502.

34. Peterson, *Arms and Armor*, 180–190. See Bivins, *Longrifles of North Carolina*, 12, for a picture of one of the Committee of Safety muskets made in Philadelphia (according to the barrel), with Philadelphia proof marks and John Nicholson's name on the gunlock, perhaps indicating that he made the gunlock, but certainly indicating that he assembled the gun.

35. Brown, *Firearms in Colonial America*, 310; Gluckman and Satterlee, *American Gun Makers, United States Muskets, Rifles and Carbines* (Buffalo, NY: Otto Ulbrich Co., 1948), 45, reproduces the entire letter, along with others on 43–46 that discuss problems of rising prices and wages preventing production of the full number of muskets required. Bishop, *History of American Manufactures*, 1:573, confirms that the commercial demand for rifles interfered with colonial contracting for muskets. See "Letter from the North Carolina Delegates to the Continental Congress," in North Carolina Colony, *Colonial Records of North Carolina*, 10:806, for confirmation of the high demand and rising wages of "workmen in every branch of the Iron manufactory."

36. Gluckman and Satterlee, *American Gun Makers*, 47–48.

37. Pennsylvania Colony, *Colonial Records of Pennsylvania*, October 27, 1775, 10:383.

38. Pennsylvania State, *Minutes of the Provincial Council of Pennsylvania* (Harrisburg, PA: 1852), 10:700; 10:523; 10:598; 10:332.

39. Pennsylvania Colony, *Colonial Records of Pennsylvania*, March 2, 1776, 10:502; Pennsylvania Colony, *Minutes of the Supreme Executive Council of Pennsylvania*, April 4, 1776, 10:535; Pennsylvania Colony, *Minutes of the Supreme Executive Council of Pennsylvania*, April 25, 1776, 10:550; Force, *American Archives*, 4th series, 3:1838.

40. Brown, *Firearms in Colonial America*, 316.

41. Gluckman and Satterlee, *American Gun Makers*, 49.

42. Fernow, *Documents Relating to the Colonial History of the State of New York*, June 9, 1775, 15:8.

43. Fernow, *Documents Relating to the Colonial History of the State of New York*, June 13, 1775, 15:8; Fernow, *Documents Relating to the Colonial History of the State of New York*, June 23, 1775, 15:9–10; Fernow, *Documents Relating to the Colonial History of the State of New York*, June 30, 1775, 15:13–14.

44. Bellesiles, *Arming America*, 191.

45. Whisker, *The Gunsmith's Trade*, 178–179.

46. Force, *American Archives*, 4th series, February 2, 1776, 4:1100.

47. Fernow, *Documents Relating to the Colonial History of the State of New York*, March 30, 1776, 15:92.

48. Force, *American Archives*, 4th series, 5:390–392.

49. Force, *American Archives*, 4th series, March 25, 1776, 5:1401; Lewis, *Gunsmiths of Manhattan*, 6.

50. Force, *American Archives*, 4th series, March 22–23, 1776, 5:1396.

51. New Hampshire State, *Documents and Records Relating to the State of New-Hampshire: During the Period of the American Revolution, from 1776 to 1783* (Concord, NH: Edward A. Jenks, 1874), 8:15–16.

52. New Hampshire State, *Documents and Records*, 10:16.

53. Hoadly, *Public Records of the Colony of Connecticut*, 15:17, 137, 317, 323, 437.

54. *Connecticut Archives, Revolutionary War Series*, 5:117–121, quoted in Kauffman, *Early American Gunsmiths*, 75.

55. Brown, *Firearms in Colonial America*, 325; Kauffman, *Early American Gunsmiths*, 41.

56. Kauffman, *Early American Gunsmiths*, 51. Lindsay, *The New England Gun*, 55, 57, describes what may be the same surviving Medad Hills musket.

57. Lindsay, *The New England Gun*, 55; Hoadly, *Public Records of the Colony of Connecticut*, 11:370–371.

58. Hartzler, *Arms Makers of Maryland*, 275.

59. Bellesiles, *Arming America*, 192.

60. Nathan Swayze, *The Rappahannock Forge* (Dallas: American Society of Arms Collectors, 1976), 1–31.

61. North Carolina Colony, *Colonial Records of North Carolina*, April 24, 1776, 10:539. An undated letter from North Carolina's delegates to the Continental Congress some months later suggests that either these public gun factories did not come into existence or that the delegates were not aware of them.

62. North Carolina Colony, *Colonial Records of North Carolina*, November 22, 1776, 10:929; North Carolina Colony, *Colonial Records of North Carolina*, December 7, 1776, 10:958; North Carolina Colony, *Colonial Records of North Carolina*, December 23, 1776, 10:1001.

63. Worthington C. Ford et al., eds. *Journals of the Continental Congress, 1774–1789*, November 4, 1775 (Washington, D.C., 1904–1937), 3:322; Ford, *Journals of the Continental Congress*, November 28, 1775, 3:388.

64. North Carolina Colony, *Colonial Records of North Carolina*, June 14, 1776, 10:630; North Carolina Colony, *Colonial Records of North Carolina*, December 21, 1776, 10:981.

65. Bivins, *Longrifles of North Carolina*, 16, 18.

66. North Carolina Colony, *Colonial Records of North Carolina*, May 3, 1776, 10:559; North Carolina Colony, *Colonial Records of North Carolina*, May 9, 1776, 10:571.

67. North Carolina Colony, *Colonial Records of North Carolina*, December 22, 1775, 10:358.

68. Brown, *Firearms in Colonial America*, 315.

69. Force, *American Archives*, 4th series, April 24, 1776, 5:1337–1338.

70. Bivins, *Longrifles of North Carolina*, 17.

71. Bellesiles, *Arming America*, 192.

72. Walter Clark, ed., *State Records of North Carolina* (Goldsboro, NC: Nash Bros., 1907), 21:168–169; Brown, *Firearms in Colonial America*, 315; Bivins, *Longrifles of North Carolina*, 16, gives a bit more detail about the location and the principals but the same reason for why the factory closed down.

73. Force, *American Archives*, 4th series, February 24, 1776, 5:580–581. Also see Force, *American Archives*, 4th series, February 25, 1776, 5:581, for an extension of their authority, including other rifle designs.

74. Force, *American Archives*, 4th series, August 2, 1775, 3:130–131.

75. Browne, *Archives of Maryland*, August 29, 1775, 11:75; Browne, *Archives of Maryland*, September 20, 1775, 11:81.

76. Browne, *Archives of Maryland*, September 1, 1775, 11:77.

77. Force, *American Archives*, 4th series, August 30, 1775, 3:448–449; Browne, *Archives of Maryland*, 11:76; Force, *American Archives*, 5th series, July 17, 1776, 1:1338; Browne, *Archives of Maryland*, May 3, 1776, 11:402; Browne, *Archives of Maryland*, January 23, 1776, 11:108; Browne, *Archives of Maryland*, July 29, 1776, 12:134.

78. Force, *American Archives*, 4th series, August 30, 1775, 3:448–449; Brown, *Firearms in Colonial America*, 351, 407, identifies Harris's place of business as Savage Town, Maryland; Browne, *Archives of Maryland*, 11:76.

79. Browne, *Archives of Maryland*, May 25, 1776, 11:444.

80. Browne, *Archives of Maryland*, October 2, 1775, 11:81–82.

81. Browne, *Archives of Maryland*, February 1, 1776, 11:127.

82. Browne, *Archives of Maryland*, October 21, 1775, 11:84–85.

83. Browne, *Archives of Maryland*, January 20, 1776, 11:99. See Browne, *Archives of Maryland*, January 17, 1776, 11:100, for more correspondence about this; Browne, *Archives of Maryland*, February 23, 1776, 11:181; Browne, *Archives of Maryland*, May 4, 1776, 11:406; Browne, *Archives of Maryland*, June 27, 1776, 11:525–526; Force, *American Archives*, 5th series, July 30, 1776, 1:667.

84. Browne, *Archives of Maryland*, October 30, 1776, 12:412.

85. Force, *American Archives*, 4th series, May 22, 1776, 5:1590–1592; Ford, *Journals of the Continental Congress*, March 13, 1777, 7:174.

86. Maryland Council of Safety to Committees of the Eastern Shore, *American Archives*, 5th series, July 16, 1776, 1:365.

87. Browne, *Archives of Maryland*, April 6, 1776, 11:314; Browne, *Archives of Maryland*, May 25, 1776, 11:444; Browne, *Archives of Maryland*, June 8, 1776, 11:472; Browne, *Archives of Maryland*, July 8, 1776, 12:10.

88. Browne, *Archives of Maryland*, April 11, 1776, 11:326; Browne, *Archives of Maryland*, June 29, 1776, 11:535.

89. Force, *American Archives*, 4th series, August 31, 1775, 3:449; Force, *American Archives*, 4th series, 3:947.

90. Browne, *Archives of Maryland*, May 31, 1776, 11:454.

91. Browne, *Archives of Maryland*, July 2, 1776, 11:544.

92. Browne, *Archives of Maryland*, July 5, 1776, 11:550.

93. Browne, *Archives of Maryland*, August 24, 1776, 12:238; Browne, *Archives of Maryland*, September 28, 1776, 12:309.

94. Force, *American Archives*, 5th series, July 27, 1776, 1:613–614.

95. Browne, *Archives of Maryland*, April 18, 1777, 16:219; Browne, *Archives of Maryland*, May 6, 1778, 21:68–69.

96. Browne, *Archives of Maryland*, August 24, 1776, 12:238.

97. Force, *American Archives*, 5th series, July 8, 1776, 1:1332; Browne, *Archives of Maryland*, September 13, 1776, 12:269; Force, *American Archives*, 5th series, July 7, 1776, 1:1331.

98. Browne, *Archives of Maryland*, 5th series, August 1, 1776, 1:707; Browne, *Archives of Maryland*, 12:159.

99. Force, *American Archives*, 5th series, August 9, 1776, 1:1352.

100. Browne, *Archives of Maryland*, September 13, 1776, 12:271.

101. Force, *American Archives*, 5th series, August 16, 1776, 3:88. There are scattered references to gunlock purchases, such as Force, *American Archives*, 4th series, January 23, 1776, 5:1526.

102. Force, *American Archives*, 5th series, September 4, 1776, 3:99–100. See a letter of July 30, 1776, to "Gun-Lock Commissioners," Force, *American Archives*, 5th series, 1:667.

103. Browne, *Archives of Maryland*, September 13, 1776, 12:271. See also Browne, *Archives of Maryland*, May 25, 1776, 11:444, directing a shipment of gunlocks from the Gun Lock Manufactory.

104. Hartzler, *Arms Makers of Maryland*, 23–24.

105. "Maryland Council of Safety to Gun-Lock Commissioners," in Force, *American Archives*, 5th series, July 30, 1776, 1:667; Browne, *Archives of Maryland*, 12:142.

106. Browne, *Archives of Maryland*, March 27, 1776, 11:293.

107. Browne, *Archives of Maryland*, May 3, 1776, 11:400–401; Browne, *Archives of Maryland*, June 14, 1776, 11:489; 45:294; Browne, *Archives of Maryland*, January 30, 1781, 45:294.

108. Force, *American Archives*, 5th series, December 1, 1776, 3:1025.

109. Browne, *Archives of Maryland*, May 4, 1776, 11:406–408.

110. Hartzler, *Arms Makers of Maryland*, 22; Browne, *Archives of Maryland*, January 31, 1776, 11:127.

111. Force, *American Archives*, 5th series, July 16, 1776, 1:1337.

112. Browne, *Archives of Maryland*, February 12, 1776, 11:155.

113. Bellesiles, *Arming America*, 186.

114. Whisker, *The Gunsmith's Trade*, 167–168.

115. Whisker, *The Gunsmith's Trade*, 168, citing Browne, *Archives of Maryland*, 11:155, and only that source, says, "64 of which had proved to be good on proof-testing, and 8 of which had failed when the barrels burst."

116. Browne, *Archives of Maryland*, February 12, 1776, 11:155.

117. Deyrup, *Arms Makers of the Connecticut Valley*, 136.

118. Browne, *Archives of Maryland*, May 31, 1776, 11:455.

119. Browne, *Archives of Maryland*, September 17, 1777, 16:377–378.

120. Bishop, *History of American Manufactures*, 1:593. See Browne, *Archives of Maryland*, July 5, 1776, 11:549, for payment to Dallam of £150 "for Musquets per Agreement." As late as August 27, 1787, we find orders to pay John Yost £123, 4s. for an unspecified debt due him from Maryland. Browne, *Archives of Maryland*, 71:215.

121. Brown, *Firearms in Colonial America*, 350–351. See Browne, *Archives of Maryland*, February 23, 1776, 11:180, for the origination of the contract; Browne, *Archives of Maryland*, April 4, 1776, 11:308; Browne, *Archives of Maryland*, July 6, 1776, 11:553; Brown, *Firearms in Colonial America*, 350–351; Browne, *Archives of Maryland*, April 16, 1776, 11:333; Browne, *Archives of Maryland*, June 19, 1776, 11:499; Browne, *Archives of Maryland*, July 5, 1776, 11:550; Force, *American Archives*, 5th series, July 16, 1776, 1:1337; Browne, *Archives of Maryland*, 12:54.

122. Force, *American Archives*, 5th series, July 27, 1776, 1:613–614; Browne, *Archives of Maryland*, 12:129. Browne, *Archives of Maryland*, June 10, 1776, 11:473, documents payment of £855 for "manufacturing Fire Arms"; Browne, *Archives of Maryland*, May 23, 1776, 11:440.

123. Force, *American Archives*, 5th series, July 16, 1776, 1:363; Browne, *Archives of Maryland*, 12:59; Browne, *Archives of Maryland*, July 23, 1776, 12:93; Force, *American Archives*, 5th series, August 11, 1776, 1:892.

124. Browne, *Archives of Maryland*, July 27, 1776, 12:128.

125. Browne, *Archives of Maryland*, April 18, 1777, 16:219.

126. Pennsylvania Colony, *Colonial Records of Pennsylvania*, March 9, 1776, 10:509; Peterson, *Arms and Armor*, 185; Bishop, *History of American Manufactures*, 1:592–593; Force, *American Archives*, 4th series, 4:725–726; Force, *American Archives*, 4th series, May 31, 1776, 11:456. See Force, *American Archives*, 5th series, September 4, 1776, 3:99–100. See a letter of July 30, 1776, to "Gun-Lock Commissioners," Force, *American Archives*, 5th series, 1:667, for more discussion of the problems of the public gunlock factory—and that they did at least make some gunlocks. Browne, *Archives of Maryland*, February 3, 1776, 11:137, contains a letter to Stephen West asking to buy gunlocks from him, but letters of February 12 and 14 at 11:154–155, 161, make it clear that he purchased these gunlocks for repairing guns and did not make them. They seem to raise the possibility that the gunlocks were made in America, "tolerable good, but not equal to the English Musket locks." Browne, *Archives of Maryland*, 11:265, documents the payment to West of £95 for the gunlocks and some knives.

127. Brown, *Firearms in Colonial America*, 315.

128. "Newark (New-Jersey) Committee to President of Congress," in Force, *American Archives*, 4th series, March 6, 1776, 5:89.

129. Kauffman, *Early American Gunsmiths*, 10. See Pennsylvania Colony, *Minutes of the Supreme Executive Council of Pennsylvania*, November 30, 1775, 10:417, for what may be this contract.

130. Brown, *Firearms in Colonial America*, 310.

131. *Pennsylvania Packet*, July 17, 1775, quoted in Kauffman, *Early American Gunsmiths*, 56; Marie Windell, "News Notes and Book Reports," *Delaware History* 5 (March 1953):3, 218–219; Ruthanna Hindes, "Delaware Silversmiths, 1700–1850," *Delaware History* 12 (October 1967):4, 256–257; Whisker, *Arms Makers of Colonial America*, 39.

132. Brown, *Firearms in Colonial America*, 314–315; Peterson, *Arms and Armor*, 207; Swayze, *The Rappahannock Forge*, 31; Kauffman, *Early American Ironware*, 116; Robert Ditchburn, "Three CPs?," *The Gun Report* (July 1962): 29.

Chapter 6

1. Bellesiles, *Arming America*, 322.

2. Bellesiles, *Arming America*, 81–82, 354, 378.

3. Bellesiles, *Arming America*, 306, 542–544n5.

4. Bellesiles, *Arming America*, 306, 542–544n5.

5. Bellesiles, *Arming America*, 306, 542–544n5.

6. George Frederick Ruxton, *Life in the Far West*, ed. Leroy R. Hafen (London: William Blackwood & Sons, 1951); John Palliser, *Solitary Rambles and Adventures of a Hunter in the Prairies* (Rutland, VT: C. E. Tuttle, Co., 1969); New Jersey Department of Labor and Workforce Development, "United States Resident Population by State: 1790–1850," accessed March 13, 2017, http://lwd.dol.state.nj.us/labor/lpa/census/1990/poptrd1.htm. Colorado, Utah, and New Mexico are all listed as "N/A."

7. David Robertson, *Reports of the Trials of Colonel Aaron Burr for Treason and for a Misdemeanor* (New York: Da Capo Press, 1969), :446–447, 582.

8. Robertson, *Reports of the Trials*, 582.

9. *Pennsylvania Gazette*, May 2, 1781, quoted in Kauffman, *Early American Gunsmiths*, 74; *Pennsylvania Journal*, November 24, 1781, quoted in Kauffman, *Early American Gunsmiths*, 71.

10. Francis Baily, *Journal of a Tour in Unsettled Parts of North America in 1796 & 1797*, ed. Augustus De Morgan (London: Baily Bros., 1856), 109.

11. Baily, *Journal of a Tour*, 127–128.

12. Baily, *Journal of a Tour*, 132–134.

13. Baily, *Journal of a Tour*, 159–160, 166, 172.

14. Baily, *Journal of a Tour*, 123, 199, 203, 208, 233, 267.

15. Edward Pole, *Military Laboratory, at No. 34* . . . (Philadelphia: R. Aitken, [1789]), in Library of Congress, Printed Ephemera Collection, Portfolio 147, Folder 9a.

16. Isaac Weld, *Travels through the States of North America, and the Provinces of Upper and Lower Canada, during the Years 1795, 1796, and 1797* (London: John Stockdale, 1807), 1:117.

17. Weld, *Travels through the States*, 1: iv, 117–119.

18. Weld, *Travels through the States*, 118–119.

19. Weld, *Travels through the States*, 1:150.

20. Weld, *Travels through the States*, 1:117–119, 234.

21. Fortescue Cuming, *Sketches of a Tour to the Western Country through the States of Ohio and Kentucky, a Voyage down the Ohio and Mississippi Rivers, and a Trip through the Mississippi Territory, and Part of West Florida, Commenced at Philadelphia in the Winter of 1807, and Concluded in 1809* (Pittsburgh: Pittsburgh Press, 1810).

22. Cuming, *Sketches of a Tour*, 156.

23. Cuming, *Sketches of a Tour*, 15, 17, 22–23, 30, 36, 54, 112, 114–115, 117–118, 126, 135, 222, 265, 273, 323, 378, 414.

24. William C. Smith, *Indiana Miscellany: Consisting of Sketches of Indian Life, the Early Settlement, Customs, and Hardships of the People, and the Introduction of the Gospel and of Schools* (Cincinnati: Poe & Hitchcock, 1867), 39, 76–77.

25. Ibid., 77–78.

26. Robert Carlton [Baynard Rush Hall], *The New Purchase: or Seven and a Half Years in the Far West* (Philadelphia: D. Appleton & Co., 1843), 1:125.

27. Ibid., 1:101; 1:175, 195, 196, 198, 200, 232–234; 2:15, 28, 73, 167, 212, 232–234, 262.

28. Carlton, *The New Purchase*, 1:85.

29. Carlton, *The New Purchase*, 1:99.

30. Carlton, *The New Purchase*, 1:122.

31. Carlton, *The New Purchase*, 1:126–127; 2:28–29.

32. Carlton, *The New Purchase*, 1:287; 2:31.

33. Carlton, *The New Purchase*, 2:255, 257, 262, 263.

34. Carlton, *The New Purchase*, 2:253–263, 290–291.

35. Carlton, *The New Purchase*, 2:29–32, 253–257, 262.

36. Abraham Lincoln, *The Collected Works of Abraham Lincoln*, ed. Roy P. Basler (New Brunswick, NJ: Rutgers University Press, 1953), 4: 61–62.

37. Michael Burlingame, *Abraham Lincoln: A Life* (Baltimore: Johns Hopkins University Press, 2008), 16.

38. Lincoln, *Collected Works*, 4:62.

39. Lincoln, *Collected Works*, 1:386–387.

40. Lincoln, *Collected Works*, 388.

41. Elias Pim Fordham, *Personal Narrative of Travels in Virginia, Maryland, Pennsylvania, Ohio, Indiana, Kentucky; and of a Residence in the Illinois Territory: 1817–1818*, ed. Frederic Austin Ogg (Cleveland: Arthur H. Clark, 1906; reprint, Chicago: Library Resources, Inc., 1970), 95–96.

42. Fordham, *Personal Narrative*, 125–126.

43. Fordham, *Personal Narrative*, 109, 205.

44. Fordham, *Personal Narrative*, 98, 213, 224, 147.

45. Fordham, *Personal Narrative*, 98, 213, 224, 147.

46. Fordham, *Personal Narrative*, 181, 200, 213, 223–225, 237.

47. Anne Newport Royall, *Letters from Alabama 1817–1822* (Tuscaloosa, AL: University of Alabama Press, 1969), 181–189, 203.

48. Milton D. Rafferty, *Rude Pursuits and Rugged Peaks: Schoolcraft's Ozark Journal 1818–1819* (Fayetteville, AR: University of Arkansas Press, 1996), 62–63.

49. Rafferty, *Rude Pursuits*, 54–55, 57, 60, 63, 68, 74.

50. Rafferty, *Rude Pursuits*, 23.

51. John Stillman Wright, *Letters from the West; or a Caution to Emigrants* (Salem, NY: Dodd & Stevenson, 1819), 21, 56, 60; Richard Flower, *Letters from the Illinois, 1820, 1821: Containing an Account of the English Settlement at Albion and Its Vicinity and a Refutation of Various Misrepresentations, Those More Particularly by Mr. Cobbett* (London: James Ridgway, 1822), 14.

52. E. Copeland Jr., "Dupont's Superior Gunpowder: A Constant Supply of Dupont's Gunpowder, Warranted of the First Quality, and Assorted Sizes . . ." (Boston: Davies, ca. 1819), from Lammont du Pont Papers (Acc. 384), Box 35-A, Hagley Museum and Library.

53. William N. Blane, *An Excursion through the United States and Canada during the Years 1822–23 by an English Gentleman* (London: Baldwin, Cradock, and Joy, 1824), 88.

54. Blane, *An Excursion Ibid*, 95–96, 145.

55. Blane, *An Excursion*, 135, 302.

56. Blane, *An Excursion*, 173–175.

57. Karl Bernhard (Duke of Saxe-Weimar Eisenach), *Travels through North America, during the Years 1825 and 1826* (Philadelphia: Carey, Lea & Carey, 1828), 1:71, 99 (describing rifle manufacturing and gunboats, respectively); Bernhard, *Travels through North America*, 2:99, 118.

58. Sandford C. Cox, *Recollections of the Early Settlement of the Wabash Valley* (Lafayette, IN: Courier Steam Book and Job Printing House, 1860), 34–35, 40, 57, 88.

59. Philip Henry Gosse, *Letters from Alabama (U.S.), Chiefly Relating to Natural History* (London: Morgan & Chase, 1859), 130–131.

60. Gosse, *Letters from Alabama*, 130–131.

61. Gosse, *Letters from Alabama*, 130–132, 226–236, 256–257, 270–272.

62. Alexis de Tocqueville, *Journey to America*, trans. George Lawrence, ed. J. P. Mayer (New York: Anchor Books, 1971), 94.

63. Tocqueville, *Journey to America*, 281.

64. Robert Baird, *View of the Valley of the Mississippi, or, the Emigrants and Traveller's Guide to the West*, 2nd ed. (Philadelphia: H.S. Tanner, 1834), 229, 246, 345.

65. Baird, *View of the Valley*, 186, 238, 306.

66. Baird, *View of the Valley*, 186.

67. Baird, *View of the Valley*, 238, 342.

68. Harriet Martineau, *Retrospect of Western Travel* (London: Saunders and Otley, 1838), 2:188

69. Gert Göbel, *Länger als ein Menschenleben in Missouri* 80–81 (St. Louis, [1877]), quoted in Walter L. Robbins, "Christmas Shooting Rounds in America and Their Background," *Journal of American Folklore* 4 (1973): 86:339.

70. Göbel, *Länger als ein Menschenleben*, 49–51.

71. Rebecca Burlend, *A True Picture of Emigration; or Fourteen Years in the Interior of North America* (London: G. Berger, 1848), 25, 29–30.

72. Frances Wright, *Views of Society and Manners in America* (London: Longman, Hurst, Rees, Orme, and Brown, 1821), 288.

73. Thomas Cather, *Voyage to America: The Journals of Thomas Cather*, ed. Thomas Yoseloff (New York: Thomas Yoseloff, 1961; reprint, Westport, CT: Greenwood Press, 1973), 132.

74. Captain Frederick Marryat, *A Diary in America*, ed. Jules Zanger (London: Longman, Orme, Brown, Green, and Longmans, 1839; reprint, Bloomington: Indiana University Press, 1960), 288–289.

75. Marryat, *A Diary in America*, 195–199, 210, 217–218, 224, 237–242, 273–274.

76. Mary Clavers [Caroline Matilda Kirkland], *A New Home—Who'll Follow? Or, Glimpses of Western Life*, 4th ed. (New York: C. S. Francis & Co., 1840), 108–109, 123, 130, 195, 201, 215–216.

77. Shirley S. McCord, *Travel Accounts of Indiana 1679–1961* (Indianapolis: Indiana Historical Bureau, 1970), 183.

78. John James Audubon, *Delineations of American Scenery and Character* (New York: G. A. Baker & Co. 1926), 3.

79. Audubon, *Delineations of American Scenery*, 6, 9, 11–12.

80. Audubon, *Delineations of American Scenery*, 26, 32–33.

81. Audubon, *Delineations of American Scenery*, 41, 44, 82.

82. Audubon, *Delineations of American Scenery*, 118–122.

83. Audubon, *Delineations of American Scenery*, 206.

84. Audubon, *Delineations of American Scenery*, 88, 93.

85. Audubon, *Delineations of American Scenery*, 68, 177, 211, 281–286.

86. Ole Rynning, *Ole Rynning's True Account of America*, ed. and trans. Theodore C. Blegen (St. Paul, MN: Minnesota Historical Society, 1926), 99.

87. Charles Augustus Murray, *Travels in North America during the Years 1834, 1835, & 1836: Including a Summer Residence with the Pawnee Tribe of Indians, in the Remote Prairies of the Missouri, and a Visit to Cuba and the Azore Islands* (London: R. Bentley, 1839), 1:118–119.

88. *Cleaveland Herald*, October 30, 1821.

89. *Cleaveland Herald*, October 30, 1821.

90. Chas H. Haswell, *Reminiscences of New York by an Octogenarian (1816 to 1860)* (New York: Harper & Brothers, 1896), 261–262.

91. Russell, *Firearms, Traps, & Tools of the Mountain Men*, 70–73.

92. Lindsay, *The New England Gun*, 113–125.

93. Bellesiles, *Arming America*, 378; *South Carolina Gazette & Public Advertiser*, October 13, 1785, quoted in Kauffman, *Early American Gunsmiths*, 23; *Federal Gazette*, September 21, 1791, quoted in Kauffman, *Early American Gunsmiths*, 14; *Pennsylvania Packet (Claypoole's American Daily Advertiser)*, April 26, 1798, quoted in Kauffman, *Early American Gunsmiths*, 66; *Pittsburgh Gazette*, December 18, 1812, quoted in Kauffman, *Early American Gunsmiths*, 45; *Somerset Whig* (Somerset, PA), January 8, 1818, quoted in Whisker, *The Gunsmith's Trade*, 155.

94. James E. Hicks, *Notes on United States Ordnance* (Mount Vernon, NY: James E. Hicks, 1940), 1:28.

95. Merrill Lindsay, *The New England Gun: The First Two Hundred Years* (New Haven, CT: New Haven Colony Historical Society, 1975), 85–91.

96. Hartzler, *Arms Makers of Maryland*, 49.

97. U.S. Congress, *Annals of Congress*, February 4, 1803 (Washington, D.C.: Library of Congress, n.d.), 7th Cong., 2nd sess., 1282.

98. Kauffman, *Early American Gunsmiths*, 69.

99. *York* (Pennsylvania) *Gazette*, August 16, 1825, quoted in Kauffman, *Early American Gunsmiths*, 58.

100. Kauffman, *Early American Ironware*, 115; S. E. Dyke, *Thoughts on the American Flintlock Pistol* (York, PA: George Shumway, 1974), 58; Whisker, *The Gunsmith's Trade*, 18, 31.

101. Bazelon, *Defending the Commonwealth*, 16–17; Hicks, *Notes on United States Ordnance*, 1:29.

102. Kauffman, *Early American Gunsmiths*, 59–60.

103. Daniel D. Hartzler, *Arms Makers of Maryland* (York, PA: George Shumway, 1977), 61. See Hartzler, *Arms Makers of Maryland*, 65–68, for photographs of a number of surviving Haslett pistols.

104. Kauffman, *Early American Gunsmiths*, 76.

105. Whisker, *The Gunsmith's Trade*, 200; S. E. Dyke, *Thoughts on the American Flintlock Pistol* (York, PA: George Shumway, 1974), 13–60.

106. *Richmond Commercial Compiler*, September 21, 1816, and October 4, 1816, quoted in Whisker, *The Gunsmith's Trade*, 163, 203–204.

107. *Whiteley's Philadelphia Annual Advertiser* (Philadelphia: Kneass & Saurman, 1820), b2; *Cleveland Herald*, May 8, 1823, quoted in Kauffman, *Early American Gunsmiths*, 4.

108. Kauffman, *Early American Gunsmiths*, 5; *Nashville Daily Republican Banner*, "Guns, Pistols, Bowie Knives," October 2, 1837–November 25, 1837: 1; *New York Morning Herald*, January 1838: 1, 3–6, 9–17.

109. *New York Morning Herald*, January 1, 3–6, 9–13, 15–17; *Free Democrat* (Huntsville, AL), "Gun and Locksmith," May 23, 1837: 1.

110. W. G. Lyford, *The Western Address Directory* (Baltimore: Jos. Robinson, 1837), 385, 418.

111. Weld, *Travels through the States*, 1:117–119, 234; 2:150.

112. Weld, *Travels through the States*, 1:234.

113. Fordham, *Personal Narrative of Travels*, 137, 155, 219–220.

114. Fordham, *Personal Narrative of Travels*, 195–196.

115. Peter Cartwright, *Autobiography of Peter Cartwright, the Backwoods Preacher* (Cincinnati: Jennings & Graham, 1856), 200.

116. Cartwright, *Autobiography*, 201, 206, 223–225.

117. Cartwright, *Autobiography*, 238.

118. *Brookville Enquirer & Indiana Telegraph*, "Communicated," January 14, 1820: 3.

119. William Oliver Stevens, *Pistols at Ten Paces: The Story of the Code of Honor in America* (Cambridge, MA: Riverside Press, 1940), 39–40.

120. Library of Congress, "A proclamation. Mayor's office, Washington Dec. 23, 1828." Printed Ephemera Collection; Portfolio 193, Folder 10.

121. Haswell, *Reminiscences of New York by an Octogenarian*, 244; U.S. Census Bureau· *Enumeration of the Inhabitants of the United States, 1830* (Washington, D.C.: Duff Green, 1832).

122. U.S. Congress, *Journal of the House of Representatives of the United States*, April 19, 1832, 25:611.

123. *North Alabamian* (Tuscumbia), "Our Town," February 24, 1837: 2.

124. *Southern Recorder* (Milledgeville, GA), "More of the Effects of Carrying Concealed Weapons," January 16, 1838: 3. The same article appears as "More of the Effects of Carrying Concealed Weapons," *Georgia Journal* (Milledgeville), January 9, 1838: 2.

125. *North Alabamian*, "Fatal Rencontre at Columbus, Geo.," February 17, 1837: 2.

126. *Nashville Daily Republican Banner*, "A Young Man by the Name of Alexander H. Dixon . . .," October 13, 1837: 2.

127. Library of Congress search URL: http://chroniclingamerica.loc.gov/search/pages/results/?state=&date1=1836&date2=1847&proxtext=pistol&x=0&y=0&dateFilterType=yearRange&rows=20&searchType=basic.

128. *Vermont Phoenix* (Brattleboro, VT), "How Jack Marland Solved a Very Stiff Problem," April 18, 1845: 1; *Camden Commercial Courier* (Camden, SC), "Scenes in Havana, in 1822," August 26, 1837: 1–2; *Columbia Democrat* (Bloomsburg, PA), "Salt-Water Bubbles," June 11, 1842: 1; *Columbia Democrat*, "The Duellists," May 7, 1842: 1.

129. *Jeffersonian* (Kosciusko, MS), "The Steward's Duel," November 30, 1844: 1.

130. *New York Herald*, March 30, 1843: 2.

131. *Daily Union* (Washington, D.C.), "Case of Wm. R. Elliott," August 22, 1845: 2.

132. *New York Herald*, "Colt's Trial," January 26, 1842: 1; *New-York Tribune*, "Colt's Trial," January 26, 1842: 1.

133. Clayton E. Cramer, "Factual Errors in the Gunning of America: Is This Scholarly History or Polemic?," http://papers.ssrn.com/sol3/papers.cfm?abstract_id=2795745, 9–11.

134. *New York Herald*, September 10, 1845: 3.

135. *Cecil Whig* (Elkton, MD), November 4, 1843: 2.

136. *Cecil Whig*, "Afternoon Session," November 4, 1843: 2.

137. *New York Herald*, March 26, 1843: 2.

138. *Camden Commercial Courier*, "Extraordinary Circumstances," August 26, 1837: 2.

139. *Columbian Fountain* (Washington, D.C.), "The New York Stabbing Case," August 27, 1846: 2.

140. *New-York Daily Tribune*, "From Florida," March 29, 1843: 2.

141. *New York Herald*, January 23, 1836: 2.

142. U.S. Congress, *House Journal*, April 24, 1844, 39:848.

143. Edward Beecher, *Narrative of Riots at Alton* (Alton, IL: 1838; reprint, New York: E. P. Dutton & Co., 1965), 14, 64, 75, 84.

144. Cassius Marcellus Clay, *The Writings of Cassius Marcellus Clay*, ed. Horace Greeley (New York: Harper & Brothers, 1848; reprint, New York: Negro Universities Press, 1969), 257.

145. *Nashville Daily Republican Banner*, "Horrid Rencontre," October 7, 1837: 2.

146. Cather, *Voyage to America*, 143–144; Marryat, *A Diary in America*, 195–196.

147. William F. Pope, *Early Days in Arkansas* (Little Rock, AR: Frederick W. Allsopp, 1895), 103.

148. Kentucky Constitutional Convention, *Report of the Debates and Proceedings of the Convention for the Revision of the Constitution of the State of Kentucky 1849* (Frankfort, KY: A. G. Hodges & Co., 1849), 822.

149. Frederick Law Olmsted, *The Papers of Frederick Law Olmsted*, ed. Charles E. Beveridge and Charles Capen McLaughlin (Baltimore: Johns Hopkins University Press, 1981), 2:232–233.

150. Generally, see Clayton E. Cramer, *Concealed Weapon Laws of the Early Republic: Dueling, Southern Violence, and Moral Reform* (Westport, CT: Praeger, 1999).

151. Bellesiles, 378. It important to note that while "handgun" and "pistol" are technically interchangeable terms, common usage today distinguishes pistols from revolvers, both of which are handguns.

152. Clayton E. Cramer, *Armed America: The Remarkable Story of How and Why Guns Became as American as Apple Pie* (Nashville, TN: Nelson Current, 2006), 204–235, provides a more detailed examination of this subject.

Chapter 7

1. Bishop, *History of American Manufactures*, 1:492, 494.

2. Bishop, *History of American Manufactures*, 1:568.

3. Cuming, *Sketches of a Tour*, 222.

4. Henry Bradshaw Fearon, *Sketches of America: A Narrative of a Journey of Five Thousand Miles through the Eastern and Western States*, 3rd ed. (London: Longman, Hurst, Rees, Orme, and Brown, 1819), 203.

5. Albert Gallatin, *A Statement of the Arts and Manufactures of the United States of America* (Washington, D.C.: A. Cornman Jr., 1814), 11. Secretary of the Treasury Tench Coxe's admission that the manufacturing census was very incomplete can be found in Margo J. Anderson, *The American Census: A Social History* (New Haven, CT: Yale University Press, 1988), 19.

6. Berkeley R. Lewis, *Small Arms and Ammunition in the United States Service, 1776–1865* (Washington, D.C.: Smithsonian Institute, 1956), 47.

7. James D. Wright, Peter H. Rossi, and Kathleen Daly, *Under the Gun: Weapons, Crime, and Violence in America* (New York: Aldine de Gruyter, 1983), 30, provides production and importation figures from which this data was calculated.

8. Gregory J. W. Urwin, *The United States Infantry: An Illustrated History, 1775–1918* (Norman: University of Oklahoma Press, 1988), 49.

9. William G. Ouseley, *Remarks on the Statistics and Political Institutions of the United States, with Some Observations on the Ecclesiastical System of America, Her Sources of Revenue, &c* (1832; reprint, Freeport, NY: Books for Libraries Press, 1970), 32. That the U.S. Army was still only 6,000 men in the 1830s is confirmed in Lorenzo de Zavala, *Journey to the United States of North America*, trans. Wallace Woolsey (Austin, TX: Shoal Creek Publishers, 1980), 23, and Murray, *Travels in North America*, 1:176.

10. Deyrup, *Arms Makers of the Connecticut Valley*, 7, n. **; Whisker, *The Gunsmith's Trade*, 47–48.

11. Whisker, *The Gunsmith's Trade*, 67.

12. The Henry Papers at the Hagley Museum, Series 2, Box 8, Folder 6, Accounts 1814–19; Henry Papers, Folder 8, John Joseph Henry III Business Accounts 1813–31.

13. Henry Papers, Series 1, Box 5, Production Records (1838).

14. Whisker, *The Gunsmith's Trade*, 47–51.

15. Whisker, *The Gunsmith's Trade*, 207.
16. Whisker, *The Gunsmith's Trade*, 225–230.

Chapter 8

1. Bellesiles, *Arming America*, 232–233.
2. Deyrup, *Arms Makers of the Connecticut Valley*, 33.
3. Whisker, *The Gunsmith's Trade*, 4–5; See also Merritt Roe Smith, *Harpers Ferry Armory and the New Technology: The Challenge of Change* (Ithaca, NY: Cornell University Press, 2015), for examination of Springfield Armory's Virginia cousin.
4. Bellesiles, *Arming America*, 232.
5. Bellesiles, *Arming America*, 232–233.
6. Deyrup, *Arms Makers of the Connecticut Valley*, vii.
7. Deyrup, *Arms Makers of the Connecticut Valley*, 5, 33.
8. Bellesiles, *Arming America*, 230.
9. Brown, *Firearms in Colonial America*, 361–362.
10. Brown, *Firearms in Colonial America*, 362.
11. Deyrup, *Arms Makers of the Connecticut Valley*, 42–43.
12. James E. Hicks, *Notes on United States Ordnance* (Mount Vernon, NY: James E. Hicks, 1940), 1:14. See *Statutes at Large*, 3rd Cong., Sess. 1, ch. 14, 1:352, for the text of the statute that authorized the purchase—though without specifying either domestic or foreign sourcing for the weapons; Hicks, *Notes on United States Ordnance*, 1:30, lists contracts, largely with the Lancaster County rifle makers, for rifles, pistols, and a few muskets in 1807 and 1808. Hartzler, *Arms Makers of Maryland*, 207–208, quotes letters from the superintendent of Indian trade to George Kreps Jr. complaining about the poor finish of rifles made by Kreps under contract.
13. See Hicks, *Notes on United States Ordnance*, 1:14–15, for details on the slow deliveries.
14. Bellesiles, *Arming America*, 232.
15. Deyrup, *Arms Makers of the Connecticut Valley*, 42–43.
16. Gluckman and Satterlee, *American Gun Makers*, 69–81.
17. Arthur Nehrbass, "Notes on Early U.S. Rifle and Musket Production," *The Gun Report* (October 1972): 25.
18. George C. Maynard, "Notes on the Manufacture of Small Arms for the United States Army by the Government and Private Makers in the Nineteenth Century," *Stock and Steel* (June 1923): 9–10.
19. Hartzler, *Arms Makers of Maryland*, 27–33.

20. Bellesiles, *Arming America*, 237.

21. Hicks, *Notes on United States Ordnance,* 1:19–23; Gluckman and Satterlee, *American Gun Makers*, 69.

22. Hicks, *Notes on United States Ordnance*, 1:19–23.

23. Bellesiles, *Arming America*, 237.

24. Bellesiles, *Arming America*, 522–523n111.

25. Hicks, *Notes on United States Ordnance*, 1:19–23, 42–43.

26. Hicks, *Notes on United States Ordnance*, 1:32–33.

27. Bellesiles, *Arming America*, 237.

28. Gluckman and Satterlee, *American Gun Makers*, 78.

29. Gluckman and Satterlee, *American Gun Makers*, 69–81.

30. Deyrup, *Arms Makers of the Connecticut Valley*, 225; Hicks, *Notes on United States Ordnance*, 1:20, for contract; Gluckman and Satterlee, *American Gun Makers*, 75, for deliveries; Gluckman and Satterlee, *American Gun Makers*, 146; Lindsay, *The New England Gun*, 92; Deyrup, *Arms Makers of the Connecticut Valley*, 226; Lindsay, *The New England Gun*, 74, 77.

31. William O. Achtermier, *Rhode Island Arms Makers & Gunsmiths: 1643–1883* (Providence, RI: Man at Arms, 1980), 21–24.

32. "Callender Irvine to John Armstrong," April 5, 1813, quoted in Gluckman and Satterlee, *American Gun Makers*, 36.

33. "Callender Irvine to John Armstrong," April 5, 1813, quoted in Gluckman and Satterlee, *American Gun Makers*, 36.

34. Bellesiles, *Arming America*, 233.

35. Bellesiles, *Arming America*, 238.

36. Gluckman and Satterlee, *American Gun Makers*, 80–81.

37. Deyrup, *Arms Makers of the Connecticut Valley*, 48.

38. Bellesiles, *Arming America*, 235.

39. Deyrup, *Arms Makers of the Connecticut Valley*, 44–47; Achtermier, *Rhode Island Arms Makers & Gunsmiths*, 23.

40. The Henry Papers, Series 1, Box 5, Production Records (1838); The Henry Papers, Series 1, Box 2, Essay of a Price Book Boulton (1815).

41. Deyrup, *Arms Makers of the Connecticut Valley*, 48–54.

42. Bellesiles, *Arming America*, 242.

Chapter 9

1. Thomas E. Holt, "Pennsylvania 1798 Contract Muskets," *American Society of Arms Collectors* 2 (November 1956): 19–20, gives the 11,200 count; Gluckman and Satterlee, *American Gun Makers*, 81–82, indicates that 20,000 muskets were contracted. The 10,000 to be made

in Britain were reallocated to American contractors, of which the contract details for only 19,000 of the original 20,000 have survived. The total of Gluckman's counts by contractor, however, total 19,200.

2. Bruce S. Bazelon, *Defending the Commonwealth: Catalogue of the Militia Exhibit at the William Penn Memorial Museum, Harrisburg, Pennsylvania* (Providence, RI: Mowbray Co., 1980), 16–17.

3. Pennsylvania Colony, *Pennsylvania Archives*, 9th series, 6:4231.

4. Lindsay, *The New England Gun*, 82, 85; Deyrup, *Arms Makers of the Connecticut Valley*, 224, lists a "Lane and Read" in Boston, 1826–1836, that might be the maker in question.

5. Bellesiles, *Arming America*, 236.

6. Giles Cromwell, *The Virginia Manufactory of Arms* (Charlottesville: University Press of Virginia, 1975), 2.

7. Bellesiles, *Arming America*, 236.

8. Cromwell, *The Virginia Manufactory of Arms*, 6–9. Whisker, *The Gunsmith's Trade*, 193–194, reports that Peter Brong, Abraham Henry, and Henry DeHuff Jr. also submitted an unsuccessful bid on the contract with the state of Virginia for pistols and long guns.

9. Cromwell, *Virginia Manufactory of Arms*, 85–87, 174.

10. Bellesiles, *Arming America*, 236.

11. Cromwell, *Virginia Manufactory of Arms*, 11–14.

12. Bellesiles, *Arming America*, 236.

13. Cromwell, *Virginia Manufactory of Arms*, 31.

14. Bellesiles, *Arming America*, 236.

15. Cromwell, *Virginia Manufactory of Arms*, 37.

16. Bellesiles, *Arming America*, 236.

17. Cromwell, *Virginia Manufactory of Arms*, 37.

18. Hartzler, *Arms Makers of Maryland*, 164.

19. Cromwell, *Virginia Manufactory of Arms*, 37.

20. Hartzler, *Arms Makers of Maryland*, 164.

21. Bellesiles, *Arming America*, 236.

22. Cromwell, *Virginia Manufactory of Arms*, 150.

23. Cromwell, *Virginia Manufactory of Arms*, 44–46, 64–65, 177–184.

Chapter 10

1. Joseph Wickham Roe, *English and American Tool Builders* (New Haven, CT: Yale University Press, 1916), 1–70, gives a history of the English development of the metal-cutting lathe and planer. Roe also

discusses the development of the use of machinery and unskilled labor to make standardized parts and the first machine mass production in the Royal Navy's shipyards. L. T. C. Rolt, *A Short History of Machine Tools* (Cambridge, MA: The MIT Press. 1965), 139.

2. Roe, *English and American Tool Builders*, 129; David Hounshell, *From the American System to Mass Production, 1800–1932: The Development of Manufacturing Technology in the United States* (Baltimore: Johns Hopkins University Press, 1984), 15–17, argues that the claims of this widespread use of the phrase are not traceable, even in documents expounding on the virtues of this system. Charles H. Fitch, *Extra Census Bulletin: Report on the Manufacture of Firearms and Ammunition*, U.S. Census Office (Washington, D.C.: Government Printing Office, 1882), 4, describes this as "the American system."

3. Joseph Wickham Roe, *English and American Tool Builders* (New Haven, CT: Yale University Press, 1916), 129–131.

4. See John Winthrop, *Winthrop's Journal: History of New England*, in *Original Narratives of American History*, James Kendall Hosmer (New York: Charles Scribner's Sons, 1908), 2:228.

5. Peter Temin, "The Industrialization of New England, 1830–1880," 111–113, in *Engines of Enterprise: An Economic History of New England*, ed. Peter Temin (Cambridge, MA: Harvard University Press, 2000).

6. Temin, "The Industrialization of New England, 1830–1880," 117; Roe, *English and American Tool Builders*, 172; Charles R. Morris, *The Dawn of Invention: The First American Industrial Revolution* (New York: PublicAffairs, 2012), 89.

7. Hounshell, *From the American System to Mass Production*, 15–25.

8. Fitch, Extra Census Report, 5; Rolt, *A Short History of Machine Tools*, 137, 147; Morris, Dawn of Innovation, 259–260.

9. N. Gregory Mankiw, *Macroeconomics*, 5th ed. (New York: Worth Publishers, 2003), 167.

10. Beth Tompkins Bates, *The Making of Black Detroit in the Age of Henry Ford* (Chapel Hill: University of North Carolina Press, 2012), 41–42; Thomas Sowell, *Economic Facts and Fallacies*, 2nd ed. (New York: Basic Books, 2011), 26; Charles Dickens, *American Notes for General Circulation* (Paris: A. and W. Galignani & Co., 1842), 1:80.

11. Morris, *Dawn of Innovation*, 95–96.

12. Dickens, *American Notes for General Circulation*, 1:82–84.

13. "Description of Colonel Colt's Fire-arm Manufactory," extracted from No. 218 of Charles Dickens's *Household Words*, May 27, 1854,

354, in Samuel Colt, *On the Application of Machinery to the Manufacture of Rotating Chambered-Breech Firearms*, 3rd ed. (London: William Clowes & Sons, 1855), 30.

14. Colt, *On the Application of Machinery*, 30; Steven Cherry, *Mental Health Care in Modern England: The Norfolk Lunatic Asylum, St. Andrew's Hospital, c. 1810–1998* (Bury St. Edmunds: St. Edmundsbury Press, 2003), 64; Liza Picard, "The Working Classes and the Poor," British Library, accessed October 6, 2016, https://www.bl.uk/victorian-britain /articles/the-working-classes-and-the-poor.

15. Richard Kurin, *The Smithsonian's History of America in 101 Objects* (New York: Penguin Press, 2013), 176; Charles T. Haven and Frank A. Belden, *A History of the Colt Revolver* (New York: William Morrow & Co., 1940), 92.

16. Haag, *Gunning of America*, 116.

17. Roe, *English and American Tool Builders*, 128.

18. "Thomas Jefferson to John Jay, August 30, 1785, United States Department of State," in *The Diplomatic Correspondence of the United States of America* (Washington, D.C.: Blair & Rives, 1887), 1:642.

19. Rolt, *A Short History of Machine Tools*, 140.

20. Morris, *Dawn of Innovation*, 138; Roe, *English and American Tool Builders*, 133; "Thomas Jefferson to James Monroe, November 14, 1801," Library of Congress, accessed October 25, 2016, https://www .loc.gov/resource/mtj1.024_1261_1261/?st=text.

21. Morris, *Dawn of Innovation*, 133, 155; Rolt, *A Short History of Machine Tools*, 143; Roe, *English and American Tool Builders*, 133–134, 136; Fitch, *Extra Census Bulletin*, 4–5.

22. Fitch, *Extra Census Bulletin*, 4.

23. Fitch, *Extra Census Bulletin*, 4.

24. Fitch, *Extra Census Bulletin*, 5.

25. Fitch, *Extra Census Report*, 6.

26. Kurin, *The Smithsonian's History of America*, ch. 24; Roe, *English and American Tool Builders*, 137; Todd Timmons, *Science and Technology in Nineteenth-Century America* (Westport, CT: Greenwood Press, 2005), 152.

27. Timmons, *Science and Technology*, 137–138.

28. Timmons, *Science and Technology*, 2.

29. Timmons, *Science and Technology*, 4–5.

30. Timmons, *Science and Technology*, 40.

31. *The Manufacturer and Builder*, "Brown and Sharpe No. 8 Milling Machine," 24(7) (July 1892): 150.

32. Timmons, *Science and Technology*, 142; Robert S. Woodbury, *History of the Milling Machine* (Cambridge, MA: Technology Press, 1960), 17–22; Morris, *Dawn of Invention*, 82–89, 89–97.

33. Richard C. Rattenbury, *A Legacy in Arms: American Firearm Manufacture, Design, and Artistry, 1800–1900* (Norman: University of Oklahoma Press, 2014), 16.

34. Woodbury, *History of the Milling Machine*, 23.

35. Roe, *English and American Tool Builders*, 142.

36. Robert S. Woodbury, *History of the Grinding Machine*, in Robert S. Woodbury, *Studies in the History of Machine Tools* (Cambridge, MA: MIT Press, 1972), 51–66.

37. Robert S. Woodbury, *History of the Gear Cutting Machine*, in Robert S. Woodbury, *Studies in the History of Machine Tools* (Cambridge, MA: MIT Press, 1972), 34–37.

38. Rolt, *A Short History of Machine Tools*, 142–143; Whisker, *The Gunsmith's Trade*, 4–5; Henry Barnard, *Armsmear: The Home, the Arm, and the Armory of Samuel Colt. A Memorial* (New York, n.p., 1866), 218.

39. Morris, *Dawn of Innovation*, 107–109, 130.

Chapter 11

1. Haag, *Gunning of America*, xiv.

2. Matt Haig, *Brand Failures: The Truth about the 100 Biggest Branding Mistakes of All Time* (London: Kogan Page, 2003), 12–15.

3. Steven Burke, "IBM Will Offer the PCjr for Further Education in Schools," *InfoWorld*, September 16, 1985: 6.

4. Thomas E. Bonsall, *Disaster in Dearborn: The Story of the Edsel* (Stanford, CA: Stanford General Books, 2002).

5. Cramer, *Armed America*.

6. Cramer, *Armed America*, xv.

7. Cramer, *Armed America*, 408n10.

8. Colt Patent Firearms Co. Colt Collection, RG103, Business File, Box 11A, Correspondence, Allies Letter Book, 1873–1880, from Hugh Harbison to Allies, October 30, 1877, p. 174 of Letter Book, Connecticut State Library.

9. Colt Patent Firearms Co. Colt Collection, RG103, Business File, Box 11A, Correspondence, Allies Letter Book, 1873–1880, from Willard and Seaver, Sec. [of Allies] to Hugh Harbison, October 17, 1877, p. 173 of Letter Book.

10. Colt Patent Firearms Co. Colt Collection, RG103, Business File, Box 11A, Correspondence, Allies Letter Book, 1873–1880, from Colt Allies to Colt Patent Fire Arms Co., June 26, 1873, p. 15 of Letter Book.

11. Colt Patent Firearms Co. Colt Collection, RG103, Business File, Box 11A, Correspondence, Allies Letter Book, 1873–1880, from Hugh Harbison to [illegible], January 24, 1874, p. 22 of Letter Book.

12. Colt Patent Firearms Co. Colt Collection, RG103, Business File, Box 11A, Correspondence, Allies Letter Book, 1873–1880, from [Allies] to Colt Fire-Arms, June 29, 1874, p. 25 of Letter Book.

13. Colt Patent Firearms Co. Colt Collection, RG103, Business File, Box 11A, Correspondence, Allies Letter Book, 1873–1880, from Colt Fire-Arms to [illegible], August 22, 1874, p. 31 of Letter Book.

14. Colt Patent Firearms Co. Colt Collection, RG103, Business File, Box 11A, Correspondence, Allies Letter Book, 1873–1880, from Hugh Harbison to Colt Patent Fire Arms, December 30, 1874, p. 39 of Letter Book.

15. Colt Patent Firearms Co. Colt Collection, RG103, Business File, Box 11A, Correspondence, Allies Letter Book, 1873–1880, from [Allies] to Colt Patent Fire Arms, December 29, 1874, p. 42 of Letter Book.

16. Colt Patent Firearms Co. Colt Collection, RG103, Business File, Box 11A, Correspondence, Allies Letter Book, 1873–1880, from Hugh Harbison to [Allies], December 31, 1874, p. 43 of Letter Book.

17. Colt Patent Firearms Co. Colt Collection, RG103, Business File, Box 11A, Correspondence, Allies Letter Book, 1873–1880, from [Allies] to Colt Patent Fire Arms, January 5, 1875, p. 44 of Letter Book.

18. Colt Patent Firearms Co. Colt Collection, RG103, Business File, Box 11A, Correspondence, Allies Letter Book, 1873–1880, from [Allies] to Colt Patent Fire Arms, February 9, 1875, p. 49 of Letter Book.

19. Colt Patent Firearms Co. Colt Collection, RG103, Business File, Box 11A, Correspondence, Allies Letter Book, 1873–1880, from [Allies] to Colt Patent Fire Arms, February 9, 1875, p. 49 of Letter Book.

20. Colt Patent Firearms Co. Colt Collection, RG103, Business File, Box 11A, Correspondence, Allies Letter Book, 1873–1880, from [Allies] to Colt Patent Fire Arms, April 10, 1875, p. 55 of Letter Book.

21. Colt Patent Firearms Co. Colt Collection, RG103, Business File, Box 11A, Correspondence, Allies Letter Book, 1873–1880, from [Allies] to Colt Patent Fire Arms, May 3, 1875, p. 63 of Letter Book.

22. Colt Patent Firearms Co. Colt Collection, RG103, Business File, Box 11A, Correspondence, Allies Letter Book, 1873–1880, from [Allies] to Colt Patent Fire Arms, June 23, 1875, p. 64 of Letter Book.

23. Colt Patent Firearms Co. Colt Collection, RG103, Business File, Box 11A, Correspondence, Allies Letter Book, 1873–1880, from [Allies] to Colt Patent Fire Arms, September 20, 1875, p. 77 of Letter Book.

24. Colt Patent Firearms Co. Colt Collection, RG103, Business File, Box 11A, Correspondence, Allies Letter Book, 1873–1880, from [Allies] to Colt Patent Fire Arms, September 20, 1875, p. 78 of Letter Book.

25. Colt Patent Firearms Co. Colt Collection, RG103, Business File, Box 11A, Correspondence, Allies Letter Book, 1873–1880, from Hugh Harbison to [illegible], January 24, 1874, p. 22 of Letter Book. See Colt Domestic MSRP Price List 2016, accessed November 1, 2016, https://www.colt.com/DesktopModules/Bring2mind/DMX/Download.aspx?EntryId=947&PortalId=0&DownloadMethod=attachment, last. ("Colt reserves the right to bid and sell to police departments, federal, state, municipal agencies, educational and other public institutions and to contract Colt products on such bids.")

26. Samuel Colt to [illegible], March 30, 1852, *The Papers of Samuel Colt*, MS28415, Connecticut Historical Society.

27. Morris, *Dawn of Innovation*, 251.

28. Haag, *Gunning of America*, 48.

29. Haag, *Gunning of America*, 419n7.

30. William B. Edwards, *The Story of Colt's Revolver* (New York: Castle Books, 1957), 264–266.

31. Edwards, *The Story of Colt's Revolver*, 264–266.

32. California Digital Newspaper Collection, search criteria: years 1853–1854; newspaper: *Sacramento Daily Union*; string "Colt's pistols"; category: ADVERTISEMENT.

33. *Daily Alta California*, December 7, 1852: 3, col. 7.

34. California Digital Newspaper Collection, search criteria: years 1853–1854; newspaper: *Daily Alta California*; string: "Colt's pistols"; category: ADVERTISEMENT.

35. California Digital Newspaper Collection, search criteria: years 1850–1859; newspapers: All; string: "Colt's pistols"; category: ADVERTISEMENT.

36. California Digital Newspaper Collection, search criteria: years 1850–1859; newspapers: All; string: "revolver"; category: ADVERTISEMENT.

37. California Digital Newspaper Collection, search criteria: years 1850–1859; newspapers: All; string: "revolvers"; category: ADVERTISEMENT.

38. California Digital Newspaper Collection, search criteria: years 1850–1859; newspapers: All; string: "pistols"; category: ADVERTISEMENT.

39. *Placer Times,* March 23, 1850: 1, col. 1.

40. *Daily Alta California,* December 22, 1851: 1, col. 4; *Daily Alta California,* November 4, 1851: 3, col. 3; California Digital Newspaper Collection, search criteria: years 1850–1859; newspapers: All; string: "'shooting gallery' Windrow"; category: ADVERTISEMENT.

41. California Digital Newspaper Collection, search criteria: years 1850–1859; newspapers: All; string: "shooting"; category: ADVERTISEMENT.

42. *Daily Alta California,* June 26, 1850: 3, col. 5.

43. *Daily Alta California,* January 9, 1850: 2, col. 4; *Placer Times,* March 23, 1850: 2, col. 1; *Placer Times,* May 24, 1850: 1, col. 4; *Daily Alta California,* July 11, 1850: 3, col. 5; *Daily Alta California,* July 17, 1850: 2, col. 3; *Daily Alta California,* July 22, 1850: 2, col. 1; *Sacramento Transcript,* July 26, 1850: 2, col. 5.

44. J. D. Borthwick, "Three Years in Calafornia [*sic*]," *Hutchings Illustrated California Magazine* 2 (October 1857): 171–172.

45. *Daily Alta California,* February 4, 1854: 2, col. 5; "The Calaveras Tragedy," *Sacramento Daily Union,* April 13, 1852: 2, col. 5.

46. Haag, *Gunning of America,* 235–236.

47. Haag, *Gunning of America,* 242–246.

48. Haag, *Gunning of America,* 240.

49. Haag, *Gunning of America,* 241–242.

50. Haag, *Gunning of America,* 255–256.

51. Haag, *Gunning of America,* 256–259.

52. Haag, *Gunning of America,* 163–178, 189; A Google search for "Juan Murietta" returns 12,300 books, https://www.google.com/search ?tbm=bks&q=Juan+Murietta#tbm=bks&q=Joaquain+Murrieta.

53. Haag, *Gunning of America,* 176.

54. Bliss *v.* Commonwealth, 13 Am. Dec. 251 (Ky. 1822); *Simpson v. State,* 13 Tenn. (5 Yer.) 356 (1833); *Aymette v. State,* 21 Tenn. (2 Hump.) 154 (1840); *State v. Reid,* 1 Ala. 612, 35 Am. Dec. 44 (1840); *State v. Buzzard,* 4 Ark (2 Pike) 18 (1842); *State v. Huntley,* 25 N.C. (3 Ired.) 418, 40 Am. Dec. 416 (1843); *State v. Newsom,* 27 N.C. (5 Ired.) 250 (1844); *Nunn v. State,* 1 Kelly 243 (Ga. 1846); *Cooper and Worsham v. Savannah,* 4 Ga. 68 (1848); *State v. Chandler,* 5 La. Ann. 489, 52 Am. Dec. 599 (1850); *State v. Smith,* 11 La. Ann. Rep. 633 (1856); *State v. Jumel,* 13 La. Ann. 399 (1858); *Owen v. State,* 31 Ala. *Smith v. Ishenhour,* 43 Tenn. 214 (1866); *Hopkins v. Commonwealth,* 66 Ky. (3 Bush) 480 (1868); *Cutsinger v. Commonwealth,* 70 Ky. (7 Bush) 392 (1870);

Andrews v. State, 50 Tenn. (3 Heisk.) 165, 8 Am. Rep. 8 (1871; *English v. State*, 35 Tex. 473, 14 Am. Rep. 374 (1872); *State v. Wilburn*, 66 Tenn. (7 Bax.) 57, 32 Am. Rep. 551 (1872); *Fife v. State*, 31 Ark. 455, 25 Am. Rep. 556 (1876); *Wilson v. State*, 33 Ark. 557, 34 Am. Rep. 52 (1878); *Salina v. Blaksley*, 72 Kan. 230, 83 P. 619, 3 L.R.A (N.S.) 168, 115 Am. St. Rep. 196, 7 Am. & Eng. Ann. Cas. 925 (1905). See Clayton E. Cramer, *For the Defense of Themselves and the State: The Original Intent and Judicial Interpretation of the Right to Keep and Bear Arms* (Westport, CT: Praeger, 1994), for a detailed history of firearms law jurisprudence.

55. Haag, *Gunning of America*, 177.

56. *Annual Report of the Secretary of the Interior on the Operations* 1:72 (Washington, D.C.: Government Printing Office, 1879).

57. David Alan Nichols, *Lincoln and the Indians: Civil War Policy and Politics* (Columbia: University of Missouri Press, 2012), 115.

58. Stephen J. Rockwell, *Indian Affairs and the Administrative State in the Nineteenth Century* (New York: Cambridge University Press, 2010), 289.

59. Haag, *Gunning of America*, 88, 179, 204.

60. "Rifles and Light Machine Guns," *Encyclopedia Britannica* (1922), 32:277

61. Tom Warlow, *Firearms, the Law, and Forensic Ballistics*, 3rd ed. (Boca Raton, FL: CRC Press, 2012), 88–89.

62. Haag, *Gunning of America*, 180–181.

63. Haag, *Gunning of America*, 179.

64. Haag, *Gunning of America*, 181.

65. Haag, *Gunning of America*, 203.

66. "Volition," Merriam-Webster.com, accessed December 29, 2016, https://www.merriam-webster.com/dictionary/volition.

Chapter 12

1. Library of Congress database search of *Chronicling America* for references to "guns" for the years 1865–1924, http://chroniclingamerica. loc.gov/search/pages/results/?state=&date1=1865&date2=1924&proxt ext=pistol&x=22&y=17&dateFilterType=yearRange&rows=20&searc hType=basic.

2. "Fall Skirt Will Have Pistol Pockets," *The Day Book*, July 30, 1913: 15.

3. *New-York Tribune*, April 16, 1916: 55.

4. *The Sun*, August 24, 1919: section 5, 59.

5. Library of Congress database search of *Chronicling America* for references to "pistol," "handgun," "rifle," "revolver," or "shotgun," http://chroniclingamerica.loc.gov/lccn/sn86063381/1918-05-22/ed-1 /seq-4/#date1=1865&index=19&rows=20&searchType=advanced&la nguage=&sequence=0&words=pistol+pistols+revolver+revolving+rifle+ rifles+shotgun&proxdistance=5&date2=1924&ortext=pistol+handgun +rifle+shotgun+revolver&proxtext=&phrasetext=&andtext=&dateFilt erType=yearRange&page=1.

6. Jeffrey L. Rodengen, *NRA: An American Legend* (Fort Lauderdale, FL: Write Stuff Enterprises, 2002), 15–21, 33–34, 39.

7. Rodengen, *NRA*, 22–29.

8. Rodengen, *NRA*, 35.

9. Rodengen, *NRA*, 41–43, 46, 48–49, 54, 56, 64.

10. Rodengen, *NRA*, 57–58.

11. Rodengen, *NRA*, 53.

12. Rodengen, *NRA*, 63–64, 69.

13. See Clayton E. Cramer, "The Racist Roots of Gun Control," *Kansas Journal of Law & Public Policy* 4(2) (Winter 1995): 17–25, for an overview of these statutes; Clayton E. Cramer, *Armed America*, 3–38, for a more detailed examination.

14. "The True Remedy for the Fugitive Slave," *Frederick Douglass' Paper*, June 9, 1854, quoted in John R. McKivigan and Heather L. Kaufman, eds., *In the Words of Frederick Douglass: Quotations from Liberty's Champion* (Ithaca, NY: Cornell University Press, 2012), 111.

15. Nicholas Johnson, *Negroes and the Gun: The Black Tradition of Arms* (Amherst, NY: Prometheus Press, 2014), 31–67; Frontispiece image from Sarah H. Bradford, *Scenes in the Life of Harriet Tubman* (Auburn, NY: W. J. Moses, 1869).

16. Johnson, *Negroes and the Gun*, 75–104.

17. Johnson, *Negroes and the Gun*, 105.

18. Johnson, *Negroes and the Gun*, 108.

19. Johnson, *Negroes and the Gun*, 122–132.

20. 65 Congressional Record 3946. The bracketed "by" appears to have been left out of the transcript.

21. "Municipal Court Has Heavy Docket," *Twin-City Daily Sentinel* (Winston-Salem, NC), November 19, 1918: 8 (19 of 20 charged with carrying concealed weapons are described as "colored."); "Pistol-Toting Decreasing," *Charlotte News* (Charlotte, NC), October 12, 1919: 4 (of 15 defendants charged, 14 are described as "colored.").

22. "No Race Trouble to Be Found in This Section," *Wilmington Morning Star* (Wilmington, NC), October 11, 1919: 5.

23. *Hunter v. Underwood*, 471 US 222, 225 (1985).

24. *Hunter v. Underwood*, 471 US 222, 228 (1985); See Clayton E. Cramer, "North Carolina's Permit to Purchase Law: The Rumble Seat of Gun Control Laws?," accessed April 12, 2017, https://papers.ssrn.com /sol3/papers.cfm?abstract_id=2759091, for a more detailed examination of the history of North Carolina's permit-to-purchase law.

25. *Watson v. Stone*, 4 So.2d 700, 703 (Fla. 1941).

26. Rebecca Tolley-Stokes, "Guns," in Bret E. Carroll, ed., *American Masculinities: A Historical Encyclopedia* (New York: Sage, 2003), 198–199.

27. James Daley, ed., *Great Speeches by American Women* (Mineola, NY: Dover Publications, 2008), 61.

28. See William J. Helmer, *The Gun That Made the Twenties Roar* (New York: Macmillan, 1970), generally for a detailed history of the Tommy gun's development and its iconic role as the weapon of Prohibition gangsters; U.S. Congress, *National Firearms Act: Hearings before the House Ways & Means Committee, House of Representatives.* 73rd Cong., 2d sess. on H.R. 9066 (Washington, D.C.: Government Printing Office, 1934), 1, 6, 7, 14, 22, 129, 99.

29. U.S. Congress, *National Firearms Act*, 19, 100.

Chapter 13

1. F. C. Ness, "Small Bore Shooting," *Fur, Fish, Game* (May 1929): 38–39.

2. "New Books Received," *Journal of Health, Physical Education, Recreation* 12 (October 1941): 495.

3. "The Rifle Club," *Journal of Health and Physical Education* 11 (January 1940): 570–571.

4. Robert Pruter, *The Rise of American High School Sports and the Search for Control, 1880–1930* (Syracuse, NY: Syracuse University Press, 2013), 123–124.

5. "Havalanta," *Journal of the American Association for Health, Physical Education, and Recreation* 21 (November 1950): 58.

6. "All the World Admires Browning," *Life*, September 27, 1954: 4.

7. Stephen Halbrook, *Gun Control in the Third Reich: Disarming the Jews and "Enemies of the State"* (Oakland, CA: Independent Institute, 2014).

8. Charles E. Cobb Jr., *This Nonviolent Stuff'll Get You Killed: How Guns Made the Civil Rights Movement Possible* (New York: Basic Books, 2015).

9. Federal Bureau of Investigation, "Federal Denials," accessed March 7, 2017, https://www.fbi.gov/file-repository/federal_denials.pdf /view.

10. Compare the National Shooting Sports Foundation's May 2014 adjusted NICS count of 974,457, accessed March 7, 2017, http://www .nssf.org/PDF/research/NICS/NSSFAdjustedNICSchartsforMay.pdf, with the FBI's 1,485,259 for the same month.

11. Federal Bureau of Investigation, "NICS Firearm Checks: Month/ Year," accessed March 7, 2017, https://www.fbi.gov/file-repository/nics _firearm_checks_-_month_year.pdf/view.

12. *Kolbe v. Hogan*, 813 F. 3d 160, 174 (4th Cir. 2016).

13. Pew Research Center, "Section 3: Gun Ownership Trends and Demographics," accessed March 19, 2017, http://www.people-press .org/2013/03/12/section-3-gun-ownership-trends-and-demographics.

14. Pew Research Center, "Why Own a Gun? Protection Is Now Top Reason," accessed March 19, 2017, http://www.people-press .org/2013/03/12/why-own-a-gun-protection-is-now-top-reason.

15. Pew Research Center, "Growing Public Support for Gun Rights," December 10, 2014, accessed March 7, 2017, http://www.people-press .org/2014/12/10/growing-public-support-for-gun-rights/#total.

16. Rasmussen Reports, "Americans Prefer Living in Neighbor- hoods with Guns," accessed March 7, 2017, http://www.rasmus- senreports.com/public_content/politics/current_events/gun_control /americans_prefer_living_in_neighborhoods_with_guns.

17. Gallup, "Guns," accessed March 7, 2017, http://www.gallup.com /poll/1645/guns.aspx.

18. Gallup, "Guns."

19. "Behind the Bloodshed," *USA Today*, accessed April 14, 2017, http://www.gannett-cdn.com/GDContent/mass-killings/index.html #explore (75 percent of mass murders involve firearms) and http: //www.gannett-cdn.com/GDContent/mass-killings/index.html#weapons (9 percent of firearm mass murders involve semiautomatic or automatic weapons).

20. Pew Research Center, "Opinions on Gun Policy and the 2016 Campaign," accessed March 7, 2017, http://www.people-press.org /files/2016/08/08-26-16-Gun-policy-release.pdf.

21. Art Swift, "In U.S., Support for Assault Weapons Ban at Record Low," accessed March 7, 2017, http://www.gallup.com/poll/196658 /support-assault-weapons-ban-record-low.aspx.

22. NORC, "Trends in Gun Ownership in the United States, 1972– 2014," accessed March 7, 2017, http://www.norc.org/PDFs/GSS%20

Reports/GSS_Trends%20in%20Gun%20Ownership_US_1972-2014 .pdf.

23. U.S. Fish & Wildlife Service, *2011 National Survey of Fishing, Hunting, and Wildlife-Associated Recreation* (Washington, D.C.: 2014), 1–4, 28.

24. U.S. Fish & Wildlife Service, *2011 National Survey*, 31.

25. Outdoor Sportsman Group, accessed March 8, 2017, http://www .outdoorsg.com/brands/hunting/petersens-hunting.

26. Outdoor Sportsman Group, accessed March 8, 2017, http://www .outdoorsg.com/brands/hunting/gun-dog.

27. Outdoor Sportsman Group, accessed March 8, 2017, http://www .outdoorsg.com/brands/hunting/north-american-whitetail.

28. Outdoor Sportsman Group, accessed March 8, 2017, http://www .outdoorsg.com/brands/hunting/wildfowl.

29. Outdoor Sportsman Group, accessed March 8, 2017, http://www .bonniercorp.com/wp-content/uploads/2015/11/FS16_MediaKit.pdf.

30. David Fessenden, *Gun Digest's History of Concealed and Defensive Handguns* (Iola, WI: Krause Publishing, 2012), 1–4; International Practical Shooting Confederation, "Welcome to IPSC," accessed March 5, 2017, http://www.ipsc.org; International Defensive Pistol Association, "Welcome to the Official IDPA Website," accessed March 5, 2017, http://www.idpa.com.

31. Single Action Shooting Society, "SASS: A Brief History," accessed March 6, 2017, http://www.sassnet.com/About-What-is-SASS-001A. php; E-mail from Misty D. Miller, CEO of the Single Action Shooting Society, March 6, 2017.

32. U.S. Civilian Marksmanship Program, *2016 CMP Annual Report*, 1–5, accessed March 6, 2017, http://thecmp.org/wp-content/uploads /CMPAnnualReport16w.pdf.

33. National Muzzle Loading Rifle Association, "National Muzzle Loading Rifle Association," accessed March 6, 2017, http://nmlra.org.

34. International Metal Silhouette Shooting Union, "International Metal Silhouette Shooting Union," accessed March 6, 2017, http://www .imssu.org/default.aspx.

35. International Handgun Metal Silhouette Association, "History of IHMSA," accessed March 6, 2017, http://www.ihmsa.org/history-of -ihmsa.html.

36. See Clayton E. Cramer and Joseph Edward Olson, "The Racist Origins of California's Concealed Weapon Permit Law" (April 27, 2015), SSRN: https://ssrn.com/abstract=2599851 or http://dx.doi.org/10.2139 /ssrn.2599851 for details of how proponents of California's current

concealed weapon law openly stated their intent to disarm Chinese and Mexicans.

37. Aaron Smith, "Only in New York: Bribing Cops for a Gun License," CNN Money, April 26, 2016.

38. See Clayton E. Cramer and David P. Kopel, "'Shall Issue': The New Wave of Concealed Handgun Permit Laws," *Tennessee Law Review* 62(3) (Spring 1995): 679–757.

39. John R. Lott, "Concealed Carry Permit Holders across the United States: 2016 (July 26, 2016)," accessed March 7, 2017, SSRN: https://ssrn.com/abstract=2814691 or http://dx.doi.org/10.2139/ssrn .2814691, 3; Wyoming Division of Criminal Investigation, Concealed Firearm Permits, accessed December 23, 2016, http://wyomingdci.wyo. gov/dci-criminal-justice-information-systems-section/concealed-firearms-permits ("A change to the Wyoming Concealed Firearm Permit State Statute in 2011 removed the requirement for Wyoming residents that wanted to carry a concealed firearm in our state from having a valid permit in order to carry a concealed firearm."); Idaho Code § 18-3302(3)(f) (2016).

40. E-mail from Dick Salzer to author, March 7, 2017; E-mail from Mobray Publishing to author, March 6, 2017.

41. U.S. Bureau of Alcohol, Tobacco, and Firearms, "Curios and Relics," accessed March 6, 2017, https://www.atf.gov/firearms/curios-relics; U.S. Bureau of Alcohol, Tobacco, and Firearms, "Is There a Specific License Which Permits a Collector to Acquire Firearms in Interstate Commerce?," accessed March 6, 2017, https://www.atf.gov/firearms /qa/there-specific-license-which-permits-collector-acquire-firearms -interstate-commerce; E-mail from FFLC@usdoj.gov to author, March 9, 2017.

42. Outdoor Sportsman Group, accessed March 8, 2017, http://www .outdoorsg.com/brands/shooting/gunsandammo; Outdoor Sportsman Group, accessed March 8, 2017, http://www.outdoorsg.com/brands /shooting/handguns; Outdoor Sportsman Group, accessed March 8, 2017, http://www.outdoorsg.com/brands/shooting/shooting-times; Outdoor Sportsman Group, accessed March 8, 2017, http://www.outdoorsg .com/brands/shooting/firearms-news.

43. Johnson, *Negroes and the Gun*, 209–284.

44. Don B. Kates, Jr., "The Necessity of Access to Firearms by Dissenters and Minorities Whom Government is Unwilling or Unable to Protect," in Don B. Kates, Jr., ed., *Restricting Handguns: The Liberal Skeptics Speak Out* (North River Press, 1979), 186.

45. NORC, "Trends in Gun Ownership in the United States, 1972–2014," 1.

46. Gary Kleck, *Point Blank: Guns and Violence in America* (Hawthorne, NY: Aldine de Gruyter, 1991), 39.

47. Johnson, *Negroes and the Gun*, 304.

48. Sarah Shannon, Christopher Uggen, Melissa Thompson, Jason Schnittker, and Michael Massoglia, "Growth in the U.S. Ex-Felon and Ex-Prisoner Population, 1948 to 2010," 7, accessed March 29, 2017, http://paa2011.princeton.edu/papers/111687.

49. Ryan Young, "African-American Gun Club Says Membership Surged in Trump Era," CNN, February 27, 2017, accessed March 18, 2017, http://www.cnn.com/2017/02/27/us/african-american-gun-club-trump.

50. Young, "African-American Gun Club."; Ben Popken, "Trump's Victory Has Fearful Minorities Buying Up Guns," NBC News, November 26, 2016, accessed March 18, 2017, http://www.nbcnews.com/business /consumer/trump-s-victory-has-fearful-minorities-buying-guns -n686881.

51. Karen I. Blu, *The Lumbee Problem: The Making of an American Indian People* (Lincoln: University of Nebraska Press, 2001), 88.

52. *State v. Cole*, 249 N.C. 733, 107 S.E.2d 732, 737 (1959).

53. Blu, *The Lumbee Problem*, 88. A detailed analysis of the subsequent court case (which went badly for the KKK) can be found in Clayton E. Cramer, *For the Defense of Themselves and the State*, 234–235.

54. Jennifer Titus, "Armed and Female: More Women Are Carrying Guns," WTSP, accessed March 18, 2017, http://www.wtsp.com/news /armed-and-female-more-women-are-carrying-guns/423414765.

55. Vincent Crivelli, "Girls with Guns: More Women Arming Themselves," WPEC, March 17, 2017, accessed March 18, 2017, http://cbs12 .com/news/local/girls-with-guns-more-women-arming-themselves.

56. Pew Research Center, "Section 3: Gun Ownership Trends and Demographics."

57. Rob Ryser, "Females and Firearms: Women Changing the Face of Gun Ownership," *Danbury News-Times* (Danbury, CT), July 11, 2016, accessed March 18, 2017, http://www.newstimes.com/local/article /Gun-ownership-more-female-than-ever-8348844.php.

58. SAW Shooting Club, accessed March 21, 2017, http://sawshootingclub .com.

59. E-mail to author from carrie@thewellarmedwoman.com, March 19, 2017, http://thewellarmedwoman.com.

60. Pink Pistols, "About the Pink Pistols," accessed April 1, 2017, http://www.pinkpistols.org/about-the-pink-pistols.

61. Evan Osnos, "Doomsday Prep for the Super-Rich," *New Yorker*, January 30, 2017; Ingrid Schmidt, "Panic, Anxiety Spark Rush

to Build Luxury Bunkers for L.A.'s Superrich," *Hollywood Reporter*, September 28, 2016; Survival Condo, accessed March 10, 2017, http://survivalcondo.com.

62. *The Economist*, "I Will Survive," December 17, 2014.

63. Federal Bureau of Investigation, *Crime in the United States 2015*, Table 11, accessed March 10, 2017, https://ucr.fbi.gov/crime-in-the-u.s/2015/crime-in-the-u.s.-2015/tables/expanded_homicide_data_table_11_murder_circumstances_by_weapon_2015.xls.

64. Federal Bureau of Investigation, *Crime in the United States 2015*, Table 3, accessed March 10, 22017, https://ucr.fbi.gov/crime-in-the-u.s/2015/crime-in-the-u.s.-2015/tables/expanded_homicide_data_table_3_murder_offenders_by_age_sex_and_race_2015.xls.

65. Federal Bureau of Investigation, *Crime in the United States 2015*, Table 1, accessed March 10, 2017, https://ucr.fbi.gov/crime-in-the-u.s/2015/crime-in-the-u.s.-2015/tables/expanded_homicide_data_table_1_murder_victims_by_race_ethnicity_and_sex_2015.xls.

66. Kevin Johnson, "Criminals Target Each Other, Trend Shows," *USA Today*, August 31, 2007.

67. Sol Stern, "Ah, Those Black Panthers! How Beautiful!" *City Journal* 16 (Winter 2006): 1, accessed May 17, 2017, http://www.city-journal.org/html/eon_5_27_03ss.html. See Tom Wolfe, *Radical Chic and Mau-Mauing the Flak Catchers* (New York: Farrar, Straus, and Giroux, 1970), for a detailed account of the Black Panther fund-raiser held by noted composer and conductor Leonard Bernstein.

68. Kate Coleman, "Souled Out," *New West*, May 19, 1980: 19.

69. "Capitol Is Invaded," *Sacramento Bee*, May 2, 1967: A1, A10.

70. "Bill Barring Loaded Weapons in Public Clears Senate 29–7," *Sacramento Bee*, July 27, 1967: A6.

71. Generally see Jeffrey Haas, *The Assassination of Fred Hampton: How the FBI and the Chicago Police Murdered a Black Panther* (Chicago: Lawrence Hill Books, 2010).

72. Dan Berger, *Outlaws of America: The Weather Underground and the Politics of Solidarity* (Oakland, CA: AK Press, 2006), 146.

73. William Graebner, *Patty's Got a Gun: Patricia Hearst in 1970s America* (Chicago: University of Chicago Press, 2008), 4.

74. Evelyn A. Schlatter, *Aryan Cowboys: White Supremacists and the Search for a New Frontier, 1970–2000* (Austin: University of Texas Press, 2006), 6–11.

75. "Behind the Bloodshed," *USA Today*.

76. "Explore the Data: U.S. Mass Killings since 2006," *USA Today*, accessed March 16, 2017, http://www.gannett-cdn.com/GDContent /mass-killings/index.html#explore.

77. Liza H. Gold, ed., *Gun Violence and Mental Illness* (Arlington, VA: American Psychiatric Association Publishing, 2016), 113.

78. See Clayton E. Cramer, "Mental Illness and the Second Amendment," *Connecticut Law Review* 46(4) (May 2014): 1301, for a detailed examination of the relationship between mental illness, murder, and deinstitutionalization. Clayton E. Cramer, *My Brother Ron: A Personal and Social History of the Deinstitutionalization of the Mentally Ill* (North Charleston, SC: CreateSpace, 2014), provides a more detailed history.

79. Gigi Douban, "Fewer People Participate in Civil War Reenactments," National Public Radio, accessed March 6, 2017, http://www .npr.org/2011/07/04/137609367/fewer-people-participate-in-civil-war -reenactments.

80. World War II Historical Re-Enactment Society, "About Us," accessed March 6, 2017, http://www.worldwartwohrs.org/AboutUs.htm.

81. Great War Association, "About Us," accessed March 6, 2017, http://www.great-war-assoc.org.

82. Reenactor.Net, "Mexican-American War," accessed March 6, 2017, http://www.reenactor.net/index.php/page.180.html.

83. Mississinewa Battlefield Society, "Mississinewa 1812," accessed March 6, 2017, http://www.mississinewa1812.com.

84. Revolutionary War Reenacting, accessed March 6, 2017, http: //www.revolutionarywarreenacting.com.

Appendix A

1. Albert W. Lindert, *Gunmakers of Indiana*, 3rd ed. (Homewood, IL: Sheffield Press, Inc., 1968); Donald A. Hutslar, *Gunsmiths of Ohio: 18th and 19th Centuries* (York, PA: George Shumway, 1973).

2. Kauffman, *Early American Gunsmiths*, 80.

3. Hartzler, *Arms Makers of Maryland*, 161.

4. Cromwell, *Virginia Manufactory of Arms*, 9.

5. Bivins, *Longrifles of North Carolina*, 155.

Appendix B

1. Pennsylvania Colony, *Pennsylvania Archives* 9th series, 2:1433–1437; 3:1730–1732, 1741–1742; Holt, "Pennsylvania 1798 Contract

Muskets," 19; Gluckman and Satterlee, *American Gun Makers*, 81–88. Holt lists several other makers as having "proposed to furnish" arms, but it is unclear whether these proposals led to contracts. He acknowledges that no such arms have come to his attention. Whisker, *The Gunsmith's Trade*, 193–194.

2. Gluckman and Satterlee, *American Gun Makers*, 69–81.
3. Gluckman and Satterlee, *American Gun Makers*, 104–116.

Bibliography

Primary Sources

Andrews, Charles M., ed. *Narratives of the Insurrections, 1675–1690.* New York: C. Scribner & Sons, 1915. Reprint, New York: Barnes & Noble, 1959.

Annual Report of the Secretary of the Interior on the Operations. Washington, D.C.: Government Printing Office, 1879.

Audubon, John James. *Delineations of American Scenery and Character.* New York: G. A. Baker & Co., 1926.

Baily, Francis. *Journal of a Tour in Unsettled Parts of North America in 1796 & 1797. Edited by* Augustus De Morgan. London: Baily Bros., 1856.

Baird, Robert. *View of the Valley of the Mississippi, or, the Emigrants and Traveller's Guide to the West.* 2nd ed. Philadelphia: H. S. Tanner, 1834.

Bank for Savings. *Fourth Report of the Bank for Savings in the City of New-York.* New York: Edwin B. Clayton, 1823.

Barnard, Henry. *Armsmear: The Home, the Arm, and the Armory of Samuel Colt: A Memorial.* New York: n.p., 1866.

Bartlett, John Russell, ed. *Records of the Colony of Rhode Island and Providence Plantations, in New England.* Providence, RI: A. Crawford Greene and Brother, 1856.

Bass, Sheila, comp. *Buffalo, Erie County, New York Directory, 1832.* Provo, UT: Ancestry.com, 2001. http://search.ancestry.com/search /db.aspx?dbid=5484. Original data: *Buffalo, New York Directory, 1832.* Buffalo, NY: L. P. Crary, 1832.

Beecher, Edward. *Narrative of Riots at Alton*. Alton, IL: George Hollon, 1838; reprint, New York: E. P. Dutton & Co., 1965.

Bernhard, Karl (Duke of Saxe-Weimar Eisenach). *Travels through North America, during the Years 1825 and 1826*. Philadelphia: Carey, Lea & Carey, 1828.

Beverley, Robert. *The History and Present State of Virginia*. Edited by Louis B. Wright. Chapel Hill: University of North Carolina Press, 1947.

Blane, William N. *An Excursion through the United States and Canada, during the Years 1822–3*. London: Baldwin, Cradock, and Joy, 1824.

Borthwick, J. D. "Three Years in Calafornia [sic]." *Hutchings Illustrated California Magazine* 2 (October 1857): 171–172.

Boston Gazette. May 30, 1720; November 17, 1741; December 8, 1741; February 2, 1742; May 11, 1742; May 18, 1742; May 25, 1742; July 13, 1742; August 10, 1742; August 24, 1742; August 31, 1742; and [September 13?], 1742.

Boston, MA. *Monthly Bulletin of the Statistics Department*. Boston: City of Boston Printing Department, 1914.

Boston, MA. *Volume of Records Relating to the Early History of Boston, Containing Miscellaneous Papers*. Boston: Municipal Printing Office, 1900.

Bradford, William. Samuel Eliot Morrison, ed. *Of Plymouth Plantation*. Edited by Samuel Eliot Morrison. New York: Alfred A. Knopf, 2002.

Brigham, William, ed. *The Compact with the Charter and Laws of the Colony of New Plymouth. . . .* Boston: Dutton and Wentworth, 1836.

Brookville Enquirer & Indiana Telegraph. January 14, 1820.

Browne, William Hand, ed. *Archives of Maryland*. Baltimore: Maryland Historical Society, 1892.

Burlend, Rebecca. *A True Picture of Emigration; or Fourteen Years in the Interior of North America*. London: G. Berger, 1848.

Camden Commercial Courier (Camden, SC). "Scenes in Havana, in 1822," August 26, 1837.

Candler, Allen D., comp. *The Colonial Records of the State of Georgia*. Atlanta, GA: Chas. P. Byrd, 1911.

Carlton, Robert [Baynard Rush Hall]. *The New Purchase, or Early Years in the Far West*. 2nd ed. New Albany, IN: Jonathan R. Nunemacher, 1855.

Cartwright, Peter. *Autobiography of Peter Cartwright, the Backwoods Preacher*. Cincinnati, OH: Jennings & Graham, 1856.

Cather, Thomas. *Voyage to America: The Journals of Thomas Cather.* Edited by Thomas Yoseloff. New York: Thomas Yoseloff, 1961. Reprint, Westport, CT: Greenwood Press, 1973.

Cecil Whig (Elkton, MD). "Trial of Palmer C. Ricketts, for Manslaughter," November 4, 1843.

Charlotte News (Charlotte, NC). "Pistol-Toting Decreasing," October 12, 1919.

Clark, Walter, ed. *State Records of North Carolina.* Goldsboro, NC: Nash Bros., 1907.

Clavers, Mary [Caroline Matilda Kirkland]. *A New Home—Who'll Follow? Or, Glimpses of Western Life. 4th ed.* New York: C. S. Francis & Co., 1850.

Clay, Cassius Marcellus. *The Writings of Cassius Marcellus Clay.* Edited by Horace Greeley. New York: Harper & Brothers, 1848. Reprint, New York: Negro Universities Press, 1969.

Cleaveland [sic] Herald (Cleveland, OH). "Jonathan Vickers informs his friends . . .," October 30, 1821.

Colt, Samuel. *The Papers of Samuel Colt.* Connecticut Historical Society.

Colt Patent Firearms Co. *Colt Collection.* Connecticut State Library.

Columbia Democrat (Bloomsburg, PA). "The Duellists," May 7, 1842 and "Salt-Water Bubbles," June 11, 1842.

Columbian Fountain (Washington, D.C.). "The New York Stabbing Case," August 27, 1846.

Commissary General of Subsistence. *Correspondence on the Subject of the Emigration of Indians.* Washington, D.C.: Duff Green, 1835.

Connecticut Colony. *Code of 1650, Being a Compilation of the Earliest Laws and Orders of the General Court of Connecticut.* Hartford, CT: Silas Andrus, 1822.

Costa, Tom, ed. "Virginia Runaways: Runaway Slave Advertisements from 18th-Century Virginia Newspapers." http://vagenweb.org/stafford/ethnic/runaway_slaves.htm. Accessed October 21, 2017.

Cox, Sandford C. *Recollections of the Early Settlement of the Wabash Valley.* Lafayette, IN: Courier Steam Book and Job Printing House, 1860.

Cuming, Fortescue. *Sketches of a Tour to the Western Country through the States of Ohio and Kentucky; A Voyage Down the Ohio and Mississippi Rivers. . . .* Pittsburgh: Cramer & Bierbaum, 1810.

Cushing, John D., ed., *The Earliest Printed Laws of North Carolina, 1669–1751.* Wilmington, DE: Michael Glazier, Inc., 1977.

Daily Alta California. "Local Matters," January 9, 1850; "By Backus and Harrison," June 26, 1850; "Sacramento Intelligence," July 11,

1850; "Local Matters," July 17, 1850; "Shooting at Stockton," July 22, 1850; "400 Bbls. Haxcall Flour," December 7, 1852; "Importations," November 4, 1851; "Van Damme & Torquet," December 22, 1851; and "Sharp's Patent Rifles!" February 4, 1854.

Daley, James, ed., *Great Speeches by American Women*. Mineola, NY: Dover Publications, 2008.

Danckaerts, Jasper. *Journal of Jasper Danckaerts: 1679–1680*. Edited by Barlett Burleigh James and J. Franklin Jameson. New York: Charles Scribner's Sons, 1913. Reprint, New York: Barnes & Noble, 1959.

Delaware Colony. *Laws of the Government of New-Castle, Kent and Sussex upon Delaware*. Philadelphia: B. Franklin, 1741.

Dwight, Theodore. *The Northern Traveller; Containing the Routes to Niagara, Quebec and the Springs*. New York: Wilder & Campbell, 1825.

Fearon, Henry Bradshaw. *Sketches of America: A Narrative of a Journey of Five Thousand Miles through the Eastern and Western States*. 3rd ed. London: Longman, Hurst, Rees, Orme, and Brown, 1819.

Fernow, Berthold, ed. *Documents Relating to the Colonial History of the State of New York*. Albany, NY: Weed, Parsons & Co., 1887. Reprint, New York: AMS Press, Inc., 1969.

Fitch, Charles H. *Extra Census Bulletin: Report on the Manufacture of Firearms and Ammunition*. U.S. Census Office. Washington, D.C.: Government Printing Office, 1882.

Flower, Richard. *Letters from the Illinois, 1820–1821: Containing an Account of the English Settlement at Albion and Its Vicinity. . . .* London: James Ridgway, 1822.

Force, Peter, ed. *American Archives: Consisting of a Collection of Authentick Records, State Papers, Debates, and Letters and Other Notices of Publick Affairs . . . 1837–53*. 4th series. Reprint, New York: Johnson Reprint Co., 1972.

Ford, Worthington C., et al., eds. *Journals of the Continental Congress, 1774–1789*. Washington, D.C., 1904–1937.

Fordham, Elias Pim. *Personal Narrative of Travels in Virginia, Maryland, Pennsylvania, Ohio, Indiana, Kentucky; and of a Residence in the Illinois Territory: 1817–1818*. Edited by Frederic Austin Ogg. Cleveland, OH: Arthur H. Clark Co., 1906. Reprint, Chicago: Library Resources, Inc., 1970.

Franklin, Benjamin. *The Papers of Benjamin Franklin*. Edited by Leonard W. Labaree. New Haven, CT: Yale University Press, 1961.

Free Democrat (Huntsville, AL). "Gun and Locksmith," May 23, 1837.

Gallatin, Albert. *A Statement of the Arts and Manufactures of the United States of America*. Washington, D.C.: n.p., 1812.

Georgia Journal (Milledgeville). "More of the Effects of Carrying Concealed Weapons," January 1838.

Gluckman, Arcadi, and L. D. Satterlee. *American Gun Makers*. 2nd ed. Harrisburg, PA: Stackpole Co., 1953.

Gosse, Philip. *Letters from Alabama*. London: Morgan & Chase, 1859.

Hall, Clayton Colman, ed. *Narratives of Early Maryland: 1633–1684*. New York: Charles Scribner's Sons, 1910. Reprint, New York: Barnes & Noble, 1959.

Hamilton, Marsha L. *Social and Economic Networks in Early Massachusetts: Atlantic Connections*. University Park: Pennsylvania State University Press, 2009.

Hamilton, Stanislaus Murray, ed. *Letters to Washington and Accompanying Papers*. Boston and New York: Houghton, Mifflin & Co., 1902.

Hart, Albert Bushnell, and Mabel Hill. *Camps and Firesides of the Revolution*. New York: Macmillan Co., 1937.

Haswell, Charles H. *Reminiscences of New York by an Octogenarian*. New York: Harper & Brothers Harper & Bros., 1896.

Heath, Dwight B., ed. *Mourt's Relation: A Journal of the Pilgrims at Plymouth*. Bedford, MA: Applewood Press, 1963.

Hening, William Waller, ed. *The Statutes at Large; Being a Collection of All the Laws of Virginia, from the First Session of the Legislature, in the Year 1619*. New York: R. & W. & G. Bartow, 1823.

Henry, William. The William Henry Papers at the Historical Society of Pennsylvania.

The Henry Papers at the Hagley Museum.

Higginson, Francis. *New England's Plantation; or a Short and True Description of the Commodities and Discommodities of That Country: Written by a Reverend Divine Now There Resident*. London: Michael Sparke, 1630.

Hoadly, Charles J., ed. *The Public Records of the Colony of Connecticut, Prior to the Union with New Haven Colony*. Hartford, CT: Brown & Parsons, 1850.

Hoadly, Charles J., ed. *Records of the Colony and Plantation of New Haven, from 1638 to 1649*. Hartford, CT: Case, Tiffany, 1857.

Hosmer, James Kendall, ed. *Original Narratives of American History*. New York: Charles Scribner's Sons, 1908.

"How Jack Marland Solved a Very Stiff Problem," *Vermont Phoenix* (Brattleboro). April 18, 1845.

Hunter v. Underwood. 471 US 222 (1985).

Jacobs, Steven, comp. *Boston City Directory, 1800.* Provo, UT: Ancestry.com, 2000. http://search.ancestry.com/search/db.aspx?dbid=4651. Original data: *Directory of Boston City Residents.* Boston: n.p., 1800.

Jacobs, Steven, comp. *Boston City Directory, 1805.* Provo, UT: Ancestry.com, 2000. http://search.ancestry.com/search/db.aspx?dbid=4813. Original data: *Directory of Boston City Residents.* Boston: n.p., 1805.

James, Sydney V., Jr. *Three Visitors to Early Plymouth.* Bedford, MA: Applewood Books, 1997.

Jameson, J. Franklin, ed. *Johnson's Wonder-Working Providence: 1628–1651.* New York: Barnes & Noble, Inc., 1959.

Jeffersonian (Kosciusko, MS). "The Steward's Duel," November 30, 1844.

Kentucky Constitutional Convention. *Report of the Debates and Proceedings of the Convention for the Revision of the Constitution of the State of Kentucky 1849.* Frankfort, KY: A. G. Hodges & Co., 1849.

Library of Congress. "Chronicling America: Historic American Newspapers." http://chroniclingamerica.loc.gov. Accessed October 27, 2017.

Library of Congress. "A proclamation. Mayor's office, Washington Dec. 23, 1828." Printed Ephemera Collection; Portfolio 193, Folder 10.

Library of Congress. "Thomas Jefferson to James Monroe. November 14, 1801." Accessed October 25, 2016. https://www.loc.gov/resource /mtj1.024_1261_1261/?st=text.

Life. "All the World Admires Browning," September 27, 1954.

Lincoln, Abraham. *The Collected Works of Abraham Lincoln.* Edited by Roy P. Basler. New Brunswick, NJ: Rutgers University Press, 1953–1955.

Lyford, W. G. *The Western Address Directory.* Baltimore: Jos. Robinson, 1837.

Mackenzie, Frederick. *A British Fusilier in Revolutionary Boston.* Edited by Allen French. Cambridge, MA: Harvard University Press, 1926.

The Manufacturer and Builder. "Brown and Sharpe No. 8 Milling Machine," Vol. 24, Issue 7 (July 1892).

Marryat, Frederick. *Diary in America.* Edited by Jules Zanger. London: Longman, Orme, Brown, Green, and Longmans, 1839. Reprint, Bloomington: Indiana University Press, 1960.

Martineau, Harriet. *Retrospect of Western Travel.* London: Saunders and Otley, 1838.

Massachusetts Provincial Congress. *The Journals of Each Provincial Congress of Massachusetts in 1774 and 1775.* Boston: Dutton and Wentworth, 1838.

McCord, David J. *Statutes at Large of South Carolina*. Columbia, SC: A. S. Johnson, 1840.

Minutes of the Supreme Executive Council of Pennsylvania. Harrisburg, PA: Theo. Fenn & Co., 1852.

Murray, Charles Augustus. *Travels in North America during the Years 1834, 1835, & 1836: Including a Summer Residence with the Pawnee Tribe of Indians, in the Remote Prairies of the Missouri, and a Visit to Cuba and the Azore Islands*. London: R. Bentley, 1839.

Myers, Albert Cook, ed. *Narratives of Early Pennsylvania, West New Jersey and Delaware, 1630–1707*. New York: Barnes & Noble, 1959.

Nashville Daily Republican Banner. "Guns, Pistols, Bowie Knives," October–November 1837.

The National Archives of the U.K. "Ledgers of Imports and Exports, America," CUST 16/1 83, 110, 171.

National Shooting Sports Foundation. May 2014. http://www.nssf.org /PDF/research/NICS/NSSFAdjustedNICSchartsforMay.pdf.

New Hampshire State. *Documents and Records Relating to the State of New-Hampshire: During the Period of the American Revolution, from 1776 to 1783*. Concord, NH: Edward A. Jenks, 1874.

New Jersey Colony. *Laws and Acts of the General Assembly of His Majesties Province of Nova Caesarea or New-Jersey . . . .* William Bradford, 1722.

New York Colony. *The Colonial Laws of New York from the Year 1664 to the Revolution . . . .* Albany, NY: James B. Lyon, 1894.

New-York Daily Tribune. "From Florida," March 29, 1843.

New York Herald. "Letter to the Editor, Jas. Watson Webb," January 23, 1836; "The Assassination of Corlis," March 26, 1843; "By Special Express," March 30, 1843; and "City Intelligence," September 10, 1845.

New York Mercury. August 29, 1763.

New York Morning Herald. "Hardware, Cutlery, Guns and Pistols," January 1838.

New-York Tribune. "Colt's Trial," January 26, 1842.

North Alabamian (Tuscumbia). February 17–24, 1837.

North Carolina Colony. *A Collection of All the Public Acts of Assembly, of the Province of North-Carolina: Now in Force and Use*. Newbern, NC: James Davis, 1751.

Olmsted, Frederick Law. *The Papers of Frederick Law Olmsted*. Edited by Charles E. Beveridge and Charles Capen McLaughlin. Baltimore: Johns Hopkins University Press, 1981.

Ouseley, William G. *Remarks on the Statistics and Political Institutions of the United States, with Some Observations on the Ecclesiastical System of America, Her Sources of Revenue, &c.* London: J. Rodwell, 1832. Reprint, Freeport, NY: Books for Libraries Press, 1970.

Palliser, John. *Solitary Rambles and Adventures of a Hunter in the Prairies.* Rutland, VT: C. E. Tuttle, Co., 1969.

Pennsylvania Colony. *Colonial Records of Pennsylvania.* Chicago: Library Resources, 1970.

Pennsylvania Colony. *Pennsylvania Archives.* Philadelphia: J. Severns & Co. et al., 1852–1935.

Pennsylvania State. *Minutes of the Provincial Council of Pennsylvania.* Harrisburg, PA: Jo. Severns & Co: 1852.

Placer Times (Sacramento, CA). "Placer Times" (rate card), March 23, 1850; "Another Affray at the Humboldt," May 24, 1850.

Pole, Edward. *Military Laboratory, at No. 34 . . . .* Philadelphia: R. Aitken, 1789. In Library of Congress Printed Ephemera Collection, Portfolio 147, Folder 9a.

Pope, William F. *Early Days in Arkansas.* Little Rock, AR: Frederick W. Allsopp, 1895.

Rafferty, Milton D. *Rude Pursuits and Rugged Peaks: Schoolcraft's Ozark Journal 1818–1819.* Fayetteville, AR: University of Arkansas Press, 1996.

Ripley, Ezra. *A History of the Fight at Concord on the 19th of April, 1775.* Concord, MA: Allen & Atwill, 1827.

Robertson, David. *Reports of the Trials of Colonel Aaron Burr. . . .* Philadelphia: Hopkins and Earle, 1808. Reprint, New York: Da Capo Press, 1969.

Royall, Anne Newport. *Letters from Alabama (U.S.), Chiefly Relating to Natural History.* London: Morgan & Chase, 1859.

Ruxton, George Frederick. *Life in the Far West*, 2nd ed. William Blackwood & Sons, 1851.

Rynning, Ole, ed. *Ole Rynning's True Account of America.* Translated by Theodore C. Blegen. St. Paul, MN: Minnesota Historical Society, 1926.

Sacramento Bee. "Capitol Is Invaded," May 2, 1967.

Sacramento Daily Union. "The Calaveras Tragedy," April 13, 1852 and "J.A. McCrea & Co.," January 1, 1853.

Sacramento Transcript. "Correspondence of the Sacramento Transcript," July 26, 1850.

Salley, Alexander S., Jr., ed. *Narratives of Early Carolina: 1650–1708.* New York: Charles Scribner's Sons, 1911. Reprint, New York: Barnes & Noble, 1959.

Saunders, William L., ed. *The Colonial Records of North Carolina.* Raleigh, NC: Josephus Daniels, 1890. Reprint, New York: AMS Press, Inc., 1968.

Schoolcraft, Henry Rowe. *Rude Pursuits and Rugged Peaks: Schoolcraft's Ozark Journal 1818-1819.* Introduction by Milton D. Rafferty. Fayetteville, AR: University of Arkansas Press, 1996: 1.

Shipton, Clifford K., ed. *Early American Imprints, 1639–1800.* Worcester, MA: American Antiquarian Society, 1967.

Shurtleff, Nathaniel B. *Records of the Governor and Company of the Massachusetts Bay in New England.* Boston: W. White, 1853–1854.

Smith, Joseph H., ed. *Colonial Justice in Western Massachusetts (1639–1702): The Pynchon Court Record, an Original Judges' Diary of the Administration of Justice in the Springfield Courts in the Massachusetts Bay Colony.* Cambridge, MA: Harvard University Press, 1961.

Smith, William C. *Indiana Miscellany: Consisting of Sketches of Indian Life, the Early Settlement, Customs, and Hardships of the People, and the Introduction of the Gospel and of Schools.* Cincinnati: Poe & Hitchcock, 1867.

Southern Recorder (Milledgeville, GA). "More of the Effects of Carrying Concealed Weapons," January 1838.

Tami, Chris. *New York City Wills.* Orem, UT: Ancestry, Inc., 1998–1999. http://www.ancestry.com.

Thomas, Gabriel. *An Historical and Geographical Account of the Province and Country of Pensilvania and West-New-Jersey.* London: A. Baldwin, 1698.

Timmons, Todd. *Science and Technology in Nineteenth-Century America.* Westport, CT: Greenwood Press, 2005.

Tocqueville, Alexis de. *Journey to America.* Translated by George Lawrence. Edited by J. P. Mayer. New York: Anchor Books, 1971.

Trumbull, J. Hammond. *The Public Records of the Colony of Connecticut, Prior to the Union with New Haven Colony.* Hartford, CT: Brown & Parsons, 1850.

Tyler, Lyon Gardiner. *Narratives of Early Virginia, 1606–1625.* New York: Charles Scribner's Sons, 1907. Reprint, New York: Barnes & Noble, 1959.

U.S. Bureau of Alcohol, Tobacco, and Firearms. "Curios and Relics." https://www.atf.gov/firearms/curios-relics. Accessed March 6, 2017.

U.S. Census Bureau. *Enumeration of the Inhabitants of the United States, 1830.* Washington, D.C.: Duff Green, 1832.

U.S. Congress. *Annals of Congress.* Washington, D.C.: Library of Congress, n.d. 7th Cong., 2nd sess., 1282.

U.S. Congress. Congressional Record 65. Washington, D.C.: Government Printing Office, 1925. 65 Congressional Record 3946.

U.S. Congress. *Journal of the House of Representatives of the United States*, 25:611.

U.S. Congress. *National Firearms Act: Hearings before the House Ways & Means Committee, House of Representatives. 73rd Cong., 2d sess. On H.R. 9066.* Washington, D.C.: Government Printing Office, 1934.

U.S. Department of State. *The Diplomatic Correspondence of the United States of America.* Washington, D.C.: Blair & Rives, 1887, 1:642.

Washington, George. *The Diaries of George Washington.* Edited by Donald Jackson. Charlottesville: University Press of Virginia, 1976.

Washington, George. *The Writings of George Washington from the Original Manuscript Sources, 1745–1799.* Edited by John C. Fitzpatrick. Washington, D.C.: Government Printing Office, 1931–1944.

Watson v. Stone. 4 So.2d 700 (Fla. 1941).

Weld, Isaac. *Travels through the States of North America, and the Provinces of Upper and Lower Canada, during the Years 1795, 1796, and 1797.* London: John Stockdale, 1807.

Whiteley's Philadelphia Annual Advertiser. Philadelphia: Kneass & Saurman, 1820.

Willard, Joseph. *Topographical and Historical Sketches of the Town of Lancaster, in the Commonwealth of Massachusetts.* Worcester, MA: Charles Griffin, 1826.

Williams, John Lee. *The Territory of Florida: Or Sketches of the Topography, Civil and Natural History.* New York: A.T. Goodrich, 1837.

Wilmington Morning Star (Wilmington, NC). "No Race Trouble to Be Found in This Section," October 11, 1919.

Winslow, Edward. *Good Newes from New England.* London: n.p., 1624. Reprint, Bedford, MA: Applewood Books, n.d.

Winston-Salem Twin-City Daily Sentinel (Winston-Salem, NC). "Municipal Court Has Heavy Docket," November 19, 1918.

Wright, Frances. *Views of Society and Manners in America.* London: Longman, Hurst, Rees, Orme, and Brown, 1821.

Wright, John Stillman. *Letters from the West; or a Caution to Emigrants.* Salem, NY: Dodd & Stevenson, 1819.

Wyoming Division of Criminal Investigation. "Concealed Firearm Permits." http://wyomingdci.wyo.gov/dci-criminal-justice-information-systems-section/concealed-firearms-permits. Accessed December 23, 2016.

Zavala, Lorenzo de. *Journey to the United States of North America.* Translated by Wallace Woolsey. Austin, TX: Shoal Creek Publishers, 1980.

Gunsmith Lists

Achtermier, William O. *Rhode Island Arms Makers & Gunsmiths: 1643–1883*. Providence, RI: Man at Arms, 1980.

Demeritt, Dwight B., Jr. *Maine Made Guns and Their Makers*. Hallowell, ME: Paul S. Plumer Jr., 1973.

Gluckman, Arcadi, and L. D. Satterlee. *American Gun Makers*. 2nd ed. Harrisburg, PA: Stackpole Co., 1953.

Hartzler, Daniel D. *Arms Makers of Maryland*. York, PA: George Shumway, 1977.

Hutslar, Donald A. *Gunsmiths of Ohio: 18th and 19th Centuries*. York, PA: George Shumway, 1973.

Lewis, Michael H. *The Gunsmiths of Manhattan 1625–1900: A Checklist of Tradesmen*. Alexandria Bay, NY: Museum Restoration Service, 1991.

Lindert, Albert W. *Gunmakers of Indiana*. 3rd ed. Homewood, IL: Sheffield Press, Inc., 1968.

Secondary Sources

Anderson, Margo J. *The American Census: A Social History*. New Haven, CT: Yale University Press, 1988.

Andrews, Matthew Page. *Tercentenary History of Maryland*. Chicago and Baltimore: S. J. Clarke Publishing Co., 1925.

Applebaum, Herbert A. *Colonial Americans at Work*. Lanham, MD: University Press of America, 1996.

Barnard, Henry. *Armsmear: The Home, the Arm, and the Armory of Samuel Colt: A Memorial*. New York: n.p., 1866.

Bates, Beth Tompkins. *The Making of Black Detroit in the Age of Henry Ford*. Chapel Hill: University of North Carolina Press, 2012.

Bazelon, Bruce S. *Defending the Commonwealth: Catalogue of the Militia Exhibit at the William Penn Memorial Museum, Harrisburg, Pennsylvania*. Providence, RI: Mowbray Co., 1980.

Bellesiles, Michael A. *Arming America: The Origins of a National Gun Culture*. New York: Alfred A. Knopf, 2000.

Bellesiles, Michael A. "The Origins of Gun Culture in the United States, 1760–1865." *Journal of American History* 83 (September 1996): 2.

Berger, Dan. *Outlaws of America: The Weather Underground and the Politics of Solidarity*. Oakland, CA: AK Press, 2006.

Bishop, J. Leander, Edwin Troxell Freedly, and Edward Young. *A History of American Manufactures from 1608 to 1860*. Philadelphia: Edward Young & Co., 1864.

Bivins, John, Jr. *Longrifles of North Carolina*. 2nd ed. York, PA: George Shumway, 1988.

Blu, Karen I. *The Lumbee Problem: The Making of an American Indian People*. Lincoln: University of Nebraska Press, 2001.

Bonsall, Thomas E. *Disaster in Dearborn: The Story of the Edsel*. Stanford, CA: Stanford General Books, 2002.

Bradford, Sarah H. *Scenes in the Life of Harriet Tubman*. Auburn, NY: W. J. Moses, 1869.

Brown, Abram English. *Beneath Old Roof Trees*. Boston: Lee & Shepard, 1896.

Brown, Kathleen M. *Good Wives, Nasty Wenches, and Anxious Patriarchs: Gender, Race, and Power in Colonial Virginia*. Chapel Hill: University of North Carolina Press, 1996.

Brown, M. L. *Firearms in Colonial America*. Washington, D.C.: Smithsonian Institution Press, 1980.

Burke, Steven. "IBM Will Offer the PCjr for Further Education in Schools." *InfoWorld*. September 16, 1985.

Burlingame, Michael. *Abraham Lincoln: A Life*. Baltimore: Johns Hopkins University Press, 2008.

Carroll, Bret E., ed., *American Masculinities: A Historical Encyclopedia*. New York: Sage, 2003.

Chartered Insurance Institute. *Journal*. London: Charles & Edwin Layton, 2005.

Cherry, Steven. *Mental Health Care in Modern England: The Norfolk Lunatic Asylum, St. Andrew's Hospital, c. 1810–1998*. Bury St. Edmunds: St. Edmundsbury Press, 2003.

Civilian Marksmanship Program. *2016 CMP Annual Report, 1–5*. http://thecmp.org/wp-content/uploads/CMPAnnualReport16w.pdf. Accessed March 6, 2017.

"Claiborne vs. Clobery et als. In the High Court of Admiralty," *Maryland Historical Magazine* 28: 26–43.

Cobb, Charles E., Jr. *This Nonviolent Stuff'll Get You Killed: How Guns Made the Civil Rights Movement Possible*. New York: Basic Books, 2015.

Coburn, Frank Warren. *The Battle of April 19, 1775*. 2nd ed. Lexington, MA: n.p., 1922. Reprint, Port Washington, NY: Kennikat Press, 1970.

Colt, Samuel. *On the Application of Machinery to the Manufacture of Rotating Chambered-Breech Firearms*. 3rd ed. London: William Clowes & Sons, 1855.

Cramer, Clayton E. *Armed America: The Remarkable Story of How and Why Guns Became as American as Apple Pie*. Nashville, TN: Nelson Current, 2006.

Cramer, Clayton E. *Concealed Weapon Laws of the Early Republic: Dueling, Southern Violence, and Moral Reform*. Westport, CT: Praeger, 1999.

Cramer, Clayton E. "Factual Errors in the Gunning of America: Is This Scholarly History or Polemic?" June 14, 2016. http://papers.ssrn.com/sol3/papers.cfm?abstract_id=2795745.

Cramer, Clayton E. *For the Defense of Themselves and the State: The Original Intent and Judicial Interpretation of the Right to Keep and Bear Arms*. Westport, CT: Praeger, 1994.

Cramer, Clayton E. "North Carolina's Permit to Purchase Law: The Rumble Seat of Gun Control Laws?" April 4, 2016. https://papers.ssrn.com/sol3/papers.cfm?abstract_id=2759091.

Cramer, Clayton E. "Mental Illness and the Second Amendment." *Connecticut Law Review* 46 (May 2014): 4.

Cramer, Clayton E. *My Brother Ron: A Personal and Social History of the Deinstitutionalization of the Mentally Ill*. North Charleston, SC: CreateSpace, 2014.

Cramer, Clayton E., and David P. Kopel. "'Shall Issue': The New Wave of Concealed Handgun Permit Laws." *Tennessee Law Review* 62 (Spring 1995): 3.

Crivelli, Vincent. "Girls with Guns: More Women Arming Themselves." WPEC, March 17, 2017. http://cbs12.com/news/local/girls-with-guns-more-women-arming-themselves.

Cromwell, Giles. *The Virginia Manufactory of Arms*. Charlottesville: University Press of Virginia, 1975.

Curtis, Edward E. *The Organization of the British Army in the American Revolution*. New Haven, CT: Yale University Press, 1926. Reprint, New York: AMS Press, 1969.

Deyrup, Felicia Johnson. *Arms Makers of the Connecticut Valley: A Regional Study of the Economic Development of the Small Arms Industry, 1798–1870*. Menasha, WI: George Banta Publishing Co., 1948.

Dickens, Charles. *American Notes for General Circulation*. Paris: A. and W. Galignani & Co., 1842.

Dickson, R. J. *Ulster Emigration to Colonial America 1718–1775*. London: Routledge & Kegan Paul, 1966.

Ditchburn, Robert. "Three CPs?" *The Gun Report* (July 1962): 26–29.

Douban, Gigi. "Fewer People Participate in Civil War Reenactments." National Public Radio, July 4, 2011. http://www.npr.org/2011/07/04/137609367/fewer-people-participate-in-civil-war-reenactments.

Dyke, S. E. *Thoughts on the American Flintlock Pistol*. York, PA: George Shumway, 1974.

The Economist. "I Will Survive." December 17, 2014.

Edwards, William B. *The Story of Colt's Revolver*. New York: Castle Books, 1957.

Federal Bureau of Investigation. *Crime in the United States 2015*. https://ucr.fbi.gov/crime-in-the-u.s/2015/crime-in-the-u.s.-2015. Accessed March 10, 2017.

Federal Bureau of Investigation. "Federal Denials." https://www.fbi.gov/file-repository/federal_denials.pdf/view. Accessed October 28, 2017.

Federal Bureau of Investigation. "NICS Firearm Checks: Month/Year." https://www.fbi.gov/file-repository/nics_firearm_checks_-_month_year.pdf/view. Accessed October 28, 2017.

Fessenden, David. *Gun Digest's History of Concealed and Defensive Handguns*. Iola, WI: Krause Publishing, 2012.

Fitch, Charles H. *Extra Census Bulletin: Report on the Manufacture of Firearms and Ammunition*. U.S. Census Office. Washington. D.C.: Government Printing Office, 1882.

Franklin, John Hope. *The Free Negro in North Carolina, 1790–1860*. Chapel Hill: University of North Carolina Press, 1995.

Gallup. "Guns." http://www.gallup.com/poll/1645/guns.aspx. Accessed March 7, 2017

Gill, Harold B., Jr. *The Gunsmith in Colonial Virginia*. Williamsburg, VA: Colonial Williamsburg Foundation, 1974.

Gluckman, Arcadi, and L. D. Satterlee. *American Gun Makers, United States Muskets, Rifles and Carbines*. Buffalo, NY: Otto Ulbrich Co., 1948.

Gold, Liza H., ed. *Gun Violence and Mental Illness*. Arlington, VA: American Psychiatric Association Publishing, 2016.

Graebner, William. *Patty's Got a Gun: Patricia Hearst in 1970s America*. Chicago: University of Chicago Press, 2008.

Great War Association. "About Us." http://www.great-war-assoc.org. Accessed March 6, 2017.

Grubb, Farley. "The Statutory Regulation of Colonial Servitude: An Incomplete-Contract Approach." *Explorations in Economic History* 37, 42–75 (January 2000).

Haag, Pamela. *The Gunning of America: Business and the Making of American Gun Culture*. New York: Basic Books, 2015.

Haas, Jeffrey. *The Assassination of Fred Hampton: How the FBI and the Chicago Police Murdered a Black Panther*. Chicago: Lawrence Hill Books, 2010.

Haig, Matt. *Brand Failures: The Truth about the 100 Biggest Branding Mistakes of All Time*. London: Kogan Page, 2003.

Halbrook, Stephen. *Gun Control in the Third Reich: Disarming the Jews and "Enemies of the State."* Oakland, CA: Independent Institute, 2014.

Hamilton, Marsha L. *Social and Economic Networks in Early Massachusetts: Atlantic Connections*. University Park: Pennsylvania State University Press, 2009.

Hamilton, T. M. *Early Indian Trade Guns: 1625–1775*. Lawton, OK: Museum of the Great Plains, 1968.

Hamilton, T. M., ed. *Indian Trade Guns*. Union City, TN: Pioneer Press, 1982.

Hansen, Joyce, and Gary McGowan. *Breaking Ground, Breaking Silence: The Story of New York's African Burial Ground*. New York: Henry Holt and Co., 1998.

Haven, Charles T., and Frank A. Belden. A *History of the Colt Revolver*. New York: William Morrow & Co., 1940.

Hicks, James E. *Notes on United States Ordnance*. Mount Vernon, NY: James E. Hicks, 1940.

Hindes, Ruthanna. "Delaware Silversmiths, 1700–1850." *Delaware History* 12 (October 1967): 4, 247–306.

Holt, Thomas E. "Pennsylvania 1798 Contract Muskets." *American Society of Arms Collectors* 2 (November 1956): 19–24.

Hounshell, David. *From the American System to Mass Production, 1800–1932: The Development of Manufacturing Technology in the United States*. Baltimore: Johns Hopkins University Press, 1984.

International Defensive Pistol Association. "Welcome to the Official IDPA Website." http://www.idpa.com. Accessed March 5, 2017.

International Handgun Metal Silhouette Association. "History of IHMSA." http://www.ihmsa.org/history-of-ihmsa.html. Accessed March 6, 2017.

International Metal Silhouette Shooting Union. "International Metal Silhouette Shooting Union." http://www.imssu.org/default.aspx. Accessed March 6, 2017.

International Practical Shooting Confederation, "Welcome to IPSC." http://www.ipsc.org. Accessed March 5, 2017.

Johnson, Kevin. "Criminals Target Each Other, Trend Shows." *USA Today*, August 31, 2007.

Journal of the American Association for Health, Physical Education, and Recreation. "Havalanta," 21 (November 1950): 58.

Journal of Health, Physical Education, Recreation 12 (October 1941): 495.

Kates, Don B., Jr., ed. *Restricting Handguns: The Liberal Skeptics Speak Out*. Great Barrington, MA: North River Press, 1979.

Katz, Stanley N., Hanna H. Gray, and Laurel Thatcher Ulrich. "Report of the Investigative Committee in the Matter of Professor Michael Bellesiles," July 10, 2002. Accessed September 27, 2016. http://www .emory.edu/news/Releases/Final_Report.pdf.

Kauffman, Henry J. *Early American Gunsmiths: 1650–1850*. New York: Bramhall House, 1952.

Kauffman, Henry J. *Early American Ironware: Cast and Wrought*. New York: Weathervane Books, 1956.

Kelly, James C., and William C. Baker. *The Sword of the Lord and Gideon: A Catalogue of Historical Objects Related to the Battle of King's Mountain*. Boone, NC: Appalachian Consortium Press, 1980.

Klay, Frank. *The Samuel E. Dyke Collection of Kentucky Pistols*. Highland Park, NJ: The Gun Room Press, 1972.

Kleck, Gary. *Point Blank: Guns and Violence in America*. Hawthorne, NY: Aldine de Gruyter, 1991.

Kurin, Richard. *The Smithsonian's History of America in 101 Objects*. New York: Penguin Press, 2013.

Land, Aubrey C. *Colonial Maryland: A History*. Milwood, NY: KTO Press, 1981.

Lewis, Berkeley R. *Small Arms and Ammunition in the United States Service, 1776–1865*. Washington, D.C.: Smithsonian Institute, 1956.

Lewis, Michael H. "An 18th Century 'American' Musket." *The Gun Report*, November 1997: 18–22.

Lewis v. United States. 445 U.S. 55 (1980).

Life. "All the World Admires Browning," September 27, 1954.

Lindgren, James. "Fall from Grace: *Arming America* and the Bellesiles Scandal." *Yale Law Journal* 111 (2002): 2195.

Lindsay, Merrill. *The New England Gun: The First Two Hundred Years*. New Haven, CT: New Haven Colony Historical Society, 1975.

Lott, John R., Jr. "Concealed Carry Permit Holders across the United States: 2016." July 26, 2016. https://ssrn.com/abstract=2814691 or http://dx.doi.org/10.2139/ssrn.2814691.

Malcolm, Joyce Lee. "Concealed Weapons." *Reason* (January 2001): 47–49.

Malcolm, Joyce Lee. "The Right of the People to Keep and Bear Arms: The Common Law Tradition." *Hastings Constitutional Law Quarterly* 10 (1983): 310.

Mankiw, N. Gregory. *Macroeconomics*. 5th ed. New York: Worth Publishers, 2003.

Matteis, Jen. "Michael Bellesiles: Bartender, Writer, History Buff." *The Day*, September 17, 2012. http://www.theday.com/article/20120917/NWS10/309209649.

Mayer, Joseph B. *Flintlocks of the Iroquois: 1620–1687*. Rochester, NY: Rochester Museum of Arts and Sciences, 1943.

Maynard, George C. "Notes on the Manufacture of Small Arms for the United States Army by the Government and Private Makers in the Nineteenth Century." *Stock and Steel* (June 1923): 5–12.

Mississinewa Battlefield Society. "Mississinewa 1812." http://www.mississinewa1812.com. Accessed March 6, 2017.

Morgan, Edmund S. "In Love with Guns." *New York Review of Books*, October 19, 2000.

Morris, Charles R. *The Dawn of Invention: The First American Industrial Revolution*. New York: PublicAffairs, 2012.

Museum of Early Southern Decorative Arts. *Index of Early Southern Artists and Artisans*. Extract of gunsmiths, January 17, 2001.

National Muzzle Loading Rifle Association. "National Muzzle Loading Rifle Association." http://nmlra.org. Accessed March 6, 2017.

National Rifle Association of America. "A Brief History of the NRA." Accessed March 18, 2017. https://home.nra.org/about-the-nra.

Nehrbass, Arthur. "Notes on Early U.S. Rifle and Musket Production." *The Gun Report* (October 1972).

Ness, F. C. "Small Bore Shooting," *Fur, Fish, Game*. (May 1929).

Neuman, George C. "Firearms of the American Revolution: Part I." *American Rifleman* (July 1967).

New Jersey Department of Labor and Workforce Development. "United States Resident Population by State: 1790–1850." http://lwd.dol.state.nj.us/labor/lpa/census/1990/poptrd1.htm. Accessed March 13, 2017.

Nichols, David Alan. *Lincoln and the Indians: Civil War Policy and Politics*. Columbia: University of Missouri Press, 2012.

NORC. "Trends in Gun Ownership in the United States, 1972–2014." http://www.norc.org/PDFs/GSS%20Reports/GSS_Trends%20in%20Gun%20Ownership_US_1972-2014.pdf. Accessed March 7, 2017.

Orwell. George. *Nineteen Eighty-Four*. New York: Alfred A. Knopf, 1992.

Osnos, Evan. "Doomsday Prep for the Super-Rich." *New Yorker*, January 30, 2017.

Outdoor Sportsman Group. http://www.outdoorsg.com. Accessed March 8, 2017.

Peterson, Harold L. *Arms and Armor in Colonial America: 1526–1783.* Harrisburg, PA: Stackpole Co., 1956.

Pew Research Center. "Growing Public Support for Gun Rights." December 10, 2014, http://www.people-press.org/2014/12/10/growing-public-support-for-gun-rights/#total.

Pew Research Center. "Opinions on Gun Policy and the 2016 Campaign." http://www.people-press.org/files/2016/08/08-26-16-Gun-policy-release.pdf. Accessed March 7, 2017.

Pew Research Center. "Section 3: Gun Ownership Trends and Demographics." http://www.people-press.org/2013/03/12/section-3-gun-ownership-trends-and-demographics. Accessed March 18, 2017.

Pew Research Center. "Why Own a Gun? Protection Is Now Top Reason." http://www.people-press.org/2013/03/12/why-own-a-gun-protection-is-now-top-reason. Accessed March 19, 2017.

Picard, Liza. "The Working Classes and the Poor." British Library. Accessed October 6, 2016. https://www.bl.uk/victorian-britain/articles/the-working-classes-and-the-poor.

Pink Pistols. "About the Pink Pistols." http://www.pinkpistols.org/about-the-pink-pistols. Accessed April 1, 2017.

Popken, Ben. "Trump's Victory Has Fearful Minorities Buying Up Guns," NBC News, November 26, 2016. http://www.nbcnews.com/business/consumer/trump-s-victory-has-fearful-minorities-buying-guns-n686881.

Pruter, Robert. *The Rise of American High School Sports and the Search for Control, 1880–1930.* Syracuse, NY: Syracuse University Press, 2013.

Randall, Richard A., Jr. "A Seventeenth-Century Account." *The American Arms Collector* (October 1958): 111–114.

Rasmussen Reports. "Americans Prefer Living in Neighborhoods with Guns." http://www.rasmussenreports.com/public_content/politics/current_events/gun_control/americans_prefer_living_in_neighborhoods_with_guns. Accessed March 7, 2017.

Rattenbury, Richard C. *A Legacy in Arms: American Firearm Manufacture, Design, and Artistry, 1800–1900.* Norman: University of Oklahoma Press, 2014.

Reenactor.Net. "Mexican-American War." http://www.reenactor.net/index.php/page.180.html. Accessed March 6, 2017.

Revolutionary War Reenacting. http://www.revolutionarywarreenacting.com. Accessed March 6, 2017.

Robbins, Walter L. "Christmas Shooting Rounds in America and Their Background." *Journal of American Folklore* 86(339) (1973): 48–52.

Rockwell, Stephen J. *Indian Affairs and the Administrative State in the Nineteenth Century*. New York: Cambridge University Press, 2013.

Rodengen, Jeffrey L. *NRA: An American Legend*. Fort Lauderdale, FL: Write Stuff Enterprises, 2002.

Roe, Joseph Wickham. *English and American Tool Builders*. New Haven, CT: Yale University Press, 1916.

Rolt, L. T. C. *A Short History of Machine Tools*. Cambridge, MA: The MIT Press, 1965.

Russell, Carl P. *Firearms, Traps, & Tools of the Mountain Men*. Albuquerque: University of New Mexico Press, 1977.

Rutman, Darrett B. *Winthrop's Boston: A Portrait of a Puritan Town, 1630–1649*. New York: W. W. Norton & Co., Inc., 1965.

Ryser, Rob. "Females and Firearms: Women Changing the Face of Gun Ownership." *Danbury News-Times* (Danbury, CT), July 11, 2016. http://www.newstimes.com/local/article/Gun-ownership-more-female-than-ever-8348844.php.

San Francisco Chronicle. "Take Another Look at Gun Rights History." September 25, 2000: A22.

Scharf, J. Thomas. *History of Western Maryland: Being a History of Frederick, Montgomery, Carroll, Washington, Allegany, and Garrett Counties from the Earliest Period to the Present Day. . . .* Philadelphia: L. H. Everts, 1882. Reprinted, Baltimore: Regional Publishing Co., 1968.

Schlatter, Evelyn A. *Aryan Cowboys: White Supremacists and the Search for a New Frontier, 1970–2000*. Austin: University of Texas Press, 2006.

Schmidt, Ingrid. "Panic, Anxiety Spark Rush to Build Luxury Bunkers for L.A.'s Superrich." *Hollywood Reporter*, September 28, 2016.

Shannon, Sarah, Christopher Uggen, Melissa Thompson, Jason Schnittker, and Michael Massoglia. "Growth in the U.S. Ex-Felon and Ex-Prisoner Population, 1948 to 2010." http://paa2011.princeton.edu/papers/111687. Accessed March 29, 2017.

Single Action Shooting Society. "SASS: A Brief History." http://www.sassnet.com/About-What-is-SASS-001A.php. Accessed October 28, 2017.

Slotkin, Richard. "The Fall into Guns." *Atlantic Monthly* (November 2000): 114–118.

Smith, Aaron. "Only in New York: Bribing Cops for a Gun License." CNN Money, April 26, 2016.

Smith, Abbot Emerson. *Colonists in Bondage: White Servitude and Convict Labor in America, 1607–1776*. Gloucester, MA: Peter Smith, 1965.

Smith, Merritt Roe. *Harpers Ferry Armory and the New Technology: The Challenge of Change*. Ithaca, NY: Cornell University Press, 2015.

Sowell, Thomas. *Economic Facts and Fallacies*. 2nd ed. New York: Basic Books, 2011.

Stern, Sol. "Ah, Those Black Panthers! How Beautiful!" *City Journal* (Winter 2006) 16: 1. http://www.city-journal.org/html/eon_5_27_03ss .html.

Stevens, William Oliver. *Pistols at Ten Paces: The Story of the Code of Honor in America*. Cambridge, MA: Riverside Press, 1940.

Stickels, George A. "The William Smith Pistols Made by Medad Hills." *The Gun Report* (September 1979): 10–12.

Swayze, Nathan. *The Rappahannock Forge*. Dallas: American Society of Arms Collectors, 1976.

Swift, Art. "In U.S., Support for Assault Weapons Ban at Record Low." Gallup, October 26, 2016. http://www.gallup.com/poll/196658 /support-assault-weapons-ban-record-low.aspx.

Temin, Peter, ed. *Engines of Enterprise: An Economic History of New England*. Cambridge, MA: Harvard University Press, 2000.

Timmons, Todd. *Science and Technology in Nineteenth-Century America*. Westport, CT: Greenwood Press, 2005.

Urwin, Gregory J. W. *The United States Infantry: An Illustrated History, 1775–1918*. Norman: University of Oklahoma Press, 1988.

USA Today. "Behind the Bloodshed." http://www.gannett-cdn.com /GDContent/mass-killings/index.html#frequency. Accessed April 14, 2017.

U.S. Fish & Wildlife Service. *2011 National Survey of Fishing, Hunting, and Wildlife-Associated Recreation*. Washington, D.C.: n.p., 2014.

Titus, Jennifer. "Armed and Female: More Women Are Carrying Guns." WTSP, March 17, 2017. http://www.wtsp.com/news /armed-and-female-more-women-are-carrying-guns/423414765.

Warlow, Tom. *Firearms, the Law, and Forensic Ballistics*. 3rd ed. Boca Raton, FL: CRC Press, 2012.

Waters, Asa H. *Gun Making in Sutton and Millbury*. Worcester, MA: Lucius P. Goddard, 1878.

Whisker, James B. *Arms Makers of Colonial America*. Selinsgrove, PA: Susquehanna University Press, 1992.

Whisker, James B. *The Gunsmith's Trade*. Lewiston, NY: Edwin Mellen Press, 1992.

Wills, Garry. "Spiking the Gun Myth." *New York Times*, September 10, 2000. http://www.nytimes.com/2000/09/10/books/spiking-the-gun-myth.html. Accessed October 28, 2017.

Windell, Marie. "News Notes and Book Reports." *Delaware History 5* (March 1953): 3, 206–221.

Wolfe, Tom. *Radical Chic and Mau-Mauing the Flak Catchers.* New York: Farrar, Straus, and Giroux, 1970.

Woodbury, Robert S. *History of the Milling Machine.* Cambridge, MA: Technology Press, 1960.

Woodbury, Robert S. *Studies in the History of Machine Tools.* Cambridge, MA, 1972.

World War II Historical Re-Enactment Society. "About Us." http://www.worldwartwohrs.org/AboutUs.htm. Accessed March 6, 2017

Worth, Robert F. "Prize for Book Is Taken Back from Historian." *New York Times,* December 14, 2002. http://www.nytimes.com/2002/12/14/business/prize-for-book-is-taken-back-from-historian.html.

Wright, James D., Peter H. Rossi, and Kathleen Daly. *Under the Gun: Weapons, Crime, and Violence in America.* New York: Aldine de Gruyter, 1983.

Young, Ryan. "African-American Gun Club Says Membership Surged in Trump Era." CNN, February 27, 2017. http://www.cnn.com/2017/02/27/us/african-american-gun-club-trump.

Index

About the Author

CLAYTON E. CRAMER teaches history at the College of Western Idaho, after having retired from a career as a software engineer. His work has been cited in U.S. Supreme Court decisions. Previous books by Mr. Cramer include *Armed America: The Remarkable Story of How Guns Became as American as Apple Pie*; *Concealed Weapon Laws of the Early Republic: Dueling, Southern Violence, and Moral Reform*; *Black Demographic Data, 1790–1860: A Sourcebook*; and *For the Defense of Themselves and the State: The Original Intent and Judicial Interpretation of the Right to Keep and Bear Arms*.